THE BEST
PLACES
TO KISS
IN HAWAII

A Romantic Travel Guide

COMPLETELY REVISED
2nd EDITION
AND UPDATED

by

Elizabeth Janda & Stephanie Bell

BEGINNING
PRESS

OTHER BOOKS IN THE

BEST PLACES TO KISS™

SERIES:

The Best Places To Kiss In The Northwest, 6th Edition $15.95

The Best Places To Kiss In Northern California, 4th Edition $13.95

The Best Places To Kiss In Southern California, 4th Edition $13.95

ANY OF THESE BOOKS CAN BE ORDERED DIRECTLY FROM THE PUBLISHER.

Please send a check or money order for the total
amount of the books, plus shipping and handling
($3 for the first book, and $1 for each additional book) to:

Beginning Press
5418 South Brandon
Seattle, Washington 98118

All prices are listed in U.S. funds.
For information about ordering from Canada or to place
an order using a credit card, call (206) 723-6300.

Art Direction and Production: Studio Pacific, Inc.
Cover Design: Studio Pacific, Inc., Deb McCarroll
Editor: Miriam Bulmer
Printing: Publishers Press
Contributors: Paula Begoun and Kristin Folsom

Copyright 1993, 1996 by Paula Begoun
Second Edition: January 1996
  2 3 4 5 6 7 8 9 10

BEST PLACES TO KISS™

is a registered trademark of Beginning Press
ISBN 1-877988-17-0

This book is distributed to the U.S. book trade by:
Publisher's Group West
4065 Hollis Street
Emeryville, CA 94608
(800) 788-3123

This book is distributed to the Canadian book trade by:
Raincoast Books
8680 Cambie Street
Vancouver, B.C.
V6P-6M9
Canada
(800) 663-5714

"As usual with most lovers in the city, they were troubled by the lack of that essential need of love—a meeting place."

Thomas Wolfe

Publisher's Note

Travel books have many different criteria for the places they include. We would like the reader to know that this book is not an advertising vehicle. As is true in all *The Best Places To Kiss* books, the businesses included were not charged fees, nor did they pay us for their reviews. This book is a sincere, unbiased effort to highlight those special parts of the region that are filled with romance and splendor. Sometimes those places were created by people, such as restaurants, inns, lounges, lodges, hotels, and bed and breakfasts. Sometimes those places are untouched by people and simply created by God for us to enjoy. Wherever you go, be gentle with each other and with the earth.

The publisher made the final decision on the recommendations in this collection, but we would love to hear what you think of our suggestions. We strive to create a reliable guide for your amorous outings, and in this quest for blissful sojourns, your romantic feedback assists greatly in increasing our accuracy and our resources for information. If you have any additional comments, criticisms, or cherished memories of your own from a place we directed you to or a place you discovered on your own, feel free to write us at:

Beginning Press
5418 South Brandon Street
Seattle, WA 98118

We would love to hear from you!

" *What of soul was left, I wonder, when the kissing had to stop?* "

Robert Browning

TABLE OF CONTENTS

THE FINE ART OF KISSING 1

Why It's Still Best To Kiss in Hawaii, The Islands, Getting Around, The Most Romantic Time To Travel, Can't We Kiss Anywhere?, You Call This Research?, Romance Warnings, Romantic Ratings, Kiss Ratings, Cost Ratings, Lodging Ratings, Romance in a Condominium, Romance in a Bed and Breakfast, A Room With a View, Love Among the Golf Courses, To Luau or Not To Luau?, The Lei of the Land, Surf's Up, Whale Watching, Sunscreen: Don't Leave Home Without It, What To Pack, Getting Married in Hawaii, and A Brief History.

OAHU. 21

MAUI 57

KAUAI 117

HAWAII—THE BIG ISLAND 165

LANAI 205

MOLOKAI 211

INDEX. 219

THE FINE ART OF KISSING

Why It's Still Best To Kiss in Hawaii

Hawaii is an exceptionally desirable place to kiss. In fact, it is probably one of *the* premier places to kiss in the world. For those of you who have never been to Hawaii, we'll begin by saying that much of it, without question, is a true tropical paradise. When you first see these jewel-like isles, it takes very little effort to imagine how they looked to the first non-native visitors to these islands over two centuries ago: unspoiled jade green hills and silvery blue waves meeting one another in all their majestic primeval glory. Today, Western and Eastern cultures have done much to change the flawless appearance of these islands, but the quintessential splendor and legendary scenery are still there in great abundance.

Paradise doesn't often mix well with modernization, and Hawaii has suffered large-scale development by both Japanese and American corporations over the past 20 years, with the greatest influx in just the last ten years. Through the 1950s, when the most prized hotel rooms rented for about $10 a night and "The Beach at Waikiki" was a popular song, the islands were relatively unmarred. Much of that had to do with accessibility. To put it mildly, the Hawaiian Islands are out in the middle of nowhere: 2,400 miles from the nearest coast (equidistant between Japan and the west coast of the United States). Back in the '50s, visiting these Polynesian playgrounds meant a long, arduous journey.

Needless to say, times have changed. Easy access from nearly every corner of the globe makes Hawaii one of the most touristed locales in the world, with the preponderance of visitors coming from the U.S. mainland and Japan. Between 7 million and 8 million vacationers a year come here searching for a taste of tropical heaven. Frequent-flyer award programs and enticing, reasonably priced vacation packages make Hawaii an affordable destination. A week's stay at a hotel or condominium, including car and round-trip airfare from the West Coast to the island of Oahu, can cost as little as $395 per person. With deals like that, the islands' exotic personality at times seems little more than a memory.

It takes some effort to find the truly enchanted, idyllic side of these South Sea islands, but it can be done. In those special places, the kissing will be as amorous as you ever dreamed possible.

The Islands

The six major islands in the Hawaiian archipelago are prime destinations for remarkably romantic sojourns. Of these, the big four, from
south to north, are the Big Island of Hawaii, renowned for the volcanic
activity of Kilauea; Maui, home to the overdeveloped but exquisite
Kaanapali Coast and growing tourism; the bustling island of Oahu,
where the heavily visited city of Honolulu and perhaps the best-known
beach in the world—Waikiki—can be found; and Kauai, a late bloomer
as a worthy destination, with some additional catching up to do after
the disastrous repercussions of Hurricane Iniki in 1992. Less known
and vastly less developed, the islands of Molokai and Lanai, nestled in
a rain shadow between Oahu and Maui, provide the ultimate in
authentic tropical seclusion; their gentle spirit is evident from the
moment you arrive.

Two other small islands complete the lineup. Nihau, just southwest of Kauai, is privately owned and restricted. Helicopter flights
to isolated parts of the island are offered, but interaction with the
natives is strictly prohibited, and the lack of amenities, expense of
the flight, and minimal local cooperation make it a pricey, joyless
getaway. There is little real reason to go, apart from fascination with
its quarantined status.

The tiny island of Kahoolawe lies slightly southwest of Maui. For
decades, the U.S. Army and Navy used it as a target for testing and
training their bombers and pilots, rendering the land desolate and virtually inhabitable. Efforts are now being made to restore and develop
the island, but how, when, and by whom is unknown at this writing.

How do you choose which island to go to? Each island has its own
personality, amenities, and landscapes. Depending on your tropical preferences, you can find an island that fits your romantic inclinations.
The chapters that follow will help you make a choice. You can settle
on just one destination, selecting a particularly secluded place to stay,
and embrace for your entire visit, or you can just as easily island hop
and experience many different aspects of the Aloha State.

If you haven't been to Hawaii before, your first thought may be to
start on the island of Oahu. Although Oahu has the fewest romantic
possibilities (it's just too crowded), you may still be curious to see this
tourist mecca for yourselves. If you do choose to visit Oahu, we recommend that you go there first. The most popular island, and the most

densely populated, it can be a jarring place to end your vacation after spending time on the comparatively tranquil islands of Kauai, Maui, Lanai, Hawaii (the Big Island), and Molokai. Peace and quiet are not the order of the day (or night) for Honolulu or Waikiki. However, if upscale designer boutiques, abundant nightlife, the excitement of city streets, and chock-full beaches are on your list of romantic amenities, whenever you schedule Oahu will be just fine. If the two of you are searching for a more relaxed, peaceful vacation, away from beach-going masses, head to any of the islands *but* Oahu.

Getting Around

There is easy access between the islands via airplane and, for some of the islands located only a few miles apart, via passenger-only ferry-boats. Three airlines provide all inter-island air service: **HAWAI-IAN AIRLINES**, (800) 367-5320; **ALOHA AIRLINES**, (800) 367-5250; and **ALOHA ISLAND AIR**, (800) 323-3345. Passenger ferry service is available from Maui to Lanai via **EXPEDITIONS**, (808) 661-3756, and from Maui to Molokai via the **MAUI PRINCESS**, (808) 661-8397.

Hawaii's main tourist office, the **HAWAII VISITORS BUREAU**, 2270 Kalakaua Avenue, Suite 801, Honolulu, Oahu, (808) 923-1811, provides information for all the islands. Phone numbers for the Visitors Bureau on a specific island are: the Big Island of Hawaii, (808) 961-5797; Kauai, (808) 245-3971; and Maui, (808) 244-3530. The islands of Molokai and Lanai do not have their own Visitors Bureau, but you can call the main tourist office on Oahu for information.

Rental cars are as much a part of the scenery on Hawaii as palm trees, although infinitely less attractive. Without a car, it is all but impossible to experience the awesome beauty hidden along winding stretches of roads and highways. Once you arrive, you are likely to understand why a rental car is a necessary evil for sightseeing activities that don't involve tours. It is less important to have a car if you plan to stay in Honolulu or near Waikiki, where excellent bus service and taxis are readily available, but even then you may want to consider a one- or two-day rental to take in Oahu's less-developed beaches and less-traveled interior.

There are some great car rental deals to be found, particularly through some of the 100 local rental companies, as opposed to the big national chains such as Hertz, Budget, Alamo Rent-A-Car, National Rent-A-Car, Thrifty, and Avis. However, while booking through a local firm can indeed be a bargain, do not wait until you get here to rent a car, particularly not during high season, when there won't be any available. If you want to compare prices, call a travel agent who can handle it for you or call a few companies on your own, including **TROPICAL**, (800) 678-6000, and **PAYLESS CAR RENTAL**, (800) 345-5230.

◆ **Romantic Suggestion:** Be sure to check whether the property you are staying at offers a package that includes a car. Many of them do.

The Most Romantic Time To Travel

As impossible as it may seem, Hawaii's beautiful weather doesn't really have an off-season. Although we wouldn't encourage anyone to visit during the near-90-degree humid heat of July and August, those months are almost as popular as the Christmas–New Year holiday season (from December 20 through January 4). Actually, families flock to the islands any time school isn't in session. In terms of perfection, perhaps the most idyllic weather conditions are to be found during fall and spring, when the weather is almost always a dry 80 degrees.

Not surprisingly, those sought-after winter dates are not only the most crowded and most expensive period, they are also dead center of the islands' rainy season. But even during this span, you are likely to encounter occasional 68-degree evenings, 75-degree afternoons, and as many sunny days as rainy ones. Conditions on each island can vary. Some sections of the islands are known for their drier conditions and may be preferable during winter. For example, on Maui, Kapalua and Hana are wetter areas in comparison to Wailea, which is more arid; Poipu Beach on Kauai is drier than the Napali Coast; and the east side of Oahu has more rain than the Diamond Head side. Staying in one of those areas doesn't mean you won't see rain during the winter, but it does improve the odds that you'll have the tropical vacation of your dreams instead of a soaking wet nightmare. Or learn to enjoy the rain. Hawaiian winters may not be sunny but they are usually warm, and the sound of the rain against the palm trees is delightful.

◆ **Romantic Note:** High season here runs from mid-December through the end of March. Low season runs from April to mid-December. The difference in hotel prices usually varies from $10 to $20 per night.

Can't We Kiss Anywhere?

You may be skeptical about the idea that one location is more romantic than another, whether it's in Hawaii or your own neighborhood. You might think, "Well, it isn't the setting, it's who you're with that makes a place special." And you'd be right. But aside from the chemistry that exists between the two of you without any help from us, some locations can facilitate and enhance the chemistry, and others can discourage and frustrate the magic in the moment. More so than any other place we've written about, this can be true for Hawaii. Hawaii's burgeoning high-rise development can literally be the other side of Eden. Perhaps the romantic expectations most couples bring to this South Pacific paradise make it all the more disappointing when a tender embrace is marred by screaming kids, slamming car doors, or a noisy exhaust fan under your private balcony. Location isn't everything, but when all the right details are shared by a loving couple, chances are undeniably better for achieving unhindered and rapturous romance.

With that in mind, here is a list of the things that we considered not even remotely romantic: places with garden or mountain views punctuated by the blare of traffic noise; hotels with impressive lobby and pool areas but mediocre rooms (particularly ones with outrageous price tags); crowded beaches; anything overly plastic or overly veneered; noisy restaurants, even if they were very elegant; most tourist spots (particularly those with facilities for tour buses); the latest to-be-seen-in night spots (romance is looking at each other, not at the people sitting across from you); and row after row of overcrowded condominium developments.

◆ **Romantic Note:** In Hawaii, sightseeing possibilities are even more abundant than condos and luaus (and that's saying something). We have highlighted the best (and worst) excursions for each island. When it comes to outdoor tours involving the water or gloriously scenic sights, it is difficult to make a mistake. The only negative may be the crowds; the water and the vistas will be just as you envisioned— ecstatically awesome. Cultural centers and museums offer a colorful, insightful perspective on life in Hawaii throughout the generations. Take advantage of these whenever you can. Although they can often feel like tourist traps, the information they offer is intriguing and thought provoking.

You Call This Research?

This book is the product of earnest interviews and careful investigation by our staff, but we have also included feedback from readers. Although it would have been nice, and from our viewpoint even preferable, kissing was not the major research method used for selecting the locations listed in this book. (And you thought this was the hottest job in town, didn't you?) If smooching had been the determining factor, several inescapable problems would have developed. First, be assured, we would still be "researching," and this book would be just a good idea, some breathless moments, random notes, overused credit cards, and nothing more. Also, depending on the mood of the moment, many kisses might have occurred in places that do not meet the requirements of this travel guide (which would have been fun, but not productive). Thus, for both practical and physical reasons, more objective criteria had to be established.

How could we be certain that a particular place was good for kissing if we did not indulge in such an activity at every location? The honest, though boring, answer is that we used our reporters' instincts to evaluate the magnetic pull of each place visited. Standard criteria of cleanliness, beauty, hospitality, architecture, comfort, quality, uniqueness, and professionalism were the most important considerations. Then, if during our visit we felt a longing for our special someone to share our discovery, we considered that longing to be as reliable as a thorough kissing evaluation.

In the final analysis, we can guarantee that if you choose to go to any of the places listed, you will find a beautiful setting, heart-stirring ambience, some amount of privacy, and the best accommodations the islands have to offer. What you do there romantically is up to you and your partner.

Romantic Warnings

Candid, genuine reviews are the hallmark of *The Best Places To Kiss* series. We understand how disappointment can affect your ability to pucker up. Even the best places can have drawbacks or failings that you need to know about. That is why we have incorporated "Romantic Warnings." Sometimes an exquisite bed and breakfast fronts a busy intersection, or an outstanding restaurant may be cursed with a belligerent wait staff. Whatever it is that might affect your interlude together, we want you to be prepared in advance. Our reviews don't always please the proprietors of the places we've included, but we are dedicated to our readers first and foremost.

On that note, we cannot emphasize the following point enough: **Many of the brochures and ads for the various hotels, resorts, and restaurants in Hawaii make them look infinitely better than they are in reality.** After reading scintillating descriptions and seeing enticing pictures, we were often shocked (as many unsuspecting tourists have been) when we arrived and none of it was evident in even the tiniest corner of the grounds or building.

Another problem we ran into repeatedly is the fact that on the islands, smoking and nonsmoking sections seem to run into one another. Because most restaurants are open-air and the trade winds are almost constant, it is hard to contain the smoke in one area. Even in hotel rooms this can be a problem, because if you leave the doors to your lanai open to enjoy the sounds of the ocean, you might end up with smoky smells that are definitely not coming from the sea. In hotels, one way to avoid this problem is to request a smoke-free room and ask whether that whole section of the hotel is smoke-free.

Romance Ratings

The three major factors we used to determine whether a place would be included were:

1. **Surrounding splendor**
2. **Privacy**
3. **Tug-at-your-heartstrings ambience**

Of the three determining factors, "surrounding splendor" and "privacy" are fairly self-explanatory. "Tug-at-your-heartstrings ambience" can probably use some clarification. Ambience, by our definition, is not limited to clean hotel rooms or tables decorated with white tablecloths and nicely folded linen napkins. Added to all that there must be a certain plushness and spaciousness, plus other engaging features that encourage intimacy and allow for affectionate discussions. For the most part, ambience was rated according to degree of comfort and number of gracious appointments, as opposed to image and frills.

If a place had all three of the qualities listed above, its inclusion was automatic. If one or two of the criteria were weak or nonexistent, the other feature(s) had to be really incredible before the place could be recommended. For example, if a breathtakingly beautiful viewpoint was situated in an area inundated with tourists and families on vacation, the place would not normally be included. However, if a fabulous hotel was beset with scores of other guests, it was included if, and only if, its interior was so wonderfully inviting and regal that the other guests no longer seemed to matter.

◆ **Romantic Note:** Hawaii is inherently romantic, but it is also a unique tourist destination. Often we found majestic scenery and sensual beaches surrounded by condominium developments and overrun by substantial crowds, or stayed at stupendous resort hotels with 500 rooms—not exactly intimate or private by anyone's standards. Our basic guideline for selecting a specific place has always been to search out smaller, more intimate, and out-of-the-mainstream spots, particularly when it comes to accommodations. Hawaii caused us to rethink our usual modus operandi. We were in a predicament: should we ignore a magnificent setting because of its current popularity or a luxurious hotel because of its size, or should we adapt our standards to the unique attributes of the Hawaiian Islands? We decided on the latter, and consequently you will read many entries that sound something like "There are too many people for this to be truly romantic, but . . ." or "This is too large to be genuinely intimate, but . . ."

Kiss Ratings

If you've flipped through this book and noticed the miniature lips that accompany each entry, you're probably curious about what they represent. Most other travel guides use stars or other symbols to rank the places they write about; for obvious reasons, we have chosen lips. The rating system notwithstanding, all the places listed in this book are special places to be; all of them have heart-pleasing qualities and are worthwhile places to visit. The tiny lips indicate only our personal preferences and the grandness of a spot. They are a way of indicating just how delightfully romantic we found a place to be and how pleased we were with the service and environment during our stay. The number of lips awarded each location indicate the following:

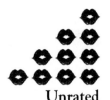

Romantic possibilities with several warnings.
Can be counted on for a satisfying experience.
Very desirable.
Simply sublime.

Unrated Not open at the time this edition went to press, but looks promising.

Cost Ratings

We have also included ratings to help you determine whether your lips can afford to kiss in a particular restaurant, hotel, or bed and breakfast (many of the outdoor places are free or charge a minimal fee for parking and entrance). The price for overnight accommodations is always based on double occupancy (otherwise there wouldn't be anyone to kiss). Eating establishment prices are based on a full dinner for two (appetizer, entrée, and dessert), excluding liquor, unless otherwise indicated. Because prices and business hours change, it is always advisable to call ahead so that your hearts and lips will not end up disappointed.

Most of the accommodations listed in this book have an extensive and diverse price list for their rooms, based mostly on the view and the time of year (high season is from mid-December through the end of March; low season is from April to mid-December.) Our cost ratings include both the lowest and the highest prices available regardless of the season, and are based on a property's published rates. They do not take into account special promotion packages or available upgrades. If you are traveling any time other than high season, you may want to consider booking the least expensive room and asking for an upgrade when you arrive. Most hotels and some condominium rental properties will be pleased to do that for you. (Although it never hurts to ask, upgrading between December 20 and January 15 is virtually impossible.)

♦ **Romantic Suggestion:** It takes an assertive tourist to locate special packages or upgrades, but it definitely beats paying the overpriced published (or "rack") rate.

Lodging Ratings

Inexpensive	$125 or less
Moderate	$130 to $175
Expensive	$180 to $225
Very Expensive	$230 to $350
Unbelievably Expensive	$350 and up

Restaurant Ratings

Inexpensive .... Under $25
Moderate .... $25 to $50
Expensive .... $50 to $80
Very Expensive.. $80 to $110
Unbelievably Expensive .... $110 and up

◆ **Romantic Warning:** Our cost ratings do not include the price that some hotels charge to park your rental car for you. If free self-parking is not available, you may get stuck paying up to $13 per day for your car to be valet parked. When booking your reservation, ask if parking is included in the daily rate for your room and if a parking lot is provided where guests can park for themselves. This way you won't be surprised by an accumulation of daily charges.

Romance in a Condominium

The number of condominiums available for rent in Hawaii is nothing less than staggering. Reviewing these properties was literally an overwhelming, albeit necessary, task. There are great advantages to staying in a condominium complex: they are generally much less expensive than the larger resort hotels; there are no extra costs such as service people to tip, phone surcharges, or pricey mini-bar treats; and they often have hotel-style front desk check-in and service. Condominiums also offer more space, fully equipped kitchens where meals can be cooked (saving the cost of repeatedly eating out), and separate dining and living room areas.

What are the negatives? Other than the lack of porters and concierges, there are very few. Of course, not all condominium complexes are created equal. Some pile people on top of each other like sardines, while others have no air-conditioning—a definite drawback on hot, breezeless nights. They tell you that the trade winds cool things off, but we can assure you it isn't always so. Another drawback can be that, for the sake of saving money, families tend to stay in condominiums, which means that the grounds and pool area may not be all that serene because of children playing. Also, because the condominiums in rental pools are privately owned, the furnishings in the individual units can vary drastically, from luxurious to absolutely tacky.

The best prices for a condominium stay are to be found on Oahu ($80 to $100 and up a night), while Maui condo rentals can start at

$120 for just average properties. We've done most of the research for you, but if you purchased a travel package and the property you have been given is not listed in this book, be sure to stipulate categorically the type of unit you want or don't want and *get it in writing*. Do not risk a spoiled vacation by finding yourselves with unsatisfactory accommodations.

Ask the following questions when attempting to rent a condominium:

♦ Is it near a main road, and if so, can traffic noise be heard?

♦ How far is it from the airport?

♦ How far *exactly* is the nearest beach, and is it safe for swimming and snorkeling?

♦ If the unit has a view, how much view is there?

♦ Does anything obstruct the view, and if so, what?

♦ What size beds are provided?

♦ How far is the property from any activity or amenity you are personally interested in, such as golf, nightlife, restaurants, an accessible jogging path, or grocery stores?

♦ Is maid service provided?

♦ Is air-conditioning and/or a phone provided?

♦ Is a rental car part of the package?

♦ **Romantic Note:** Speaking of condominiums, at some point during your visit in Hawaii you are very likely to receive a sales pitch from a time-share salesperson. In exchange for sitting through a presentation, you will be offered a free rental car for one day, a dinner sail, a visit to a wax museum, or some other attraction (many of which are not very romantic or even very interesting). There is a great deal of consumer information about time-shares you should know before you deal with a provocative sales performance (and these people are pros). Do your homework before you inadvertently get involved with something you may be better off resisting.

Romance in a Bed and Breakfast, Hawaii-Style

Professionally run bed and breakfasts are hard to find in Hawaii. It's not that they don't exist, it's just that the vast majority of them are represented exclusively by bed-and-breakfast agencies, and these companies don't make it easy for travel writers (they are very protective, and dislike giving out names and numbers without a booking). Also, licensing is very complicated and political, so a vast number of

bed and breakfasts are run illegally. Additionally, most bed and breakfasts don't advertise, and only a handful are listed in the phone book.
That means we often couldn't scope out a property before booking.
But booking and then assessing is a highly inefficient way to weed
through literally hundreds of bed and breakfasts. Usually we seek out
potential candidates, eliminate all but the best, and then book before
we do a final review for inclusion. Given the number of establishments, with descriptions that often sound infinitely better than they
actually are, it can take an amazing amount of time to distinguish
between the merely ordinary and the truly superb when staying is the
only way to discover that.

Bed and breakfast Hawaii-style is more informal (and vastly less
expensive) than what you may be used to in, say, Northern California
or New England. Many of the hosts work at other jobs, have families, or are retired, and it can feel more like a home stay with a
relative than anything else. But a wide variety of accommodations
are available—everything from separate cottages to apartments
located on your own floor of an oceanfront home. We did our best
to uncover as many of the more professionally run, comfortable,
and plush places as we could. Given the limited number we've
included, if you prefer bed-and-breakfast accommodations (something we wholeheartedly endorse), using a local agency is the best
way to go. Be specific about your requirements, expectations, and
needs, and get everything *in writing*. Your lips (and pocketbooks)
will be eternally thankful if you do.

◆ **Romantic Note:** The only bed-and-breakfast agency we found with
consistently high standards for the properties it chooses to represent was
HAWAII'S BEST BED AND BREAKFASTS, (808) 885-0550, (800)
262-9912 (from the mainland). Their office is located on the Big Island,
but they handle properties all over the state.

A Room With a View

Incredibly sensual views abound in Hawaii, and the very thought
of its rocky cliffs, sun-drenched beaches, and opalescent blue ocean
can be enough to fill your heads and hearts with anticipation even
before you start packing. Most people go to Hawaii with the expecta-
tion of seeing as much of these spectacles as possible. It isn't surprising
to discover that the better the view and the proximity to the water, the

steeper the price tag for your room. Most hotels add sizable price incre-
ments as the view improves from a peekaboo glimpse of the Pacific to
the most coveted prize, an unobstructed, full frontal vista of the rolling
surf. Be aware that sometimes an expensive ocean view is visible only
through thick foliage, way off in the distance, or over a massive rooftop, or may be glimpsed from a window or lanai above a noisy pool.
When you ask for a specific room or certain features, make your request
and get an answer *in writing.* Do not settle for the words "ocean view"
on your confirmation. There is a lot of leeway in that description, and
that could set you up for a burn that isn't from the sun.

Is a room with a view necessary? That depends primarily on your
budget. Many lovely properties that have minimal water views or magnificent mountain views (sans cars) and a beach nearby are wonderful
places to stay. But it would be misleading to say that waking to the
sound of the waves surging against the shore and a view of the endless
oceans isn't more romantic and breathtaking, because it is. Balancing
the quality of various accommodations against view and beach accessi-
bility was a major factor in all our lodging reviews.

◆ **Romantic Warning:** Expensive doesn't always mean most desirable, and hotel properties with well-known names can have their drawbacks, such as a mountain or garden view highlighted by a well-trafficked
street or parking lot, or rooms in need of renovation. Read our recommendations carefully; sometimes reputations die hard, which can make
for some lackluster kissing places.

Love Among the Golf Courses

Almost as big a draw as the beaches and exquisite scenery are the
assortment of world-class golf courses in Hawaii. Set on hillsides, bor-
dering the ocean, wrapped around premier resort properties, these links
make the islands a golfer's utopia. Golf tournaments abound, golf carts
circle about in the distance, and you are as likely to overhear conversa-
tions discussing the layout of a course and the great shots of the day as
praise for the beautiful beaches. This book is not about golfing, but we
would be remiss not to mention this attraction for affectionate couples
who together or separately may want to go for one or more under par.
All of the islands have several excellent courses to choose from, and
the more popular ones are listed for each individual island or town

area. Even if you are not fond of golf, these courses are so magnificent that you may find yourself drawn to this sport that has so many island visitors so firmly under its spell.

To Luau or Not To Luau?

More luaus take place on the Hawaiian Islands today than ever took place in all of the islands' combined pre-statehood history. Every major hotel and even some minor ones as well as large and small restaurants host luaus on a nightly basis. There are even special restaurants with incredible outside settings dedicated only to luaus. No matter which one(s) you choose to attend (and we mention a couple of possibilities), you will behold a totally contrived, artificial reenactment of a once time-honored Hawaiian ritual. The rampant commercialization of this tradition has dashed whatever authenticity might have existed. Although we recommend avoiding luaus, the lure to attend at least one will be hard to resist. So if you're in the mood, go anyway, although one should be plenty. You will find the dancing colorful enough, and the music can be quite entertaining (performance quality varies greatly). The traditional *kalua* pig (a whole pig cooked in an *imu*, or underground pit) is often very good, but you don't get very much of it because there usually isn't enough to go around. The dinner is served buffet-style, which means a large crowd lining up at the same time for usually mediocre food (including coleslaw, potato salad, overly sweet punch, and standard white cake with coconut frosting). It isn't very Hawaiian, but it's not all that easy to find the *real* Hawaii anymore.

The Lei of the Land

Many package deals include a lei greeting at the airport, and although it is a wonderful welcome, a lei is most appreciated when given by one loved one to another. The custom of presenting a sweetly scented garland of tropical flowers is one of Hawaii's most endearing expressions of aloha. The tradition is said to have begun when the earliest explorers brought flowering plants, to be used for adornment, along with their food supplies, but that may not be the whole story. It seems that during a USO show that took place in Honolulu during World War II, a female singer, prodded to kiss an enlisted man, gave him a lei and a kiss on the cheek, announcing this to be an old Hawaiian custom. That was enough to popularize the tradition.

Since then, the creation of leis has become quite an art form. Leis can be made from simple plumeria blossoms, beautifully woven jasmine flowers, trailing vines, sweet-smelling pikake, or rare (and very expensive) niihau shells. Except for the intricate, multistrand niihau shell leis that can cost thousands of dollars, leis are available almost everywhere on all the islands (we even saw them at convenience stores), at prices ranging from $3 to $30. Downtown Honolulu's Chinatown has the greatest profusion of lei shops, some of which have been family owned and operated for many generations.

Surf's Up

Please read this section carefully together. Water safety can never be emphasized too much. Just ask any hospital emergency room staffer in Hawaii about respect for the power of the ocean. The water beckons with a siren's call that cannot be ignored, and the desire to rush hand-in-hand into the surf will be intense, absolute, and easy to do with nary a wince or shrug: after all, the water temperature is an optimal 75 to 80 degrees year-round. But the brilliant blue of the water can mask the turbulence and force of the surf and tides. Although the ocean may appear calm or flat when you enter, moments later you are likely to confront a crashing set of waves that can tumble you out of control back onto the beach. The following are specific guidelines to consider whenever you are tempted to re-create that beach scene in *From Here To Eternity*:

- ◆ Waves come in sets, and even though all you presently see are small waves, bigger ones may be on the way.
- ◆ Never turn your back on the ocean. Watch for what is coming your way.
- ◆ If you do encounter a breaking wave, do not try to outswim it or ride it ashore. Your best option is to duck or dive under it. The waves pass over you rather quickly, but be ready: the next one is on its way.
- ◆ Remember that tidal undertow can pull you farther out than you want to go.
- ◆ Never swim alone (besides, alone isn't romantic).
- ◆ If you can't swim, do not play in high, rolling waves. At first the water may seem only knee-deep, but it can become 15 feet deep in the blink of an eye.

◆ Distances over water can be deceiving. Judge your endurance conservatively.

◆ Do not step barefoot on coral reefs (coral cuts are painful and can become infected) or on rocky ground where sea urchins and eel bites are prevalent.

◆ It is best to watch surfers from high ground. Avoid being in the water at the same time with a group of surfers if you are not savvy to surfer etiquette. You can easily get hit by a surfer or a runaway surfboard.

◆ There are sharks in these waters, but they prefer fish to humans. Shark attacks are infrequent and rarely result in a fatality. If you do see a shark, do not panic; swim quietly away, get out of the water, and tell a lifeguard of your sighting.

◆ **Romantic Note:** When you are snorkeling, the temptation to remove some of the sea's alluring natural gifts can be hard to resist, but be strong and keep your hands off. The ocean is not a gift shop, and what you remove is not easily replaced. Be respectful of nature's wonders and leave them there for the next couple to enjoy.

◆ **Second Romantic Note:** The beaches in Hawaii are some of the most spectacular in the world. They are often somewhat difficult to reach around the massive hotel properties and private homes here, but they are accessible. Remember, *all beaches in Hawaii are public*. No beach can be privately owned; they are all available for use by everyone. Signs may not be visible or might not exist at all, but that doesn't mean you can't use the beach.

Whale Watching

If you have always secretly longed to witness first-hand the passage of whales on their yearly migration to warmer waters (where the humpback whales give birth to their young), the Hawaiian Islands are a great place to live out your fantasy. December to April is the best time to witness this odyssey, particularly when the weather conditions are clear and sunny. Be sure to start your search early, about the time when the sun is radiantly warming the cooler morning air. As you stand at the edge of the shore, scanning the Pacific realm, you will have a tremendous view of the open waters. Find a comfortable sandy spot or grassy knoll, snuggle close together, and be patient. This performance is intermittent at best and requires careful observation and diligence. But be prepared for an amazing encounter.

Imagine the scene. You are slowly studying the calm, azure waters. Suddenly, in the distance, breaking the still of a silent, sun-drenched Hawaiian winter morning, a spout of bursting water explodes from the surface. A giant, arched black profile stands out boldly against the blue sea, followed by an abrupt tail slap and then stillness once more. It's hard to explain the romance of that moment, but romantic it is. Perhaps it's the excitement of seeing such an immense creature gliding effortlessly through the water with playful agility and ease. Or perhaps it's the chance to celebrate a part of nature's mysterious aquatic underworld together. Whatever it is, discover it for yourselves if you have the chance.

◆ **Romantic Note:** There are good whale-watching spots on many of the islands, but the southern shores of Maui are particularly prime. Boat excursions can take you out for more intimate viewing from all the islands. On Maui, the most enlightening whale-watching cruises are sponsored by the **PACIFIC WHALE WATCHING FOUNDATION**, (808) 879-8811, (800) WHALE-11, with daily departures from Maalaea Harbor and Lahaina Harbor. The guides are authorities from the foundation, and they fill the two-and-a-half-hour expedition with everything you ever wanted to know about whales and more. Prices start at $30 per person for a two-hour trip.

Sunscreen: Don't Leave Home Without It

Nothing can destroy a romantic holiday or your ability to kiss faster than a sunburn, and the Hawaiian sun can burn fast and furiously. If you pack nothing else, you must pack a sunscreen with an SPF (sun protection factor) of at least 12 to 15. It doesn't have to be expensive as long as it has a high SPF rating. (Because of FDA regulations, all sunscreens protect from the sun equally based on the SPF number.) For total protection from both UVA and UVB rays (broad spectrum protection), you may want to consider a nonchemical sunscreen. Not only do these new sunscreens provide more protection, they are also virtually irritant-free (no more burning eyes). Look for the words "chemical free" or "nonchemical" on the label if you are interested in this type of protection.

Be sure to apply sunscreen at least 20 minutes before you go out in the sun. You can get burned just in the time it takes to walk from your car to the beach and spread out your blanket. Apply sunscreen evenly and generously, covering every inch of exposed skin. Don't forget the tops of your feet, thin hair spots, the hairline, where your hair parts, ears, and eyelids. It is also essential to reapply sunscreen after you swim or exercise. Try to purchase a sunscreen before your departure: the hotels and stores in Hawaii charge a hefty fee in comparison to what you would pay in a drugstore on the mainland.

What To Pack

As many times as we've been to Hawaii, we still engage in a never-ending discussion about what we should and shouldn't pack. It seems self-evident, yet it is of great concern given the variety of experiences and attractions available and the inevitable heat. Obviously a lot depends on your itinerary, but we offer some basic suggestions to help lighten your luggage.

Be assured that shorts and a short-sleeved shirt of any kind are acceptable at 99 percent of the places you will visit. Even tank tops for both women and men are fine in most casual restaurants and shops. We were often surprised at what is considered acceptable. These islands have an amazingly nonchalant, laid-back temperament. However, the dress code does change when you go out for a posh evening of dining and dancing. Many of the finer restaurants require women to wear nice resort wear and men to wear jackets. But don't worry about bringing a jacket along—almost all of the fancier restaurants have jackets you can borrow while you dine, and some are much less strict than their policy implies. If you choose to attend a luau or other evening entertainment, the dress depends on the type of place. The fancier the venue, the more clothes you have to wear.

During the winter months, nights can get a bit on the cool side. For Hawaii that means in the low 70s or high 60s. A lightweight cotton sweater or jacket is all you should need to ward off the slight evening chill. Cotton slacks are also a good idea on those occasions. As far as footwear goes, given the varied number of hiking trails available and your own level of endurance, good hiking boots can be an asset, particularly on the island of Kauai.

◆ **Romantic Note:** We always pack our own snorkels, fins, and beach towels so we can indulge our urge for the surf at a moment's notice without worrying about rentals. But don't be concerned if you don't have your own; there are plenty of rental places all over the islands (prices range from $5 to $10 per day).

Getting Married in Hawaii

One of the most auspicious times to kiss is the moment after wedding vows have been exchanged. Locations for your wedding can vary from a lush garden perched at the ocean's edge to a specially built chapel at an elegant beachfront hotel to a private suite in an exclusive condominium. As an added service to those of you in the midst of prenuptial arrangements, we have provided brief wedding information. Right after the cost ratings we've indicated whether a place offers wedding facilities and how many people can be accommodated. For more specific information about which facilities and services are offered and the cost, please call the establishments directly. They should be able to provide you with menus, prices, and all the details needed to make your wedding day as spectacular as you have ever imagined.

Many of the more notable island hotels increasingly specialize in weddings and renewals of vows, and some of them handle more than 60 weddings a month. These noteworthy packages are gaining popularity because the hotels make it so easy for you, and they can be surprisingly affordable. Some resorts have romance directors or wedding organizers whose sole job is attending to the details of your nuptials, no matter how simple or complex the event. If you do decide to utilize the exotic surroundings of Hawaii for one of the most romantic interludes of your life, there are plenty of options available. Simply choose a hotel from the listings that follow, ask for their wedding or romance planner, and tell them your budget. They'll take it from there; you just need to bring the wedding dress, the tux, and the rings. It really is that simple.

◆ **Romantic Suggestion:** For a free wedding brochure with information about getting married in Hawaii, write to the **HAWAII VISITORS BUREAU**, 2270 Kalakaua Avenue, Suite 801, Honolulu, HI 96815, or call (808) 923-1811.

A Brief History

Beginning about A.D. 1200, when the first Polynesian settlers (believed to be Tahitian) arrived on these islands, and culminating in the multibillion-dollar tourist industry of today, Hawaii's history is a fascinating and spellbinding saga. Because of Hawaii's geographic location and exotic tumultuous past, its identity and culture are distinctly different from the mainland's, but Hawaii was associated with the United States long before it became the 50th state in 1959.

Although the islands are often characterized as a peaceful, untroubled corner of the world before missionaries and colonists came bringing sickness, Western religion, and capitalism, that is not a totally accurate or complete depiction. Before the European discovery of these islands by Captain Cook in 1788, the tribes here were continually at war, vying for position and dominance; human sacrifice was a customary religious practice; and there was a caste system (*kapu*) in place that made life miserable for some and luxurious for others.

It wasn't until the arrival of Western civilization that human sacrifice was stopped, the *kapu* system was eliminated, and the population was educated. However, Western civilization also changed the unspoiled glory of the land forever, bringing intense foreign commerce through whaling in the 1840s, agriculture in the form of sugar and pineapple plantations in the 1850s and 1860s, and the elaborate and virtually overflowing tourist industry of the present.

Perhaps the most notorious and controversial interaction between the United States and Hawaii occurred in 1893, when Queen Liliokalani, after trying to reinstate her rightful control over the islands, was overthrown by American Republican forces in Honolulu. Seven years later Hawaii became a territory of the United States, and the monarchy was officially defunct.

Over the past 20 years the plantation fields of pineapple and sugarcane have slowly lost their financial productivity and been superseded by high-rise hotels and condominiums. Almost all of the local population to one degree or another, directly or indirectly, works for the massive tourist industry.

From ancient Polynesians crossing the oceans more than 800 years ago to the jam-packed streets of Waikiki today, there is much to discover regarding the history of Hawaii. We encourage you to take the time to delve more into this remarkable chronicle. It would be a shame to come all this way and not find the real Hawaii, because it does exist—not on the beaches or at tourist attractions, but in the history books.

Oahu

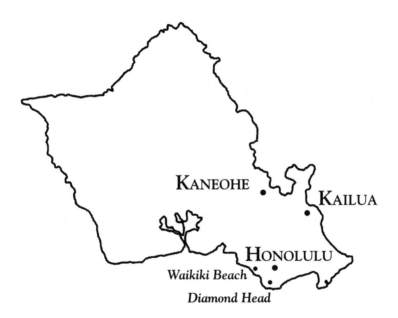

KANEOHE

KAILUA

HONOLULU

Waikiki Beach

Diamond Head

*"Her lips on his could tell him better
than all her stumbling words."*
Margaret Mitchell

OAHU

Eighty percent of Hawaii's population calls Oahu home, with most of the population concentrated in Honolulu, primarily encompassing Waikiki Beach. Waikiki, with its white sandy beaches, busy streets, and immense high-rise hotels, its numerous shopping centers dotted with designer boutiques, its myriad restaurants and clubs, is certainly where the action is, but visitors who concentrate their energy and time only in this vicinity are missing out. Decidedly an island of contrasts, Oahu offers as much tropical beauty as the less populous islands, and much, much more.

You can escape the crowds to some degree by heading east to **DIAMOND HEAD**, where the hotels thin out and elite residential areas are the rule. The sandy beaches here are gorgeous (one is even called **SANDY BEACH**) but popular with local surfers, so this isn't the spot if you want a lot of privacy. Nevertheless, it is definitely less crowded than Waikiki, which can be a considerable kissing advantage.

Sunsets on the northwest shore are extraordinarily majestic. You can park your car and walk along any number of astonishingly beautiful beaches; **SUNSET BEACH** and **WAIMEA BEACH** are particularly stupendous. These areas are also celebrated surfing spots, with awesome thundering waves, and no crowds. Farther south, near **KAENA POINT STATE PARK**, glorious scenery abounds, and a formidable surf crashes against rocks interspersed with patches of sand. Although this part of Oahu is primarily residential and undeveloped (sans hotels and condominiums), much of it is run-down, with communes of makeshift houses scattered along the coast.

Head due north for a beautiful drive between the **WAINAE AND KOOLAU MOUNTAIN RANGES**, rising imperially on either side of you. An expansive series of residential neighborhoods lines the north shore, which means the beach is obscured by homes. But remember, *all* of the beaches on *all* of the island are public (even if they look private), so keep your eyes open for access paths. You are more likely to find an empty stretch of beach in this area than almost anywhere else on Oahu. Even if you don't, you are guaranteed to find fewer crowds than you would in Waikiki.

Popular locations such as 1,800-acre **WAIMEA FALLS PARK**, (808) 638-8511, and the **POLYNESIAN CULTURAL CENTER**,

(808) 293-3333, make interesting day trips and provide entertaining insights into the history of the Polynesian people, but be ready for busloads of people and a theme-park atmosphere. Crowds of tourists flock to these places every day, so while they may be fun and educational, they are of little to no romantic interest.

◆ **Romantic Note:** Although we don't often recommend tourist attractions, we do urge you to take the time to see the **ARIZONA MEMORIAL**. Poignant and affecting, it is dedicated to the U.S. military lives lost during World War II's Pearl Harbor attack.

◆ **Romantic Warning:** As with any city anywhere in the world, even a city in paradise, you must be careful to never leave any valuables in your rental car. Enough said.

West Oahu

While much of Oahu has been heavily developed, the west coast has barely been touched and retains much of its pristine natural beauty. Developers intend to create an upscale resort atmosphere here, one that is much more reserved (and hopefully less paved and concrete) than Waikiki. At this point there is only one place to stay, but that surely will change. Regardless of where you stay, the beaches and sights are worth a day trip, not only to see the island's varying landscape of volcanic shores and drier hillsides, but to escape the city life of Waikiki. If you're really lucky, you may even spot a pod of spinner dolphins offshore as you drive up the Farrington Highway (Highway 930).

Kapolei

Hotel/Bed and Breakfast Kissing

IHILANI RESORT AND SPA, Kapolei   ❤ ❤ ❤ ❤
Ko Olina Resort, 92-1001 Olani Street
(808) 679-0079, (800) 626-4446
Very Expensive to Unbelievably Expensive and Beyond
Wedding facilities are available for a maximum of 600 people.

From westbound H-1, take the Ko Olina exit, which leads directly to the main entrance of Ko Olina Resort. The guard on duty will direct you to Ihilani.

The Ihilani Resort and Spa's location might be too far from city lights and liveliness for some (it's about 30 minutes outside of Waikiki), but if privacy and calm are part of your romantic agenda, this exclusive getaway is made for you. As the first of three intended hotels on the 642-acre Ko Olina Resort, Ihilani stands alone, with a tranquil lagoon on one side and the crashing Pacific on the other.

No expense was spared in the 387 sophisticated rooms, and the effect is stunning. From the generous lanais to the high-tech electronic systems to the spacious marble bathrooms, you won't be disappointed. Plush bedspreads, teak furnishings, and soft taupes or pale greens complement each room. The majority of the rooms are ocean-front (facing the crystal-clear lagoon and the lovely swimming pool) or ocean-view (facing the open ocean). Views from both sides are remarkable, but if you're hoping to savor as many amazing Hawaiian sunsets as possible, request an ocean-view room. For those who can afford to splurge (and we mean *really* splurge), the luxury suites are the way to go—each is wonderfully opulent, and several have whirlpool tubs and outdoor Jacuzzis.

Little gifts from the **IHILANI SPA**, such as a soothing foot gel, are left on your pillow each night with turn-down service. The 35,000-square-foot spa has six tennis courts, a fitness center outfitted with the latest equipment, a lap pool, and enough therapeutic treatments and services to make you feel totally pampered. Finally, we must mention the one-and-a-half-mile-long beach walk that begins just beyond the hotel's pool. If you time your stroll properly, you can begin walking early in the evening and catch the sun dropping into the ocean as you head back to your sweet oasis.

◆ **Romantic Note:** The hotel's fairly casual, poolside **NAUPAKA RESTAURANT** is great for breakfast or lunch, but save room for dinner. **AZUL** (reviewed in "Restaurant Kissing") is one of the best fine dining experiences on Oahu.

Feedback from readers is one of the ways we find out if an establishment is living up to its lip rating. Please send us your comments; a "Kiss and Tell" form is provided at the end of this book.

Restaurant Kissing

AZUL, Kapolei   ❖ ❖ ❖ ❖
Ko Olina Resort, 92-1001 Olani Street, at the Ihilani Resort and Spa
(808) 679-0079, (800) 626-4446
Very Expensive

From westbound H-1, take the Ko Olina exit, which leads directly to the main
entrance of Ko Olina Resort. The guard on duty will direct you to Ihilani.

We considered ordering a whole grilled Maine lobster the night we
dined at Azul, but this is not the kind of place where you'd feel comfortable using your fingers or making a mess of your napkin. Genteel
and elegant, Azul has mastered the art of refined dining, with the
emphasis on refined. Soft-hued murals depicting Mediterranean sea-
scapes enrich the dimly lit, handsome dining room, accented with dark
wood and choice white linens. Exceedingly proper, attentive waiters
address you by name and cater to your every need over the course of
the long, savory, multicourse meal. All entrées include appealing Mediterranean starters, such as seafood risotto with saffron. The innovative
menu varies nightly, with tantalizing items like sautéed jumbo tiger
prawns with crispy risotto in a light tomato or garlic cream, and island
chicken with eggplant and smoked mozzarella served on a light cream
of white truffle, butter, and porcini mushrooms. Take the time to linger
over dessert and coffee; like everything else here, they are superb.

Honolulu/Waikiki

In the south-shore area of Waikiki, they really did "pave paradise
and put up a parking lot." All of this development services millions of
tourists a year who want some semblance of tropical bliss without for-
going convenience and the excitement a big city can provide. Nearly
perfect year-round temperatures and the famous beach at Waikiki, with
its vast aqua blue shallow waters and silky ivory sand, are what draw
masses of people here. But Waikiki is so densely covered with tourists
(about 80,000 daily) that it isn't really most people's idea of paradise
anymore. Actually, kissing on the beach at Waikiki can be problem-
atic—if you close your eyes for a moment and move ever so slightly,

you may end up kissing someone you don't know. On a warm day, the shoulder-to-shoulder lineup of bodies is staggering. However, at night, when the crowds are across the street shopping at the endless prom-enade of stores and markets or sampling the varied nightlife offerings, this warm and exquisite beach is virtually private.

The **INTERNATIONAL MARKETPLACE** is one of the most popular places to shop on the Waikiki strip. You are likely to get good deals on just about anything, but you'll also be cornered by deter-mined salespeople. A more relaxed shopping area (if such a thing exists) is the **ALOHA TOWER MARKETPLACE**, just a couple of miles west of there. This open-air shopping center features designer boutiques, art galleries, casual eateries, and a more leisurely pace. Parking can be tricky and expensive, but a trolley runs back and forth from the central part of Waikiki for only $1 each way.

Hotel/Bed and Breakfast Kissing

ASTON WAIKIKI BEACH TOWER, Waikiki
2470 Kalakaua Avenue
(808) 926-6400, (800) 922-7866 (mainland)
Very Expensive to Unbelievably Expensive
Wedding facilities are available for a maximum of 30 people.

On Kalakaua Avenue at Liliuokalani Avenue.

Exotic white flowers cover an enclosed, trellised walkway, drawing you into this small but lovely hotel set just across the street from Waikiki Beach. It's easy to bypass this diamond in the rough, hidden among the sky-rise hotels on busy Kalakaua Avenue. Koa wood, hand-painted Asian antiques, a beautifully detailed mural, and bouquets of tropical flowers adorn the handsome lobby. All are telltale signs of the comfort that awaits you in the upstairs guest rooms. Each floor houses four suites, which makes the hotel feel unusually intimate. Best of all, these suites are exceptionally spacious, appointed with modern furnishings and pretty pastel color schemes. Sizable lanais open to views of the ocean, and full (albeit dated) kitchens and stocked wet bars add to your com-fort. Most of the simple but attractively furnished bedrooms also enjoy an ocean view, which improves the higher up you go. If you can tear yourselves away from the view, sneak downstairs to splash each other in the small, heated outdoor pool or the whirlpool tub. And don't worry about crowds: this is one of the best-kept secrets in this part of town.

◆ **Romantic Note:** Parking for registered guests is free of charge, a rarity in Waikiki, and a definite romantic plus.

ASTON WAIKIKI BEACHSIDE HOTEL, Waikiki   ◖◗ ◖◗ ◖◗
2452 Kalakaua Avenue
(808) 931-2100, (800)922-7866 (mainland)
Moderate to Very Expensive

On Kalakaua Avenue, between Uluniu and Liliuokalani avenues.

In many ways this is one of the most unusual hotel properties on Oahu, or on any of the Hawaiian Islands, and it is a welcome change of pace. As you leave busy Kalakaua Avenue and venture into the elegant marble lobby filled with carefully chosen antiques, you seem to enter an entirely different world. Only 79 rooms (most on the small side) fill this boutique hotel. Intimate and cozy, each room features European and Asian detailing, pastel peach fabrics and walls, hand-painted Oriental screens, plush furnishings, attractive marble baths, and twice-daily maid service. A complimentary continental breakfast is served in the hotel's small but charming parlor area, and special touches like candles and champagne waiting in the room can be arranged in advance for honeymooners (or for anyone, for that matter).

Overall, the ambience is refined, and you won't miss the overbearing, impersonal atmosphere found in the countless other hotels that line the Waikiki strip.

◆ **Romantic Note:** Since the hotel is set directly across the street from the beach, ocean-view rooms are preferred. The other rooms tend to be quieter, but that is because they face a cement wall or have no windows at all (a situation more claustrophobic than romantic, in our opinion).

HALEKULANI, Waikiki
2199 Kalia Road
(808) 923-2311, (800) 367-2343
Very Expensive to Unbelievably Expensive and Beyond
Wedding facilities are available for a maximum of 320 people.

From Kalakaua Avenue, turn toward the water onto Lewers Street. The hotel will be directly in front of you.

Without a doubt, this is the most desirable place to stay in all of Waikiki. Halekulani means "house befitting heaven" and this aptly named luxury hotel stands alone as a tranquil, serene oasis in the heart of downtown Waikiki. Quiet splendor and the fragrant scent of jasmine enfold you as you step from the busy street into an open-air lobby replete with glimpses of the ocean, small waterfall-fed pools, imported marble pillars framing gracious corridors, and lovely garden landscaping. A beautifully tiled oceanside swimming pool beckons to you, flaunting a brilliant white painted orchid under the shimmering surface of the blue water. Upon arrival, you are greeted in gracious aloha style and ushered to the privacy of your own room to register. Moments later, a complimentary basket of tropical fruits and chocolates (and sometimes champagne, if it happens to be a special occasion, so tell them you're celebrating) arrives at your doorstep.

All 456 guest rooms face the hotel's secluded oceanside courtyard, and each suite surrounds you in white, from the plush carpet and crisp bed linens to the sparkling bathroom tiles. Brilliant orchids embellish the decor with streaks of color. Throw back the shutters and step out onto your spacious lanai, where you can survey the courtyard below and the ocean beyond. Views of the water are also available from the vantage point of a sunken soaking tub in the beautiful marble bathroom, if you slide open the partitioned doors or shutters. Discerning attention to simple details adds the final romantic touch to every room; in place of chocolates, you'll find seashells and poems on your pillows in the evening.

Although Halekulani's prices might at first sound steep, they are surprisingly comparable with those of Oahu's less luxurious properties. In fact, Halekulani's rates feel much more reasonable in light of the hotel's extraordinary accommodations and service.

◆ **Romantic Note:** Halekulani's two restaurants, the exorbitant and sophisticated **LA MER** and the more casual **ORCHIDS** (both are reviewed in "Restaurant Kissing"), offer efficient, attentive service, unpretentious settings, and a refreshing amount of open-air drama.

HILTON HAWAIIAN VILLAGE, Waikiki
2005 Kalia Road
(808) 949-4321, (800) 221-2424
Moderate to Unbelievably Expensive and Beyond
Wedding facilities are available for a maximum of 2,000 people.

On the corner of Ala Moana Boulevard and Kalia Road.

You could live here for quite some time and never have to leave the property to fulfill your every need. More than the "village" its name states, the Hilton is for all intents and purposes a city unto itself, providing guests with everything from a full-size post office to a grocery store.

One of the largest resorts in the state of Hawaii, the Hilton can be, to say the least, overwhelming. Situated on 20 acres of prime but crowded beachfront property, the Hilton boasts fantastic ocean views from its unbelievable 2,542 guest rooms in four sky-rise towers. In addition to multitudes of boutiques and cafes, the village provides three outdoor swimming pools, over 20 restaurants and lounges, and live entertainment such as Charo and the "Magic of Polynesia" show. The "super pool," a 10,000-square-foot pool surrounded by thundering lava rock waterfalls and tropical landscaping, would be of particular interest if it weren't also surrounded by many excited, noisy children. Family vacations are a Hilton specialty.

Although guest rooms in each of the hotel's four towers have all the necessary amenities and are renovated on an ongoing basis, the decor and furnishings are fairly nondescript and standard. For the best ocean views, we recommend rooms on the 15th floor or higher—a real bargain at these prices. In spite of the crowds, service is still efficient, and the hotel can arrange everything from on-site car rentals to baby-sitting. An additional plus: the private health and fitness spa with pool, sauna, whirlpool, and massage rooms.

◆ **Romantic Suggestion:** Dinner at either of the Hilton's well-known restaurants, **BALI BY THE SEA** and **GOLDEN DRAGON** (both are reviewed in "Restaurant Kissing"), is an absolute must.

HYATT REGENCY, Waikiki
2424 Kalakaua Avenue
(808) 923-1234, (800) 233-1234
Expensive to Unbelievably Expensive and Beyond
Wedding facilities are available for a maximum of 600 people.

On Kalakaua Avenue, between Koa and Uluni streets.

Directly across the street from the beach at Waikiki stands this massive twin-towered hotel complex, which rises 40 stories above the water. Centered around a large atrium lobby with a cascading waterfall, the hotel's ground floor is a full-scale shopping mall, complete with more boutique and jewelry stores than you can shake a pineapple at.

Those who have more than shopping in mind will appreciate the Hyatt's spacious guest rooms, located upstairs above the mall. Recently renovated, each of the pleasing 1,230 rooms is appointed with attractive wood furnishings, stylish brightly colored linens, and a private lanai. Amenities like coffee makers, VCRs, and mini-bars are nice extras. If water views are at the top of your agenda, keep in mind that the higher up you go, the closer you are to a bird's-eye view of the scintillating tropical city scenery. Guests who are willing to pay extra also have exclusive use of sun decks perched at the top of both tall towers.

◆ **Romantic Suggestion:** We wholeheartedly recommend only one of the Hyatt's six restaurants for affectionate dining. **CIAO MEIN,** (808) 923-CIAO, (Moderate to Expensive), boasts several semi-casual, fun dining rooms. Although the black-and-white Italian motif looks slightly out of place beside Chinese sculptures and hand-painted vases filled with exotic flowers, the unusual blend of Chinese and Italian cuisine is a big success. The unique menu items are all artistically presented and well executed, from the sesame asparagus and black mushrooms with oyster sauce appetizer to the mouthwatering meringue dessert appropriately called Double Happiness.

MANOA VALLEY INN, Honolulu
2001 Vancouver Drive
(808) 947-6019, (800) 535-0085
Inexpensive to Expensive
Wedding facilities are available for a maximum of 30 people.

Call for directions.

Professionally run bed and breakfasts are rare commodities in Hawaii. The Manoa Valley Inn is the only historical inn of its kind on Oahu, which is the primary reason we included it. Those who like the personal touches of a bed and breakfast will appreciate this three-story gabled country inn set in a relatively quiet residential neighborhood. It once reveled in ocean views, but now Waikiki's high-rise skyline looms in the distance—not so alluring in the daytime, but lovely at night when the city lights twinkle in the darkness. Eight

rooms are available: seven in the main house and one separate cottage. The three rooms on the top floor share a bath, which is rather
unromantic, but the others, which have private baths, are possibilities. These rooms feature weathered black-and-white photographs,
massive antique carved wood or iron beds, patterned wallpaper, and
marble-topped dressers, all in need of renovation, but retaining
touches of Victorian charm.

Continental breakfast is served on the expansive covered backyard
lanai, definitely the coziest spot for two at any time of day. Although
the other common rooms house interesting and authentic antiques,
they are timeworn and somewhat dreary. Still, this is a unique, historical alternative to the luxury hotels in Waikiki.

OUTRIGGER HOTELS HAWAII   ❤ ❪
Various locations
(800) 462-6262
Inexpensive to Expensive

Call for directions and reservations at any of the Outrigger properties.

You can't mention "Hotel Kissing" on Hawaii without at least com-
menting on the Outrigger hotels. This well-known island chain has 30
hotels scattered across the four main islands, 20 of them on Oahu, yet
once you've seen one, you have virtually seen them all. Outriggers offer
welcome budgetary relief from Waikiki's otherwise exorbitant prices, while
providing standard hotel accommodations, good service, and even the
occasional ocean view for relatively reasonable prices. Generally well
kept and conveniently located, Outrigger hotels are ideal for tourists
who want to enjoy Waikiki but don't want to spend a lot of money for
luxury (or a lot of time in their rooms).

ROYAL GARDEN HOTEL, Waikiki
440 Olohana Street
(808) 943-0202, (800) 367-5666
Inexpensive to Unbelievably Expensive

At the corner of Olohana Street and Ala Wai Boulevard.

Major renovations have transformed this previously nondescript hotel
into a lovers' oasis. Located just blocks from the ocean in the heart of
downtown Waikiki, the Royal Garden is worthy of romantic praise. Crys-

tal chandeliers illuminate a luxurious marble lobby filled with exotic bouquets, where guests can cozy up in cushion-laden couches and appreciate the melodies of a self-playing grand piano. A complimentary continental breakfast is served buffet-style in this relaxing spot every morning.

Elegant hallways and brass-trimmed doors contrast with the Royal Garden's Standard and Moderate rooms, which feature unimpressive, mismatched furnishings. But you won't find fault with any of the 17 reasonably priced Deluxe Suites or slightly more expensive Royal Suites. Many of these gracious rooms enjoy peekaboo views of the nearby canal or distant glimpses of the ocean. Decorated in peach and cream or Pacific blue and white color schemes, each of these suites sports a wet bar, a marble bathroom, lovely wood antiques, and plush carpeting and bed linens. French doors separate the bedroom from the living room, creating a feeling of ample space as well as optimum privacy.

Although the Royal Garden caters primarily to businesspeople, guests with amorous agendas can turn this fact to their advantage. During business hours, you're likely to be the only ones using the two outdoor swimming pools, whirlpool, sauna, or fitness room.

◆ **Romantic Suggestion:** You're missing out if you don't have lunch or dinner at the Royal Garden's lovely poolside restaurant, **CASCADA BY THE WATERFALL** (reviewed in "Restaurant Kissing"), which features delicious Mediterranean cuisine.

THE ROYAL HAWAIIAN, Waikiki
2259 Kalakaua Avenue
(808) 923-7311, (800) 782-9488
Unbelievably Expensive and Beyond
Wedding facilities are available for a maximum of 500 people.

Heading east on Kalakaua Avenue, pass the Royal Hawaiian Shopping Center and the hotel is on the right.

For obvious reasons, this hotel is commonly referred to as the "Pink Palace of the Pacific." You can't miss this conspicuously bright pink building on your way down Kalakaua Avenue. Dating back to 1927, the formidable, colorful exterior has endured the decades with glamour and panache. You can virtually feel the history as you walk through the tasteful, luxurious lobby and meander down the tropical, tree-lined pathways. The only potential mistake in booking a stay here is if you are misguided into thinking that the newer oceanfront tower has the better accommodations. Although these are the only units with lanais, most of these rooms are rather small, with standard bathrooms and mediocre furnishings. Go for the original, historic wing instead, where you'll never want for space, luxury, or style. Intricately hand-carved wooden doors open into rooms with high ceilings, lush fabrics, unique moldings, attractive baths, and interesting antiques. To compensate for the lack of a lanai, open your windows and let the fresh ocean air drift through your room.

Not many restaurants or bars sit directly on the beach at Waikiki, but the Royal Hawaiian boasts two: the **SURF ROOM** and the **MAI TAI BAR**. Although the Surf Room can get crowded and the food is just OK, the expanse of beach is beautiful and Sunday brunch here is lively and pleasant. And with a ringside view of the water, the Mai Tai Bar is a wonderful casual setting for sipping cocktails as the day dramatically ebbs into night.

◆ **Romantic Note:** The pool area is unusually small for a hotel this size and can get beyond crowded, to near bursting, at the height of the afternoon. Although the pool area opens to the beach, the crowds on the sand are no less daunting.

SHERATON MOANA SURFRIDER, Waikiki
2365 Kalakaua Avenue
(808) 922-3111, (800) 782-9488
Expensive to Unbelievably Expensive
Wedding facilities are available for a maximum of 260 people.

Heading east on Kalakaua Avenue, pass the Royal Hawaiian Shopping Center and the hotel is on the right. Enter on the second driveway.

Dating back to 1901, the Moana Surfrider was Waikiki's first hotel property. Sparkling crystal chandeliers hang from the ceiling in the historic lobby, flanked by white columns, extravagant tropical bouquets, and elegant winding staircases. All suggest that this elegant, plantation-style property has been restored to its original grandeur. Sadly, the Sheraton's 793 air-conditioned guest rooms have not retained much, if any, of the stunning lobby's old-world charm and intimacy. In spite of ongoing renovations, even the hotel's historic wing is surprisingly disappointing, with dowdy bedspreads, dated color schemes, and standard hotel furniture. The Moana's nostalgic past, impressive lobby, and prime beachfront location are the only real reasons these rooms are worth your affectionate consideration. Still, for many people, this is reason enough.

Outside, afternoon tea is served on a lovely wraparound porch called the **BANYAN VERANDA** (reviewed in "Restaurant Kissing"), where a magnificent, towering banyan tree shades the oceanfront courtyard.

◆ **Romantic Suggestion:** We highly recommend a romantic dinner for two at the Moana's reputable **SHIP'S TAVERN** (reviewed in "Restaurant Kissing"). It's a perfect place to savor delectable Pacific Rim cuisine and spectacular ocean views.

WAIKIKI JOY HOTEL, Waikiki
320 Lewers Street
(808) 923-2300, (800) 922-7866 (mainland)
Inexpensive to Expensive

On Lewers Street, between Kuhio and Kalakaua avenues.

Inexpensive accommodations are hard to come by in Waikiki, unless you plan to settle for little more than four walls, a bed, and (with luck) a window. But in our search for economical luxury, we stumbled gratefully over the threshold of the Waikiki Joy Hotel, an affordable find. The modest, attractive open-air lobby is enhanced by Italian marble, stately white pillars, and a small waterfall pond. A tiny swimming pool awkwardly located next to the lobby offers little to no privacy, but unless a swimming pool is essential to your idea of escaping the heat, you won't mind once you've seen the upstairs rooms, which all feature large Jacuzzi soaking tubs. The suites themselves are not extravagant, but they are nicely appointed with wicker furnishings and pale tones of pink, blue, and gray. Some include a full kitchen and wet bar. Continental breakfast, served on the first-floor veranda area, is included with your room.

The only real drawback here is that you might miss the beach, because the views from the lanais are primarily of neighboring rooftops, but be reassured it is only a few blocks away. Considering the price (and the lack of competition in this price range), the Waikiki Joy is an affectionate surprise that lives up to its name.

WAIKIKI PARC HOTEL, Waikiki
2233 Helumoa Road
(808) 921-7272, (800) 422-0450
Moderate to Very Expensive

Heading east on Kalakaua Avenue, before you reach the Royal Hawaiian Shopping Center, turn right onto Lewers Street, then left onto Helumoa Road. The hotel is on the right.

A sister of the elegant Halekulani across the street, the Parc lacks its sibling's oceanfront drama and opulence, but don't let that deter you from booking a reservation here. You can't find rooms, ocean views, and service of this caliber anywhere else in Waikiki at such reasonable rates. Situated above a modest but comfortable lobby, each of the Waikiki Parc's 298 rooms is beautifully decorated with a soft white and Pacific blue color scheme, simple bamboo furnishings, ceramic tile floors, plush carpeting, and white shutters that open onto a cozy lanai with partial ocean views. (As usual, the higher the floor, the better the view.) Fortunately, the pool on the eighth floor sits high enough to have a view of the water, and for some reason it is often yours alone.

♦ **Romantic Note:** Connected to the Waikiki Parc Hotel, and a magnet for sushi lovers, is **KACHO** (Inexpensive). This petite restaurant, elegantly though sparsely appointed, serves fresh udon and even fresher sushi.

Restaurant Kissing

ALAN WONG'S RESTAURANT, Honolulu
1857 South King Street
(808) 949-2526
Moderate to Expensive

On South King Street, between Punahou and McCully Street. The restaurant is located on the fifth floor. Valet parking is available for $2.

Bottles of soy sauce and chile oil sit on the tables in the place of salt and pepper at this innovative new restaurant, but you won't need them. The kitchen makes sure that the magnificently presented Pacific Rim dishes are perfectly spiced and seasoned. Da Bag, steamed clams with *kalua* pig, shiitake mushrooms, and spinach, is a particularly memorable appetizer because it is brought to the table in what looks like a large foil balloon that is broken open for you. Steam and wonderful aromas rise from it—it's sort of like your own miniature luau. Choosing an entrée is difficult, since everything sounds (and is) so wonderful. The shrimp and clams in a spicy but light lemongrass–black bean sauce, served on perfectly al dente penne pasta, is delectable, and the grilled mahimahi with stir-fried vegetables and a wasabi sauce is equally satisfying.

Alan Wong's intriguing cuisine is served in an upbeat atmosphere with modern track lighting, island-print table coverings, and wicker-and-iron chairs. Not exactly romantic, but the main reason to come here is the magnificent food. Because this restaurant is geared primarily toward groups, the room can become more and more noisy with voices and the laughter of celebrations as the evening progresses. Service is professional, but still warm and welcoming.

◆ **Romantic Note:** A five-course chef's tasting menu is available for $65 per person. Yes, that does fall into our Unbelievably Expensive category, but if you're celebrating a special occasion that comes only once a year and you're true connoisseurs of Hawaiian cuisine, this is the perfect place to indulge.

BALI BY THE SEA, Waikiki
2005 Kalia Road, in the Hilton Hawaiian Village
(808) 941-2254
Inexpensive to Expensive
Wedding facilities are available for a maximum of 224 people.

On the corner of Ala Moana Boulevard and Kalia Road.

Ocean views are guaranteed no matter where you sit at this sophisticated open-air restaurant, set above the waterfront and offering unforgettable sunsets as a backdrop. Warm tropical breezes waft through the plush, sage green dining room, where you will want to linger by candlelight long after your meal is done. Breakfast and lunch are slightly less formal (and much less expensive), although the menu is still impressive, with a focus on regional Hawaiian fare. Dusk is undeniably the most romantic time to enjoy this setting, and the evening menu includes favorites like lasagna with eggplant and roasted peppers, and a Pacific Northwest salmon fillet baked in rice paper. Desserts change nightly and never disappoint.

BANYAN VERANDA, Waikiki

2365 Kalakaua Avenue, in the Sheraton Moana Surfrider Hotel
(808) 922-3111
Expensive

Heading east on Kalalaua Avenue, pass the Royal Hawaiian Shopping Center and the hotel is on the right. Enter on the second driveway.

A white banister encloses this idyllic wraparound terrace dining room, which fronts the sapphire blue Pacific. From any angle it is one of the most enticing spots on the island for breakfast, Sunday brunch, or afternoon high tea. High-backed wicker chairs, teak floors, and open-air seating create an authentic island setting, and a harpist enhances the breezy mood as light winds blow through the venerable banyan tree in the courtyard. White-glove service from a polite staff can be gracious but a little on the haughty side. If you don't mind the formality, you will relish the romance that overflows from this picturesque setting.

CASCADA BY THE WATERFALL, Waikiki

440 Olohana Street, in the Royal Garden Hotel
(808) 945-0270
Moderate
Wedding facilities are available for a maximum of 200 people.

On Olohana Street, near Ala Wai Boulevard.

Set next to a waterfall that tumbles into a swimming pool, this suitably named country French dining spot gently murmurs as the sound of cascading water drifts through open sliding doors. Beautiful wood-and-iron chandeliers shed light on well-spaced tables set beneath a floral frescoed ceiling. Hawaiian bouquets and tiled murals lend a tropical feeling to the otherwise semiformal interior, accented with white linens and plaid chair coverings. Renowned for his culinary talents, Cascada's chef is wonderfully adept in the kitchen. Lunch offerings range from an eggplant-zucchini soufflé on a bed of fresh tomato sauce to ricotta-spinach gnocchi; dinner items are equally tasty and innovative, especially the royal crab cakes with a blend of peppers and the tofu dumplings laced with oyster sauce. Service is impressive.

THE CONTEMPORARY CAFE, Honolulu
2411 Maikiki Heights Drive, at the Contemporary Museum
(808) 523-3362
Inexpensive

Located on Maikiki Heights Drive. Lunch is served Tuesday through Saturday from 11 A.M. to 2 P.M., and on Sunday from noon to 2 P.M. Desserts and beverages are served from 2 P.M. to 3 P.M. Tuesday through Sunday. The cafe is closed on Mondays.

You wouldn't guess it, but this is one of the more interesting places to kiss in Hawaii. It is so close to Waikiki, yet it feels so far away. A winding drive up through the venerable Maikiki Heights neighborhood brings you to the Contemporary Museum, a spectacular 1920s estate that now houses modern art exhibitions and a surprisingly gourmet lunch room. It is still just a casual cafe, but the unique location away from hordes of tourists, the stylishly spartan decor, and the fabulous menu make it worth mentioning. We recommend a light lunch of baked Brie served with fruit and a warm baguette, or the Malaysian shrimp salad of succulent tiger prawns, green papaya, and leafy lettuce in a tasty peanut dressing. When you've finished your meal, enjoy a walk through the three and a half acres of beautifully landscaped Japanese gardens dotted with massive, unusual sculptures. All your senses will feel fully enlivened.

◆ **Romantic Note:** Take the time to peruse the museum's exhibits. The $5 admission fee applies even if you only come for the cafe, but most likely you'll be glad to have paid when you see the noteworthy shows.

GOLDEN DRAGON, Waikiki
2005 Kalia Road, in the Hilton Hawaiian Village
(808) 949-4321
Inexpensive to Expensive

On the corner of Ala Moana Boulevard and Kalia Road.

Harbored on an oceanfront marina, this series of luxurious, open-air dining rooms resembles the interior of a mansion, brimming with exquisite Oriental antiques, shoji screens, and Chinese statues. Candles flicker at well-spaced tables draped in white, set off by mahogany floors and wood pillars. Despite the enticing, potentially pretentious surroundings, service is decidedly friendly. The sizable menu includes standard Cantonese favorites such as wonton soup and potstickers, in addition to more unusual dishes like jellyfish with sesame shoyu and ocean scallops seared with lychees (a must if you've never tried this interesting tropical fruit). Our *only* complaint was that the scallops were slightly undercooked, but that wouldn't dissuade us from recommending the Golden Dragon again and again for the enchanting ambience.

HANOHANO ROOM, Waikiki
2255 Kalakaua Avenue, in the Sheraton Waikiki
(808) 922-4422
Very Expensive
Wedding facilities are available for a maximum of 150 people; call for details.

On Kalakaua Avenue behind the Royal Hawaiian Shopping Center.

The view is the attraction at the Hanohano Room, and the major, if not only, reason to mention this established restaurant. Ensconced on the 30th floor of the Sheraton Waikiki, you can dine amidst vast, majestic views of the ocean, mountains, and endless sky. Prices are fairly astronomical in light of the kitchen's failings, and there is nothing distinctive about the interior. Yet, there is that view. Sunset can be quite an experience from up here if you stick to just cocktails and snacks served in the small bar area, which has fine access to the view and a pianist who plays gently into the night.

HARLEQUIN RESTAURANT, Waikiki
1956 Ala Moana Boulevard, in the Alana Waikiki Hotel
(808) 951-3138
Moderate
Wedding facilities are available for a maximum of 70 people.

On Ala Moana Boulevard, between Kalakaua Avenue and Hobron Street.

Harlequin has parted with several different chefs in the recent past, so we hope the current one is here to stay. Our meal here was truly memorable and savory. We're still raving about the guava wood-smoked swordfish topped with tasty mango salsa and the ginger-crusted ahi with shichimi butter sauce. Why such a modest rating for such lip-smacking Pacific Rim cuisine? In spite of the kitchen's talents, the dining room's small size makes it impossible to keep smoke from the back of the room from drifting toward tables in the nonsmoking section. Anybody who is slightly sensitive to smoke will have difficulty appreciating the praiseworthy cuisine and simple, modern ambience.

INDIGO, Honolulu
1121 Nuuanu Avenue
(808) 521-2900
Inexpensive to Moderate
Wedding facilities are available for a maximum of 87 people.

In historic Chinatown, on Nuuanu Avenue, between South Beretania and Hotel streets.

Now we know why everyone is talking about Indigo, a relatively new Eurasian restaurant nestled in the heart of Waikiki's historic Chinatown. It's fabulous! Provocative modern art and authentic Chinese antiques contribute to an intriguing atmosphere in the first of several dining rooms, but hold out for a table in the open-air brick courtyard, where the real romance awaits. Here, you will feel as if you've been transported across the globe to another time and place. Tiki torches illuminate two-person tables cozied next to a genuine Chinese pond teeming with goldfish and floating water lilies. A second handful of larger tables overlook a small, melodic rock waterfall in the adjacent neighborhood park. (Views of the park are most pleasant at nightfall, when nearby construction ceases and gatherings have thinned out.)

There is nothing Indigo's chef doesn't do right. Bao buns with Okinawan potatoes and sun-dried cherries are a sweet, unique beginning, and almost as delicious as the lobster potstickers with soy-ginger sauce. Norwegian salmon cakes with smoked chipotle mayonnaise and stir-fried asparagus with black bean–butter sauce are sublime and artistically presented on lovely platters with pickled vegetables, chutney and salsa, and chive pillow noodle cakes. Leave room for the appropriately named "Explosions to Heaven"—fried bananas with coconut gelato. It's a gala event for your palate.

Reserve your rental car in advance. During high season,
cars may not be available when you arrive.

KAHALA MOON CAFE, Honolulu
4614 Kilauea Avenue, Suite 102
(808) 732-7777
Moderate to Expensive
Wedding facilities are available for a maximum of 95 people.

On Kilauea Avenue, in the Kahala Mall.

After a brief recess due to a kitchen fire, the Kahala Moon Cafe is back again, and in rare form. Loyal patrons crowded the restaurant on its second opening night, and we felt privileged to be among them. There is nothing remotely cafe-ish about this lovely, contemporary restaurant, appointed with modern Hawaiian art, pale mint walls, tall leafy plants, and a spectacular koa wood bar. Candlelit tables draped in white linen are arranged strategically in two adjacent dining rooms. (The handful of two-person tables facing a cushioned bench that runs the length of one dining room can feel a little too close for kissing comfort.) Everything on the menu is fresh and enticing, especially the chilled sweet tomato soup with shrimp dumplings and Thai basil pesto. Our medallions of mahimahi with garlic-potato puree, sautéed spinach, and saffron vinaigrette were excellent. Service was extremely gracious and efficient, although the staff was still in the process of fine-tuning the valet parking (to several parties' dismay, this service wasn't optional).

KEO'S THAI CUISINE, Waikiki
625 Kapahulu Avenue
(808) 732-2593
Inexpensive to Moderate
Wedding facilities are available for a maximum of 150 people.

At the corner of Kapahulu Avenue and Date Street.

Every celebrity imaginable has eaten at the Kapahulu Avenue Keo's, and then some. The proof is on the wall. Peruse the gallery of pictures as you enter and see how many stars *you* recognize. This is definitely Waikiki's to-be-seen-in hot spot, and if you eat here you're likely to see at least one famous person—even if you don't recognize him or her. If you don't care about who's who, come anyway, just to experience the intriguing surroundings and out-of-this-world Thai cuisine.

The dining room bursts with exotic floral arrangements and abundant greenery; colorful paintings of flowers and landscapes add to the lush (somewhat crowded) surroundings. Several tables nestled snugly throughout the room are shaded by umbrellas and separated by white partitions to enhance privacy. Service is professional and swift, and you won't mind the tight squeeze once you've tasted the food. Delight in creatively prepared Thai entrées, such as roll-your-own spring rolls, spicy green seafood curry, or their unique Evil Jungle Prince, a medley of vegetables and spices in a rich coconut sauce. Indulge in a smooth fresh mango daiquiri or try a Thai iced tea—your kisses will taste sweeter than ever. Reservations are recommended and a must on Friday and Saturday nights.

◆ **Romantic Suggestion:** Keo's has several locations, but the other one of romantic interest is **KEO'S THAI BAR & GRILL**, 1486 South King Street, Waikiki, (808) 947-9988, (Inexpensive to Moderate). The food is just as good, and although you may not be able to stargaze, the slower-paced, slightly quieter dining room could inspire you to gaze into each other's eyes instead.

LA MER, Waikiki
2199 Kalia Road, in the Halekulani Hotel
(808) 923-2311
Very Expensive to Unbelievably Expensive
Wedding facilities are available for a maximum of 35 people.

From Kalakaua Avenue, turn toward the water onto Lewers Street. The hotel will be directly in front of you.

Housed on the second floor of what was originally a private beachfront estate at Halekulani, this dining room is characterized by subdued etched paneling and delicious ocean views. Fresh ocean air (and the sound of next-door evening entertainment) spills into the elegant dining room. Guests are greeted with glasses of champagne, then escorted to elegant, secluded tables topped with flickering candles. Although the menu offers delectable, award-winning Pacific Rim selections, prices can be absurdly expensive. To get the most for your money, choose one of the three available prix fixe dinners. This is a slightly more affordable (yet still Unbelievably Expensive) way to taste a little bit of everything.

NICHOLAS NICKOLAS, Waikiki
410 Atkinson Drive, in the Ala Moana Hotel
(808) 955-4466
Expensive
Wedding facilities are available for a maximum of 250 people; call
for details.

The Ala Moana Hotel is just off Ala Moana Boulevard, on Atkinson Drive.
Valet parking is available for $3, and the club is on the 36th floor.

Looking for a sexy nightspot where you can observe Waikiki's twinkling city lights from 36 floors up? Vamp your way to Nicholas Nickolas.
Tables for two, adorned with white linens and single red roses, hug the
supper club's window-lined perimeter, but cozy leather booths are also
available. The mostly American-style cuisine is just average—a major
disappointment considering the prices. Service is attentive to the point
of being ludicrous, unless you are comfortable with a parade of tuxedoed
men waiting on you. Still, Nicholas Nickolas is one of the few intimate
late-night options in Waikiki, and it is a prime place to kiss. Just come
for drinks, dancing, and maybe dessert (bananas Foster is a deliciously
sweet option).

NICK'S FISHMARKET, Waikiki
2070 Kalakaua Avenue, in the Waikiki Gateway Hotel
(808) 955-6333
Expensive
Wedding facilities are available for a maximum of 225 people.

On Kalakaua Avenue, between Kalaimoku and Olohana streets.

Nick's Fishmarket has been serving great fresh fish for as long as
anyone can remember, and it still holds its own against competition
from the highly touted chefs flocking to Waikiki. The dimly lit dining
rooms are a tad old-fashioned and a bit too dark for some tastes, but the
snug leather booths and adequately spaced tables with high-backed
chairs offer a surplus of cozy spots for two. Service is friendly yet professional, and the kitchen takes time and care with every item on its enormous menu, down to the fresh-baked, hot-out-of-the-oven dinner rolls.
(Watch out—it's easy to fill up on these!) Large portions of Hawaiian
fish are presented in a variety of remarkably tasty sauces. The calamari

Provencal, sautéed with tomato, basil, mushrooms, and garlic butter, was lip-smacking good (pun intended).

◆ **Romantic Warning:** Half of this restaurant is a nightclub in the late evening, with an open bar, a dance floor, and live entertainment. Sounds from the bar definitely carry into the restaurant and can be a romantic deterrent if you're not in the mood for the evening's musical selections.

ORCHIDS, Waikiki
2199 Kalia Road, in the Halekulani Hotel
(808) 923-2311
Moderate to Expensive
Wedding facilities are available for a maximum of 22 people.

From Kalakaua Avenue, turn toward the water onto Lewers Street. The hotel will be directly in front of you.

Halekulani does everything to perfection, and their Orchids restaurant is no exception. Provocative floral arrangements and white linens fill the terraced, open-air oceanfront dining room, which is graced by eucalyptus hardwood floors. Scintillating views counterpoint a gala of flavors and tastes, from the appetizers all the way through to dessert. Savor the fresh seafood, the open ravioli with smoked duck and shiitake mushrooms, and the lightly smoked pink snapper steamed in ti leaf with a papaya and Maui onion relish. All your senses will be filled to overflowing by the end of your perfect evening at Orchids.

◆ **Romantic Alternative:** If you want to admire views of Halekulani's grounds and the ocean in a more casual atmosphere, gaze and graze at the hotel's **HOUSE WITHOUT A KEY**, (808) 923-2311, (Inexpensive to Moderate). The poolside terrace dining room serves a small but eclectic assortment of ethnic cuisines. Simple combinations or a delicious chicken fajita salad are relatively reasonable, and the service is sheer perfection.

SHIP'S TAVERN, Waikiki
2365 Kalakaua Avenue, in the Sheraton Moana Surfrider
(808) 922-3111
Very Expensive
Wedding facilities are available for a maximum of 200 people.

Heading east on Kalakaua Avenue, pass the Royal Hawaiian Shopping Center and the hotel is on the right. Enter on the second driveway.

Tavern is a misnomer for this elegant dining room. Named after the old-fashioned luxury liners that used to spend several weeks at sea en route to Waikiki, Ship's Tavern is the Sheraton Moana Surfrider's "flagship" restaurant. Linen-cloaked tables arranged with romantic privacy in mind line an expanse of windows that overlook sultry ocean sunsets and twinkling city lights. Colorful bouquets of exotic flowers lend the formal setting a tropical flair. The steamed onaga Oriental with shiitake mushrooms and snow peas, and the seared ahi on eggplant-tomato relish are two tasty examples of the restaurant's creative Hawaiian cuisine. A dessert of poached pear in red wine with ginger-pear sorbet is guaranteed to make your dreams sweeter.

Outdoor Kissing

HONOLULU MAUKA TRAIL SYSTEM, Honolulu

Call Oahu's Division of Forestry, (808) 587-0166, for maps and descriptions of all the hikes in the Honolulu Mauka trail system. To reach the various trailheads for most of the hikes, follow Round Top Drive up to its highest point, where it becomes Tantalus Drive; parking lots on the road indicate where to stop.

If you are one of the many who believe that Oahu's natural beauty has been diminished by overbuilding and overpopulation, you need to venture into the Honolulu Mauka trail system. An afternoon in the Tantalus area will restore your faith in the power of nature. Fertile stands of lush bamboo and fragrant eucalyptus line the **PUU OHIA TRAIL**, which rambles through groves of wild fruit trees among other tropical treasures. Sections of this three-quarter-mile hike are steep but not too difficult—if you have proper shoes (*proper* is the operative word here). If you still long for more natural wonders once you reach the highest point of this trail, you can take the **MANOA CLIFF TRAIL**, which it crosses, then continue on the **AIHUALAMA TRAIL** and make the gorgeous descent into **MANOA VALLEY**.

◆ **Romantic Suggestion:** There are so many intersections and varying trails that you really need to get a map and specific descriptions of each hike from the Division of Forestry, (808) 587-0166, in advance.

LYON ARBORETUM, Honolulu
3860 Manoa Road
(808) 988-3177
No admission fee, but donations are accepted ($1 suggested). Open Monday through Saturday, 9 A.M. to 3 P.M.

Drive north on University Avenue, which turns into Oahu Avenue after you pass the University of Hawaii campus. Pass East Manoa Road, then turn right onto Manoa Road. Signs will first direct you to Paradise Park, then Lyon Arboretum.

If you've been curious about the names of the exotic flora that seems to envelop the Hawaiian Islands (and you're looking for slightly cooler air), Lyon Arboretum is the place to go. Every imaginable kind of tropical flower, plant, and tree is exhibited in this enchanting public garden set deep in the lush folds of the Manoa Valley. As you linger in the arboretum's 124 verdant acres, the scent of the aromatic flowers, the sight of the varied blossoms and foliage, the sounds of chirping birds, and the feel of your beloved's hand in yours will delight and refresh your senses.

Diamond Head

Go ahead—close your eyes. The chances of accidentally kissing a stranger on the beach are much slimmer here than on the beach at Waikiki. Diamond Head summons you away from the crowds and mayhem of urban Waikiki. You won't be totally alone, but you'll have a lot more room to enjoy the surf, sand, and sunshine.

There isn't a better place to witness spectacular views of Waikiki's shoreline and cityscape (or to kiss) than the top of **DIAMOND HEAD CRATER.** Early morning is really the only time that the heat isn't too unbearable for the steep hike, but once you reach the top, you'll be glad you made the less-than-an-hour-long trek. Strong legs and shoes with good traction are advised. If you would like additional guidance (and a certificate proving that you conquered the great crater), the **NEW OTANI KAIMANA BEACH HOTEL** (reviewed in "Hotel/Bed and Breakfast Kissing") offers organized hikes up the crater. Call the hotel, (808) 923-1555, (800) 733-7949, for details.

Hotel/Bed and Breakfast Kissing

COLONY SURF HOTEL, Diamond Head   ◆ ◆ ❮
2895 Kalakaua Avenue
(808) 923-5751, (800) 252-7873 (mainland U.S.)
Expensive to Very Expensive
Wedding facilities are available for a maximum of 154 people; call
for details.

*Follow Kalakaua Avenue through Waikiki, past Kapiolani Park, and watch
for a Colony Surf Hotel sign on the right.*

The Colony Surf is one of several desirable, semi-moderately priced
hotels harbored on this tiny stretch of beach. Outside appearances may
be discouraging—the two white towers are timeworn and separated by
an unattractive parking lot—but have faith: a welcome surprise awaits
you in the main, waterfront tower (but only that one). Your apprehensions will wane once you are checked into an open, airy, white and
pastel one-bedroom suite, awash in sunlight and accented by white
wicker furnishings. Each suite has two double beds, which is a little
odd for one couple, but the prices are right and you will be thrilled
with the spaciousness. Enjoy the convenience of a fully equipped
(although dated) kitchen and a small, standard private bath.

Views of Diamond Head or the ocean and Waikiki are yours from
the vantage point of a window seat (instead of a lanai) set beneath bay
windows that run the entire width of the room. Sunsets here are truly
remarkable. There is no air-conditioning, but you can open the shutters to allow the sound of the gentle surf below and the refreshment of
a warm ocean breeze to sweep through the room.

◆ **Romantic Note:** The majority of the units at the Colony Surf
are private condominiums (only about 20 suites are available for overnight guests), which explains the blend of services for both homeowners
and hotel guests.

KAHALA MANDARIN ORIENTAL HOTEL,
Diamond Head   **Unrated**
5000 Kahala Avenue
(808) 734-2211, (800) 367-2525
Expensive to Unbelievably Expensive

Call for reservations and directions.

Formerly the Kahala Hilton, this well-known, gorgeous site is being completely renovated and is set to reopen in early 1996 as the Kahala Mandarin Oriental Hotel. We can't make any promises on exactly what the future holds, but the unmarred stretches of sandy beach, the verdant rolling hills of the surrounding Waialae Country Club Golf Course, and the clusters of palm trees should still enfold this luxury oceanfront resort in hushed seclusion. What we can say is that if the duration of the renovation (a full year) is any indication of the grandeur the new owners have in mind, this will be a romantic's dream come true.

THE NEW OTANI KAIMANA BEACH HOTEL, Diamond Head
2863 Kalakaua Avenue
(808) 923-1555, (800) 356-8264
Inexpensive to Unbelievably Expensive
Wedding facilities are available for a maximum of 120 people; call for details.

Follow Kalakaua Avenue into Diamond Head and watch for signs to the hotel on the right.

As travel writers, we have learned never to judge a book solely by its cover (so to speak), and the New Otani is a case in point. Pulling into the hotel's narrow driveway and crowded parking lot, you may initially doubt that romantic possibilities can be found here, but put your worries aside. Although the hotel's exterior and hallways are a little the worse for wear, each of the guest rooms (except the standard ones that face the neighboring condo complex) and suites has the makings for a blissful getaway. Private balconies, expansive floor-to-ceiling windows, and pastel fabrics and wall coverings create an inviting atmosphere. Many of the rooms have impressive views of the churning blue ocean, while others face neighboring Kapiolani Park. We prefer (and recommend) the ocean-view rooms since pedestrian traffic practically disappears on the beach at night, and this is not the case in the park. Either way, downtown Waikiki sparkles in the distance—far away enough for you to enjoy peaceful nights and quiet mornings.

◆ **Romantic Suggestion:** Of special amorous interest are the five spacious, beautifully designed suites situated on the hotel's top floor. Sensually appointed with Jacuzzi tubs and boutique furniture, they leave little doubt that the extra expense (minimal in comparison to other hotels in the area) will provide an experience you and yours will fully appreciate.

Restaurant Kissing

HAU TREE LANAI, Diamond Head
2863 Kalakaua Avenue, in the New Otani Kaimana Beach Hotel
(808) 921-7066
Moderate
Wedding facilities are available for a maximum of 40 people.

Follow Kalakaua Avenue into Diamond Head and watch for signs to the hotel and restaurant on the right.

Share sunset beneath a sprawling hau tree at this lovely beachside terrace restaurant. Ocean breezes drift past cozy tables covered with white tablecloths and shaded by pink umbrellas. After night falls, tiki torches glow, the glorious tree is lit with twinkling white bulbs, and soft classical guitar music accompanies your meal. Choose from a menu offering grilled steak, lobster, and various fresh seafood dishes—pretty standard fare, but the main reason to come here is the setting, not culinary wizardry. The atmosphere is best described as informal, with breakfast and lunch the most casual as swimmers and sunbathers pass by. We think it's a quaint, ambrosial place for holding hands and dining any time of day.

MICHEL'S, Diamond Head
2895 Kalakaua Avenue, in the Colony Surf Hotel
(808) 923-6552
Expensive
Wedding facilities are available for a maximum of 150 people.

Follow Kalakaua Avenue through Waikiki, past Kapiolani Park. Turn right into the parking lot when you see signs for the New Otani Hotel. The Colony Surf is next door.

Remember, all beaches are public in Hawaii. As long as you can find public access, you are welcome to enjoy the beaches everywhere.

The ambience here is unquestionably sensual. In fact, it would be hard to find more amorous surroundings. The plush open-air dining room is nestled directly on the beach and offers panoramic views of the ocean surf and Waikiki beyond. The three connecting dining rooms exude elegance at every turn. Cozy, candlelit tables for two are draped in white linens, adorned with hand-painted plates, and set beneath dimly lit crystal chandeliers and gilded mirrors.

Unfortunately, the kitchen's talents are not as impressive as those of the interior decorator. French cuisine may be a welcome change for those who are tired of the Pacific Rim rage, but the menu is not nearly as innovative as we had hoped it would be (especially at these prices), and the service is disappointing. Breakfast is probably the most romantic time to be here (before the beach is full), and the kitchen does a better job then.

Southeast Oahu

Hawaii Kai

Restaurant Kissing

ROY'S RESTAURANT, Hawaii Kai
6600 Kalanianaole Highway
(808) 396-7697
Moderate
Wedding facilities are available for a maximum of 80 people.

On Kalanianaole Highway, in the Hawaii Kai Corporate Plaza.

Oahu is buzzing about Roy's. Although the ambience is a bit too loud and lively for an intimate interlude, most of the people who frequent this Euro-Asian restaurant are couples. It must be the stellar reputation of the owner and the skilled chefs that keeps them coming back again and again. An open kitchen is the centerpiece of this second-floor dining room, and vivid modern art graces the walls. Window seats do look out to palm trees and the ocean beyond, but the view also takes in the busy highway. Brightly adorned tables are packed in rather tightly, and since this restaurant is almost always booked, don't expect any privacy. What you can expect is good professional service and well-executed dishes. The shiitake-spinach ravioli is a nice starter, and the spicy rimfire shrimp in a sweet chili sauce with Asian vegetables is delectably light.

◆ **Romantic Note:** Reservations are recommended, but if you call too late and the dining room is already full, the first-come, first-served lower level is devoted to those who don't plan ahead. The same menu is offered in the casual bar and outdoor patio area, plus live Hawaiian-style entertainment (steel guitars and soft melodies).

◆ **Romantic Alternative:** Roy's next-door neighbor is **HANATEI BISTRO**, 6650 Kalanianaole Highway, Hawaii Kai, (808) 396-0777, (Moderate), serving a mixture of Japanese and Italian food. For the most part, the Japanese dishes, such as a spicy unagi roll, are better than the Italian choices, which include a bland pasta primavera that leaves much to be desired. Service is somewhat awkward, and most of the tables are set up for groups. Still, a harmonious jazz trio performs softly in the corner of the restaurant, and the sun setting over the ocean makes the closer view of the rushing highway traffic almost disappear.

Outdoor Kissing

KOKO HEAD DISTRICT PARK
(808) 395-3096, (808) 973-7250

On Oahu's southeast shore.

Due east of Diamond Head is the rugged terrain and breathtaking shoreline of Koko Head District Park. **HANAUMA BAY**, a volcanic crater open to the sea on one side, is the big attraction on this side of the island. The crater features prime snorkeling among some of the most abundant, amazing, and colorful sea creatures you will encounter anywhere. The number of visitors is now strictly limited in order to protect the marine life that calls Hanauma Bay home, so save snorkeling for another day and drive through this park for the views and the chance to experience as much of Oahu as possible. Every turn of the road brings new panoramas of deep blue waves turning to white mist as they crash against the rocky volcanic shoreline. You won't be all alone on this drive, but the crush of tourists does seem to thin out over here. There are plenty of lookout points where you can stop, linger over the view, take pictures, and, most important, share a kiss or two.

◆ **Romantic Note:** Even though the number of sea-life enthusiasts has been reduced at **HANAUMA BAY**, the area can still seem loaded. However, this is still the best place to snorkel on Oahu. While you must deal with the crowds when you first arrive, once submerged you enter a totally different, much more peaceful world of bright fish and shapely coral. Access to the bay is limited, based on parking spots available. Come in the morning (except on Wednesday, when it is closed until noon), as early as 6 A.M., when the sun is not too blistering and others haven't arrived. Admission price for nonresidents is $5 per person.

Kailua

Located about 40 minutes east of Waikiki is the town of Kailua, which goes about its business at a drastically different, far less hectic pace. You won't see a single high-rise here. The drive through the Koolau Mountain Range via the Pali Highway is reason enough to at least check out this charming residential area and its excellent beaches. *Condé Nast Traveler* recently named **KAILUA BEACH PARK** the third-best beach in the country. (A couple of Florida beaches were ranked numbers one and two, but we firmly believe the kissing is much better in Hawaii than almost anyplace else on earth.)

Hotel/Bed and Breakfast Kissing

MANU MELE BED AND BREAKFAST, Kailua
153 Kailuana Place
(808) 262-0016
Inexpensive

Call for specific directions.

Travel to Oahu's windward side for an attractive alternative to the Waikiki scene. Manu Mele (it means "bird song") is a handsomely renovated bed and breakfast with two simply but attractively appointed guest rooms. Both rooms open to a pool area and well-tended garden courtyard, and each is totally self-sufficient, with a microwave, coffee maker, refrigerator, television, and fresh fruit and muffins. A nearby path leads to a sweeping, fairly empty stretch of sun-kissed sand at Kailua Bay. The only drawback to this kissing bargain is the adjacent thoroughfare. Cars whiz by and the sound is less than idyllic, but the price, the closeness of the beach, and the owners' professionalism and attention to detail more than make up for this urban drawback.

Outdoor Kissing

LANIKAI BEACH

This beach is just south of Kailua, in front of Mokulua Drive. Watch for walkways and signs stating "PUBLIC RIGHT-OF-WAY TO BEACH."

Soft, warm waves lap against the sandy white shore, and the water is crystal clear. Two small islands (seabird sanctuaries) dot the horizon. The scene looks like an impossibly perfect picture in one of those brochures advertising a tropical paradise. Located at the edge of an affluent neighborhood, Lanikai Beach is no secret, but those who spend time here come to enjoy the serenity and peacefulness of the pale aqua ocean, not to see or be seen as in Waikiki.

◆ **Romantic Suggestion:** If you can muster the energy for an extremely early morning, try to experience at least one sunrise here. It is an event never to be forgotten.

North Shore

Kaneohe

Hotel/Bed and Breakfast Kissing

HALE O'HONU, Kaneohe
(808) 247-6821
Expensive to Very Expensive

Call for reservations and directions.

If you've got your heart set on a dream vacation rental home, look no further. Sheltered on Oahu's spectacular North Shore, this self-sufficient beachfront house is prettier than a postcard. Set overlooking crystal blue Kawela Bay (one of the few remaining feeding grounds for endangered Hawaiian green sea turtles) and a white sand beach, the contemporary two-story home feels relatively secluded, with neighbors on only one side.

Ample windows allow for cool breezes and lovely water views on the home's lower floor, where you'll find two bedrooms, a fully stocked kitchen, and a cheerful, airy living room appointed with blonde hard-wood floors and comfortable wicker furnishings. Unfortunately, during summer's peak the upstairs master bedroom is suffocatingly hot, even when the windows are open and the ceiling fan is running at high speed. If it's just the two of you, consider sleeping in one of the down-stairs bedrooms, although you'll want to take advantage of the large glass-enclosed soaking tub upstairs in the master bathroom. When the sun has gone down completely, watch the stars emerge in the night sky from the steamy privacy of the outdoor hot tub in the backyard.

◆ **Romantic Note:** From January through August, a seven-night minimum stay is required. September through mid-December, five nights are required, and during Christmas and New Year's, ten days are required.

"Kisses are like grains of gold or silver found
upon the ground, of no value themselves,
but precious as showing that a mine is near."
George Villiers

Maui

KAANAPALI

PAIA

LAHAINA

KIHEI

HANA

WAILEA

*"I don't know how to kiss, or I would kiss you.
Where do the noses go?"*
Dudley Nichols

MAUI

All of the idyllic words used to describe practically anyone's concept of paradise are associated with this wondrous corner of heaven. Surely the garden of Eden looked something like Maui—well, at least the Maui of 20 or more years ago. Maui's glory is no longer a secret, and the island's increasing popularity and growth have unfortunately left their mark, especially in the sprawling condominium complexes that dot (and occasionally overwhelm) the sunniest, sandiest beaches. Even so, the scenery is still graced with plenty of lush tropical forests, green fields of sugarcane, azure waters, and pristine beaches. Yes, the handful of mostly single-lane main roads that circle the island are usually filled with cars, creating slow-moving, frustrating traffic jams. But if you change your focus and concentrate on the scenery, the warm air, and each other, everything is forgivable.

Besides being the second-largest island in the Hawaiian chain, Maui has the dubious status of being considered the island of the well-heeled. There are more millionaires per capita here than anywhere else in the United States. In alliance with that statistic, Maui also has some of the most expensive, prestigious hotel rooms in the world: e.g. two suites at the Grand Wailea that go for $10,000 a night. (We won't describe what you get for that; it would only cause you a great deal of envy and potential kissing distress.) Despite the preponderance of costly properties with stupendous places to stay, there are also less prohibitive places that can feel almost as indulgent and grand.

If you have never visited Maui before, and even if you come again and again, certain tourist activities (requiring only a car and the appropriate gear) are mandatory on any romantic (or nonromantic) itinerary: climbing up above the clouds to witness a sublime sunrise or sunset from **HALEAKALA CRATER**; hiking **IAO VALLEY STATE PARK** to discover the 2,250-foot rocky spire of **IAO NEEDLE**; driving two and a half hours through lush tropical rain forest, navigating more than 600 hairpin turns, to the remote, scenic town of **HANA** and the dramatic **SEVEN POOLS** waterfall just outside of Kipahulu; viewing colorful marine inhabitants while snorkeling off **BLACK ROCK** in Kaanapali; strolling through the old whaling village of **LAHAINA**; watching windsurfers skim back and forth over the waves at **HOOKIPA PARK** on the north side of the island; and being treated like royalty while enjoying a leisurely Sunday brunch at any of the half dozen or so phenomenal hotel developments that hug exquisite sections of the island. This side of Maui is well known, extremely impressive, and, for the most part (except for brunch), free.

If your vacation budget is generous, you can also consider bicycling down Haleakala on an organized biking trek (about $100 per person); taking a helicopter to Hana or just sightseeing (about $95 and up per person); taking a boat ride out to the extinct volcanic crater of **MOLOKINI** (see the next Romantic Warning) or other less public snorkeling spots (about $65 to $95 per person); taking scuba diving lessons (rates vary widely, but top out at about $150 for three hours); or savoring a gourmet dinner at one of the island's select romantic restaurants (about $100 to $150 for two).

While all of the paid-for outdoor activities are well organized, fun, and provide extraordinary experiences in extraordinary places, if you have to choose only one, we suggest going on some type of boat ride that includes snorkeling or on a romantic sunset sail. For specific information on Maui and all of the activities on the island, call the **MAUI VISITORS BUREAU** at (808) 244-3530. To receive a Maui Vacation Planner, call (800) 525-MAUI.

The reviews that follow will help you indulge your romantic inclinations in less touristy, more intimate ways.

◆ **Romantic Warning:** Be forewarned that snorkeling cruises to Molokini are extremely popular, and the area is crowded. The trip out is wonderful, but the crescent-shaped rocky rim can resemble a parking lot for boats. In fact, the fish are so overfed here they often appear nonchalant about your food offerings.

◆ **Romantic Historical Note:** Maui is the name of the Hawaiian deity who created all the Hawaiian Islands. The story goes something like this: At the beginning of time, Maui used his legendary rope to hook and haul up the land submerged under the seas, forming the islands. After accomplishing this mythic feat, Maui then attempted to lasso the sun god, La, to bring light to the islands. Their great struggle took place at the top of Haleakala. Maui emerged victorious. In a dire effort to obtain his freedom, the enslaved La promised to travel slowly across the heavens to forever warm the people and their harvests. It is for these benevolent acts that the god Maui came to have an island named after him.

West Maui

Kapalua

Quite literally the end of the road on the westernmost tip of Maui, Kapalua is the last developed place on this side of the island (and likely to stay that way). You can't exactly call this town remote, but the traffic and the crowds thin out immensely up here, especially compared to other areas on Maui. The West Maui mountains, 23,000 acres of pineapple fields, and a rugged shoreline define this lush, majestic domain. Depending on your preferences, there are many things that can make this a desirable area and a few things that might make it disappointing.

Among Kapalua's virtues are its truly remote, unmarked beaches (all but three are a bit of a hike to get to), ideal for playing in the surf; the incredibly scenic drive (somewhat inaccessible without a four-wheel-drive vehicle) from Honokahua to Kahakuloa; and a welcome feeling of relative seclusion. One minor drawback is that this is the wettest section of the island. (What that really means are a few more clouds and an extra couple of hours of precipitation during the rainy season, but that's about it.) Kapalua's only other potential letdown for some travelers is what makes it wonderful to the rest: it isn't where to find the action on Maui. Instead you will find serenity, seclusion, and quiet, all things that should lead to a more amorous vacation.

Hotel/Bed and Breakfast Kissing

KAPALUA BAY HOTEL AND VILLAS, Kapalua
One Bay Drive
(808) 669-5656, (800) 367-8000 (mainland)
Expensive to Unbelievably Expensive
Wedding facilities and services are available for a maximum of 180 people.

From Highway 30, follow signs and turn west into Kapalua. Signs will lead you to the hotel.

In its prime, the Kapalua Bay Hotel was a sight to behold. The massive open lobby, spectacular oceanfront location, and truly ample rooms with large, sensual baths made it a rarity along these shores. Now it pales in comparison to some of Maui's newly built, more extravagant properties, but the comparatively affordable prices have enabled it to keep up with increasing competition.

Situated on 18 luscious acres of prime oceanfront property, the Kapalua Bay Hotel is surrounded by swaying palm trees and landscaped gardens. You won't want for space in the 2,500-square-foot guest rooms, which feature high ceilings, roomy lanais, attractive (although sometimes dated) linens and artwork, and large marble bathrooms. Many rooms offer ocean views; others overlook the hotel's well-groomed gardens and sweeping lawns.

◆ **Romantic Note:** Complimentary afternoon tea service is offered daily, and the hotel also features two great restaurants: **THE GARDEN RESTAURANT** and **THE BAY CLUB** (both are reviewed in "Restaurant Kissing"). Be sure to plan a hand-in-hand walk at sunset on nearby **KAPALUA BEACH**, one of the better beaches on Maui.

◆ **Romantic Alternative:** For optimum privacy, stay in one of the hotel's condominium villas scattered over the Kapalua Resort. **THE KAPALUA VILLAS** (reviewed elsewhere in this section) also rent condominiums and exclusive vacation homes throughout the resort, but despite the nearly identical names, these are two different companies.

THE KAPALUA VILLAS, Kapalua
500 Office Road
(808) 669-8088, (800) 545-0018 (mainland)
Moderate to Unbelievably Expensive

From Highway 30, turn west onto Office Road and follow signs to the Kapalua Villas office.

High atop the scintillating Kapalua coastline, you can dwell in the lap of luxury at any of the units managed by The Kapalua Villas. Stay in one of three separate developments (the Bay, Ridge, and Golf villas), or rent a stunning Pineapple Hill home if your budget allows.

Generally, privately owned condominium units are difficult to recommend, regardless of the property, because individual owners have different tastes and budgets. Such a dilemma does not exist here. Simply stated, if someone can afford to purchase a condo in this neighborhood in the first place (it's the most expensive real estate on Maui), they can (and do) invest in furnishing it beautifully.

Units in the Golf Villas are the lowest priced because the ocean view is distant and interrupted by other properties' rooftops. Still, these lodgings may be the best value because it isn't an unbearable view by any means, and the spacious one- or two-bedroom units have designer kitchens and are very well kept up. Four pools are shared by guests and tenants, so your chances of having a swimming spot all to yourselves can be pretty good.

Considerably closer to the ocean are the pricey "oceanfront" Bay Villas, set on a hillside up from the water, and the "ocean-view" Ridge Villas behind them. Interiors of both Bay and Ridge villas are gorgeous. With their stylish overstuffed couches, beautiful furnishings, exquisite artwork, expansive lanais, enviable kitchens, vaulted ceilings, loft bedrooms, and a virtual wall of windows facing spectacular views of Molokai and the deep blue Pacific, these are accommodations you won't want to (or have to) leave.

Finally, the private, gated community of Pineapple Hill contains the most exclusive and grandest options. Ample room between each of these homes guarantees supreme privacy. Every house has its own tiled swimming pool or large outdoor Jacuzzi tub, modern kitchen and bathroom, sumptuous furnishings, and sensational views. Yes, the price tag is steep (and we mean *steep*), but you won't be disappointed with this once-in-a-lifetime getaway filled with opulent romantic opportunities.

◆ **Romantic Warning:** Some units in the Bay Villas and Ridge Villas do not have air-conditioning. Trade winds blow through here on many days, but if you don't want to be at the mercy of the weather report, it is essential to request air-conditioning in advance.

◆ **Romantic Note:** A free on-call shuttle service can take you wherever you need to go throughout the Kapalua Resort, which is extensive. Take advantage of this service and go to the neighboring **RITZ-CARLTON** (reviewed elsewhere in this section). Complimentary use of Ritz facilities is included with your stay.

THE RITZ-CARLTON, Kapalua
One Ritz-Carlton Drive
(808) 669-6200, (800) 262-8440
Very Expensive to Unbelievably Expensive
Extensive wedding facilities are available, including a historic wedding chapel; maximum capacity of 60 people in the chapel, up to 800 outside.

From Highway 30, turn west onto Office Road and follow the signs to the hotel.

In some ways this is just another Ritz-Carlton, but that says a lot about the kind of elegance you can expect. As you cross the threshold into the impressive lobby, you enter a world where luxury and finesse are paramount. With 37 acres sloping downward to the ocean, and 550 rooms, this is the second-largest Ritz in the chain (there are 29 internationally). Perhaps the magnitude is what makes the service here seem less personal and a little more lax than at other Ritz-Carltons. (Don't be disappointed when the valet doesn't show up in typical Ritz attire, including top hat and white gloves, with a cheery greeting.) Overall, the service isn't a major problem, but it is something to be aware of since you're still paying typical Ritz rates.

European refinement (a Ritz trademark) is evident in all of the formal fabrics and gilt-edged furnishings. The rooms, mostly upscale hotel-basic with large marble bathrooms, are filled with light and more than comfortable. Color schemes vary from subtle rose to pastel blue, and tasteful Hawaiian art adorns the walls. Most of the adequately sized lanais, equipped with wrought-iron railings and furniture, look out toward the ocean over the golf course or beyond the three cascading pools, while the rest face the emerald Maui mountains.

Amenities such as truly outstanding restaurants, a gorgeous pool area, and spectacular sandy **FLEMING BEACH** (reviewed in "Outdoor Kissing") are all must-see's and must-do's during your stay. As amazing as it seems, *all* of the restaurants deserve unusually high praise. One of the absolute best dinner destinations on the island is **THE GRILL** (reviewed in "Restaurant Kissing"). For a more casual repast, try **THE BANYAN TREE** (also reviewed in "Restaurant Kissing") for lunch, or **THE BEACH HOUSE**, which features a small selection of sandwiches and salads along with a full bar, and is splendidly located directly on Fleming Beach, with comfortable white tables and chairs set on the edge of a sandy bluff. Whatever you want or need, as a guest at the Ritz-Carlton you shouldn't have to leave the property to get it.

Pick up a disposable underwater camera if you go snorkeling or if you take a boat ride and don't want to risk getting your "real" camera wet. These take surprisingly good photos.

◆ **Romantic Note:** Another special spot on the Ritz property is the historic **KUMULANI CHAPEL**, built by plantation families as their place of worship in the 1950s. Sunday-schoolers still come every week, but this charming little white steepled church is a gorgeous site for brides and grooms to make or renew their vows. Helpful wedding and honeymoon planners are on-site, and various wedding packages are available. Couples inspired by the tranquillity, warmth, and romance of Maui have made impromptu weddings a fairly common occurrence here.

Restaurant Kissing

THE BANYAN TREE, Kapalua
One Ritz-Carlton Way, in the Ritz-Carlton
(808) 669-6200, (800) 262-8440
Moderate

From Highway 30, turn west at Office Road and follow signs to the hotel.

For a stylish, relaxed oceanfront lunch, venture quickly to The Banyan Tree, and enjoy Mediterranean fare that is simply sensational. An ornate iron chandelier hangs from the high redwood-beamed ceiling, marking the center of the room. Tables and chairs made of the same lovely redwood are dispersed throughout the dining area, and a slate floor enhances the casual ambience. The entire restaurant has the potential to be open-air, but winds are usually strong enough to keep the sliding glass doors shut. Tables are also available outside, where glass partitions and canvas umbrellas effectively buffer the wind.

Incredible ocean views from nearly every seat make up for proximity to the mostly sedate crowd gathered around the nearby pool. Tempting lunch entrées include gourmet thin-crust pizzas, sandwiches like the mahimahi club, and a variety of salads. Pizzas and sandwiches are consistently good, but the salad dressings can be too heavy—to be safe, ask for it on the side. The restaurant is open for lunch every day, and serves pupus (Hawaiian for appetizers) and cocktails in the early evening.

THE BAY CLUB, Kapalua
One Bay Drive, adjacent to the Kapalua Bay Hotel
(808) 669-5656
Very Expensive
Wedding facilities are available for a maximum of 80 people.

From Highway 30, take the Kapalua exit and follow the signs for the Kapalua Bay Hotel. The restaurant is adjacent to the hotel.

The sound of the surf accompanies the leisurely meals served at this handsome open-air restaurant situated on a small bluff just above the water's edge. Views of palm trees and the vast ocean take your mind off (but don't compensate for) the very standard seafood served here. We recommend sticking to cocktails or dessert at sunset, when the surf is accompanied by a pianist's soothing melodies.

THE GARDEN RESTAURANT, Kapalua
One Bay Drive, in the Kapalua Bay Hotel
(808) 669-5656
Moderate to Expensive

From Highway 30, take the Kapalua exit and follow the signs to the Kapalua Bay Hotel. The restaurant is on the lower level of the hotel.

In spite of the big hotel setting, this airy ocean-view restaurant feels surprisingly secluded and quaint. A towering wall of French doors opens to let warm tropical breezes caress the interior. Water cascades down one wall of the dining room, trickling into a koi pond and a stream that winds through the restaurant. The menu features Hawaiian cuisine, reasonably priced and beautifully presented. We particularly enjoyed the fresh Pacific salmon and ahi served with wasabi and a red pepper coulis.

THE GRILL, Kapalua
One Ritz-Carlton Way, in the Ritz-Carlton
(808) 669-6200, (800) 262-8440
Expensive to Unbelievably Expensive

From Highway 30, turn west onto Office Road and follow the signs to the Ritz-Carlton.

This bastion of exquisite dining deserves a less understated name. The service is flawless, the formal setting simply stunning, and the food the most tantalizing and brilliantly presented on the island. There is little to inhibit a leisurely romantic evening. Begin your night out in the stately lounge adjacent to the restaurant, where handsome love seats and plush armchairs invite you to snuggle close while you listen to light jazz performed by a pianist and singer. Once you are seated for dinner, the menu works its own seduction. Don't even try to resist the silky smooth lobster and ginger consommé, whole Thai snapper, or caramelized salmon in an orange shoyu glaze. Every dessert is a master-piece, and the sweet sensations are sheer ecstasy.

PINEAPPLE HILL RESTAURANT, Kapalua
1000 Kapalua Drive
(808) 669-6129
Expensive

Turn west off Highway 30 at the sign for Kapalua and follow the signs to the restaurant.

If it weren't for the exceptional views from this historically signifi-cant old plantation home, we wouldn't even mention Pineapple Hill Restaurant, and we certainly would not recommend it. But it is set high atop a hill over Kapalua, making it the best place in all of West Maui to watch the glowing sun dropping into the sea. The restaurant is desperately understaffed, and the decor borders on (and sometimes crosses into) tacky, with old ceiling fans, orange lightbulbs, cheap-looking wood paneling, and worn multicolored carpet. As for the food, you'd get the same overcooked, oversauced steak and seafood entrées at the Denny's in Lahaina, but pay a lot less for them. The view makes up for some of the kitchen's failings, but you'd be better off just having dessert, coffee, and the sunset.

PLANTATION HOUSE RESTAURANT, Kapalua
2000 Plantation Club Drive
(808) 669-6299
Moderate to Expensive
Wedding facilities are available for a maximum of 250 people.

Follow Highway 30 to just north of the Kapalua entrance and watch for signs for Plantation Club Drive on the right. Turn right onto Plantation Club Drive, then follow signs for the restaurant.

Perched high on a hill with breathtaking views of the water, the distant isle of Molokai, and surrounding emerald fields, this restaurant is romantically recommended for its vantage point alone. Thankfully, though, the chef makes sure there is more reason to come here. The ambience during breakfast and lunch tends to be more social and friendly than intimate (most of the tables are set for larger groups); however, the view, the efficient professional service, and the attractive interior of pale wood, high beamed ceilings, upholstered chairs with pineapple-carved backs, massive fireplace with marble hearth, and open-air windows, more than make up for the golfing state of mind.

Dinner here is a must, when the sun is making its daily descent behind Molokai or into the ocean (depending on the time of year). Most of the entrées from the Mediterranean–Pacific Rim menu are excellent. Roasted tomato-basil bisque with focaccia and pine nuts is a delicious starter, and the catch of the day, available in various preparations, is always fresh and moist. We enjoyed mahimahi pan-seared in mirin (rice wine) and macadamia nuts with jasmine risotto and caramelized chili-sesame sauce. If you're still waiting for the sun to set (or even if you're not), linger over dessert—they're all good.

Outdoor Kissing

THE DRIVE FROM HONOKAHUA
TO KAHAKULOA

From Kihei, follow Highway 30 past Kapalua and beyond. When you come clear of the high-rise hotels and see nothing but water and trees, you'll know you're in the right place.

Just north of the many high-rise hotels of Kapalua, you'll come to the northwestern section of Highway 30. When you get here, be prepared to take turns driving: the scenery along this minimally traveled road is so spectacular, your natural inclination will be to keep your eyes *off* the road and *on* the unbelievably beautiful surroundings.

Along the way, on the ocean side of the road, you'll find many accessible viewing spots with innumerable photo opportunities of the breathtaking seascape. Waves crash dramatically up against the sharp rocks, and the brick red clay cliffs set next to the deep blue water are as bright as colors in a child's crayon box. Stunning vistas of sea and sky unexpectedly appear around every turn as the road continues on. Small villages dot the way, with no provisions for travelers, but that is a clear reminder of what it was like on Maui before it was overrun with hotels and T-shirt shops.

When you come to the end of the road you'll know it. Deep pot-holes and gravel mark the highway when the pavement ends, and we recommend turning around at this point (although there are brave souls who carry on, even though car-rental places don't allow it). Hopefully, on the return trip you'll get to see the panoramic sunset, which is certainly a celestial sight to behold.

FLEMING BEACH, Kapalua

The beach is accessible from Highway 30, north of the Ritz-Carlton, after you've passed the Kapalua sign.

You *must* visit this remarkable stretch of beach. Although it is rather small, it is arguably one of the most beautiful in the world. The silky soft sand is edged with rocky outcroppings, and rolling green hills glow in the distance. Depending on the weather, the surf either rolls in lazily or surges several feet in the air and comes crashing down in a rush of white water.

The Ritz-Carlton's Beach House and Banyan Tree restaurants are close by, so you can enjoy a mai tai, pina colada, or delicious pupus after you've played in the rolling waves.

HONOLUA BAY, Kapalua

The beach is accessible from Highway 30, about three miles north of Kapalua.

Cars parked on either side of the road are the only obvious marker at this extraordinary snorkeling bay. Unfortunately, they are also a signal that you won't be alone (which truly would be too much to ask for at such a wonderful spot). A short, steep walk through forest brings you to the inviting rocky beach. Swim alongside colorful tropical fish and, partial to this spot, large sea turtles. It is fascinating to watch these gentle giants swim in and out of their caves.

♦ **Romantic Note:** Two catamarans can capture the breeze in their sails to whisk you here in style. The Hyatt Regency's **KIELE V**, (808) 661-1234, extension 4720, offers afternoon or early evening tours, as does the **TERALANI**, (808) 661-0365. Both depart from Kaanapali Beach, and the price, ranging from $35 to $70 per person, includes snorkel gear plus appetizers and drinks on some sails. About 40 other eager snorkeling enthusiasts will join you, but the trip is a wonderful opportunity to see the island from the water. If you're going by car, try to come before or after the boat excursions arrive (before 11 A.M. or after 3 P.M.).

Napili

Buried between the high-rent districts of Kapalua and Kaanapali, Napili has a plethora of condominium developments and hotels piled one on top of the other, without much breathing room or beachfront. There are some bargains to be found here, but the sacrifice often includes air-conditioning and privacy. This isn't our favorite section of Maui, but it is only a stone's throw from its neighbors' more remarkable beaches and restaurants. The decision is yours.

Hotel/Bed and Breakfast Kissing

HONOKEANA COVE, Napili Bay
5255 Lower Honoapiilani Road
(808) 669-6441, (800) 237-4948 (mainland)
Inexpensive to Moderate
Wedding facilities are available for a maximum of 200 people.

Just north of Kaanapali, turn west off Highway 30 at the Napili turnoff, which becomes Honoapiilani Road. The condos are on the left.

Upon pulling up to this low-rise building you may be apprehensive; the weathered brown exterior doesn't look very inviting. Those in the know (now including you) realize this is just the back of the building, which gives no indication of the ample space and openness found in the units (especially the lofts). Like many other condominium units along the coast, these do feel like someone else's home, full of their trinkets and artwork, but condos in this part of the world often double as part-time rental unit, part-time someone else's vacation home. When you see this location, near the water's edge, looking out to the island of Molokai, we think you'll be glad the owners decided to share.

Each unit has a private lanai facing the water, petite fully equipped kitchen area, nice-sized living room with comfortable furnishings, and small, rather lackluster baths. What they don't have is air-conditioning. (Laundry facilities are available on-site, but not in the units.) Some of the furnishings are dated, but the price is right and, overall, things are kept nice and clean. The pool sits at the edge of a rocky bluff, and a relatively secluded cove below has great snorkeling. A short walk away is a sandy beach with rolling waves to play in. There is a three-night minimum, but prices get better the longer you stay. Tempting, isn't it?

ONE NAPILI WAY, Napili
5355 Lower Honoapiilani Road
(808) 669-2007, (800) 841-6284 (mainland)
Inexpensive to Expensive

Just north of Kaanapali, turn west off Highway 30 at the Napili turnoff, which becomes Honoapiilani Road. The condos are on the left.

One Napili Way is a clean, comfortable, and affordable option for a romantic retreat. Sans views but attractively appointed, this unusually small condo complex has only 14 units. Each features a towering wood-beamed ceiling, contemporary cane furniture, a nicely sized kitchen with a large refrigerator and all the appliances you'll need, attractive baths with a small whirlpool tub, television with VCR, ceiling fans in every room (no air-conditioning), and plentiful windows. These bright, roomy rentals are available with one, two, or three bedrooms. Well-tended gardens and swaying palm trees front the units, and a small but crystal-clear pool with an outdoor spa is set out back. It may not be beachfront, but access to Napili Bay is nearby.

◆ **Romantic Note:** This property has minimum-stay requirements for the high (five nights) and low (four nights) seasons.

Kahana

Restaurant Kissing

ROY'S KAHANA BAR AND GRILL, Kahana
4405 Honoapiilani Highway
(808) 669-6999
Moderate to Expensive
(See following entry for review)

ROY'S NICOLINA, Kahana
4405 Honoapiilani Highway
(808) 669-5000
Moderate to Expensive

Just off the Honoapiilani Highway, between Kaanapali and Napili. Both restaurants are on the second floor of the Kahana Gateway shopping center.

That's right: same address, same owner, same lip rating, but these are two separate establishments right next door to each other. What's the difference? It is easier to begin by explaining the similarities. Both restaurants were opened by Roy Yamagouchi, chef and restaurateur extraordinaire; both have an upbeat ambience; both feature out-of-this-world delicacies; both have an outstanding wait staff. Hawaiian cuisine is the main focus, but the executive chef at Roy's Kahana Bar and Grill sticks to Roy's original Euro-Asian–inspired dishes, while the chef at Roy's Nicolina specializes in Pacific Rim dishes with a Southwest flair. The ever-changing nightly specials sheets, offering over 20 inventive and uniquely prepared items, allow each chef to really shine.

For those with romance as well as excellent cuisine on their minds, the only drawbacks are the boisterous atmosphere (these dining rooms are always packed) and the location in a roadside shopping mall with views of a parking lot. Then again, if Roy's restaurants were waterfront, it would be impossible to get a reservation (it's hard enough as it is). Whether you take a table at either Roy's Kahana or Roy's Nicolina, your lips and palate won't be disappointed.

Kaanapali

A few years back, the Kaanapali coast was considered the premier enchantment of Maui. Two miles of soft sandy beach with gentle rolling waves made it the most desirable of Hawaiian areas. Unfortunately, the proliferation of high-rise condominiums and mega-resort hotels has changed this once-serene location to a crowded mess. Do not expect calm here, particularly during high season.

All of the properties in this area tout rooms that are referred to as having a garden or mountain view. You might very well see beautiful gardens and mountains from them, and the prices may sometimes be reasonable, but you will also see (and hear) a barrage of traffic. The noise can be maddening. (Of course, the restaurants and the ocean-view rooms are free from this offense, but carry the requisite steep price tag.) Please note that all of the "Hotel/Bed and Breakfast Kissing" recommendations in this area are only in consideration of the location. Even the most beautiful property can become intolerable if a romantic interlude or a dreamy morning in your room is marred by slamming car doors and screeching brakes.

Surprisingly, the beach is still radiant, and because the hotel and condominium properties all have great pool areas, it is relatively uncrowded. For swimming and soaking up the sun, this is a great location. For romance—well, you may have to wait until after dark to really be alone.

Hotel/Bed and Breakfast Kissing

EMBASSY SUITES, Kaanapali
104 Kaanapali Shores Place
(808) 661-2000, (800) 462-6284
Expensive to Unbelievably Expensive
Wedding facilities are available for a maximum of 800 people.

At the north end of Kaanapali Beach, just off Highway 30.

Judging from the wild pink exterior and funky tiered balconies, you would never guess this towering 12-story hotel holds some of the most spacious and attractive suites in town. But that is exactly what Embassy Suites offers. Every one of the 413 rooms is a large (over 800 square feet), beautifully appointed suite. A 35-inch television, VCR, stereo system, comfortable sitting and dining area, tiny kitchenette with microwave and refrigerator, and a sizable lanai grace each unit. The bathrooms are surprisingly sensual, with corner bathtubs big enough for two and separate glass-enclosed showers framed in white tile. Some rooms have a cheery feel, with crisp blue-and-white furnishings, while recent refurbishments have given others a more subdued, refined beach theme, with shell-print fabrics and peach-and-taupe-striped furniture. Renovations are ongoing, and eventually all of the rooms will be redecorated, but the rooms that have not yet been done aren't in pressing need and are quite nice. In addition to the extra space, you also receive a generous cooked-to-order complimentary breakfast buffet, and there is an early-evening cocktail hour (also complimentary).

The pool area opens to a sandy beach with tranquil surf. All this, plus the open-air lobby and the water views from many rooms, makes the Embassy, to borrow a phrase from the management, one "suite deal." In fact, in comparison to other oceanfront hotels and considering the size of the rooms, the prices are downright reasonable. The only drawback is that you'll have to travel off the property (but not too far) for good food. The Embassy's on-site restaurants are, sadly, a major letdown.

HYATT REGENCY MAUI, Kaanapali
200 Nohea Kai Drive
(808) 661-1234, (800) 233-1234
Very Expensive to Unbelievably Expensive
Wedding facilities are available for a maximum of 1,500 people inside or 2,500 people outside; call for details.

On Kaanapali Beach, just off Highway 30.

Six years ago, when we first visited the Hyatt Regency on Kaanapali Beach, it was an outstanding experience, one we will never forget. The towering building encircled an open courtyard filled with tropical plants, palm trees, and flowing streams. A jungle-like pool area with a delightful three-story slide only steps away from the ocean made the Hyatt a fantasy escape unlike any other.

In many ways, nothing has changed: the grounds are still absolutely enchanting. What *has* changed is the development of even more spectacular hotel properties that make the Hyatt Regency seem more ordinary. It is still a premium resort, and the restaurants here (particularly the **SWAN COURT**, reviewed in "Restaurant Kissing") are first-class, but the rooms are pretty much standard hotel issue, and despite recent renovations they show a little more wear and tear than you would expect (especially in the rooms that allow smoking). Still, the Hyatt remains romantic when you consider the long stretch of sandy beach out front and the trails that wander through the lush landscaping. Both are especially romantic at night.

◆ **Romantic Notes:** If you're interested, the Hyatt's **DRUMS OF THE PACIFIC LUAU** ($55 per adult) is considered one of the best on the island. Even if you are not interested, if your room is in the Lahaina Tower you will hear the show every night (except Sunday), from about 7 P.M. until about 8:30 P.M., making rest and relaxation nearly impossible.

A much more desirable (and quieter) option, for $10 each, is the Hyatt's **TOUR OF THE STARS**. On top of the hotel's roof is an elaborately assembled telescope where you can see and learn about the stars. A closer acquaintance with various heavenly bodies could put romantic ideas in your head. If you still need some guidance, have no fear: the Hyatt is prepared with a computer program for couples called **DISCOVERIES IN ROMANCE**, to help spice things up if you are having trouble deciding what to do with all of this intimate time alone. It's sure to at least provoke some interesting discussions and give you some good ideas of where to go on the island.

KAANAPALI ALII, Kaanapali
50 Nohea Kai Drive
(808) 667-1666, (800) 642-6284
Expensive to Unbelievably Expensive
Wedding facilities are available for a maximum of 60 people.

On Kaanapali Beach, between the Westin Maui and the Maui Mariott.

As many savvy travelers have learned, most hotel and condominium properties have extensive grounds and exteriors but small, standard guest rooms. This may be your first concern when you approach the four massive, 11-story buildings that envelop Kaanapali Alii's large pool area and palm tree–covered grounds. But don't jump to the wrong conclusion; all 210 of these one- and two-bedroom units are huge. In fact, they are some of the most spacious condominiums on the island (1,500 to 1,900 square feet, to be exact).

Hardwood-floored foyers in every unit provide a pleasant welcome. Interiors range from Hawaiian wicker and bamboo to Japanese simplicity, but every unit is clean, comfortable, air-conditioned, and, don't forget, spacious. Expect a large, fully equipped tiled kitchen, separate dining and living rooms, an ample lanai, washer and dryer, and a jetted master bathtub. Compared to what you find in other hotels and condo complexes, this is a real bargain. All of the amenities of a big hotel are available except for on-site restaurants, but you won't have to go far. **SOUND OF THE FALLS RESTAURANT** (reviewed in "Restaurant Kissing") is right next door, and **SWAN COURT** (also reviewed in "Restaurant Kissing") is just two buildings over.

◆ **Romantic Note:** The size of these rooms makes Kaanapali Alii most popular for family vacations (including children): good to know if you're planning to take the kids, but be forewarned if you're not.

MAHANA AT KAANAPALI, Kaanapali
110 Kaanapali Shores Place
(808) 661-8751
(800) 922-7866 (mainland), (800) 321-2558 (inter-island)
Inexpensive to Very Expensive

On Kaanapali Beach, two buildings south of Embassy Suites.

For the price, you can't beat what Mahana at Kaanapali condominiums have to offer. Every unit is oceanfront, and we *mean* oceanfront—you can't put a building much closer to the water's edge or it would fall right in. Various studios and one- and two-bedroom units are available. The studios feel like standard hotel rooms because the bed is in the would-be living room, but the one- and two-bedroom units are spacious and still a good deal (especially for two couples traveling together). Although each condo is decorated differently, you can count on finding pastel tones and Hawaiian-style furnishings (cushioned rattan or cane couches and chairs), fully equipped kitchens, and air-conditioning. A nice pool area, set between the two towers of units, faces the Pacific, and a little strip of sandy beach awaits out front.

MAUI KAI, Kaanapali
106 Kaanapali Shores Place
(808) 667-3500, (800) 367-5635
Inexpensive to Expensive

On Kaanapali Beach, next door to Embassy Suites.

Hugging the Kaanapali coastline is this relatively small condominium building of affordable one-bedroom units. They aren't fancy—in some ways they are rather plain, and the exterior is quite weathered from the salt air—but they are all oceanfront units with wonderful eight-foot-deep lanais, ample windows, central air-conditioning, and comfortable (sometimes homey) furnishings. A small fenced-in pool area with accompanying Jacuzzi is situated strangely in the parking lot, but the unparalleled views from the units and a sandy beach next door make this a mentionable romantic option.

◆ **Romantic Note:** A two-night minimum stay is required.

ROYAL LAHAINA RESORT, Kaanapali
2780 Kekaa Drive
(808) 661-3611, (800) 44-ROYAL
Moderate to Unbelievably Expensive
Wedding facilities are available for a maximum of 300 people.

On Kaanapali Beach, just off Highway 30.

A one-lip rating might not seem all that exciting, but the hotel's location, at the north end of Kaanapali Beach, takes it out of the rush of things, while the oceanfront cottages are actually quite spacious, near the sound of the surf, and probably deserve another lip or two. It remains a "one-lipper" because the entire hotel, and its restaurants, are in desperate need of restoration. Recent minor renovations spruced up the aforementioned oceanfront cottages, but they were already lovely due to their location. The rest of the standard, worn (but still pricey) units in the tower need help.

Three terraced pools provide a place to desalinate after a day of ducking in and out of waves. Venture into the heart of Kaanapali or Kapalua for your dining pleasures, because the Royal Lahaina's restaurants are not recommended.

THE WESTIN MAUI, Kaanapili
2365 Kaanapali Parkway
(808) 667-2525, (800) 228-3000 (mainland)
Very Expensive to Unbelievably Expensive
Wedding facilities are available for a maximum of 500 people.

On Kaanapali Beach, just off Highway 30.

If only more of the Westin's lower-priced rooms (in the Moderate range) weren't so disappointing, this would be a remarkable place to stay. The luxury and splendor of the lobby and the hotel's restaurants (**SOUND OF THE FALLS RESTAURANT** is reviewed in

"Restaurant Kissing") are legendary, and they more than live up to their acclaim. An exceptionally delightful multilevel pool area, complete with slides, waterfalls, and grottos, borders the exquisite Kaanapali Beach.

Unfortunately, you can't sleep in these gracious common areas. Some of the rooms could stand a bit of sprucing up; most are simply standard hotel rooms. Many of the suites have mountain views that have to contend with a fairly busy parking lot and entryway, something the brochure forgets to mention. A lot of the units with views of the water are set back from the shore and focus on the lobby and pool. The more desirable (and most expensive) rooms are in the Beach Tower. These are by far the most attractively appointed, with the best views and the highest tariffs.

◆ **Romantic Note:** Ask about the Westin's Romance Packages and Wedding Packages. They include everything you can think of, including the minister.

Restaurant Kissing

SOUND OF THE FALLS, Kaanapali
2365 Kaanapali Parkway, in the Westin Maui
(808) 667-2525, (800) 228-3000 (mainland)
Expensive

On Kaanapali Beach, just off Highway 30.

Perhaps not quite as breathtaking as the **SWAN COURT** (also reviewed in this section), its romantic neighbor down the road, Sound of the Falls is still a lovely setting for an open-air dinner, and the kitchen here produces better meals. The dining room, appointed with tall columns, faces a striking pond where cascading waterfalls tumble down a rocky embankment into the clear water, and flamingos perch on man-made islands with palm trees. Black and coral marble floors, napkins, and glasses echo those long-necked birds. Just behind the pond, the ocean stretches grandly; the counterpoint woven by the

---

Never leave valuables in your rental car. Just because you're in paradise doesn't mean you don't have to be city smart.

falls, the surf's gentle surging rhythm, and the pianist's soothing melodies is true water music. The cuisine is a blend of continental and
island dishes, including Hawaiian-style Caesar salad with wok-seared
sashimi, and vegetable-wrapped opakapaka in shredded phyllo. Service is professional and attentive.

SWAN COURT, Kaanapali
200 Nohea Kai Drive, in the Hyatt Regency
(808) 661-1234, (800) 233-1234
Expensive to Unbelievably Expensive

On Kaanapali Beach, just off Highway 30.

It doesn't get much more romantic than this. If only the dinners here
lived up to the ambience, Swan Court would rate ten lips. The atmosphere is sumptuous, and the service exemplary. A towering wall of open-
air windows looks out to a dramatic pond where gracefully poised black
and white swans glide by with the ocean in the background, enhancing
the elegantly sensuous mood. The grand menu reads like a symphony,
but the performance is on the bland side, lacking seasoning and finesse,
until the finale. The desserts are perfectly exquisite, particularly the mango
soufflé with ginger crème anglaise ladled in the middle.

◆ **Romantic Note:** Like many other hotel restaurants in Hawaii,
the Swan Court serves a daily breakfast/brunch, but the similarity
ends there. This one is truly romantic, excellently prepared, and reasonably priced at $16.25 per person.

Outdoor Kissing

KAANAPALI BEACH

Located off Highway 30, just north of Lahaina.

Without question, this magnificent stretch of soft sandy beach would
be the beach of choice on Maui if it weren't for the array of towering
hotels and condominiums lining it. The flip side is that guests of the
hotels and condos generally spend time by the properties' pools rather
than the beach, so it is never jam-packed. And at sunset, or even after
dark, the beach is superior for long walks and wave dodging. Black
Rock, at the north end of the beach, is an extraordinary place to snorkel and possibly meet a sea turtle face to face.

Lahaina

Founded in the 1600s, Lahaina was once the capital of the Hawaiian Islands. Royalty was the focus of the town back then, with all the commensurate traditions and rituals. Later, from 1840 to 1860, Lahaina was an enterprising whaling port, with rowdy sailors and hundreds of ships coming and going yearly. Today, it is hard to imagine those times as you walk along the crowded, compact streets of this small village. Lahaina's monarchs and mariners are long gone, and the once-quaint community and energetic port is filled with a hodgepodge of T-shirt stores, jewelry boutiques, art galleries, clothing shops, trendy eateries, oceanfront restaurants, and sightseeing boats. Visit anyway. There are several excellent restaurants here, and the views of the water and harbor are exciting. Accent your exploration with a mai tai or a pina colada in one of the many establishments along Front Street.

◆ **Romantic Note:** Many whale-watching charters depart from Lahaina between December and March, to witness the yearly migration of the humpback whales. It is almost impossible not to have a sighting, but even if you don't, you are likely to spot dolphins, sea turtles, and other "see-worthy" sights.

Hotel/Bed and Breakfast Kissing

LAHAINA INN, Lahaina
127 Lahainaluna Road
(808) 661-0577, (800) 669-3444
Inexpensive

From Highway 30, turn west onto Lahainaluna Road.

The Lahaina Inn demands a little romantic bookkeeping. Debits: Lahaina's hectic town center pulses right outside the door, you don't have even a glimpse of the ocean, and the nearest beach is several miles up the road in Kaanapali. Assets: Once you enter your room, there is little evidence that the outside world even exists, letting you concentrate on each other in luxurious bliss.

> *Always ask hotels about their package deals and "romance packages."*
> *These special offers can sometimes save you a lot of money.*

Victorian elegance is a rare commodity in Hawaii, but it exists in abundance at the Lahaina Inn. A stunning, authentic renovation has turned this 13-room inn into a fascinating, sumptuous place to stay. Each room is affectionately decorated with floral wallpaper, lace draperies, stately antiques, eyelet bedspreads, crystal decanters filled with port wine, and attractive tile and marble bathrooms. Private balconies overlook the bustling downtown—not exactly romantic, but a fact of life in this area. Some of the less expensive rooms are on the snug side, but still beautifully appointed. A simple continental breakfast is served buffet-style in the common area. Trays are provided to take back to your room for a truly intimate repast.

LAHAINA SHORES BEACH RESORT, Lahaina
475 Front Street
(808) 661-4835, (800) 628-6699
Inexpensive to Expensive

From Highway 30 in the town of Lahaina, turn west onto Dickenson Street, drive until it dead-ends at Front Street, and turn right.

Sheltered on a wide sandy beach, this attractive plantation-style resort is located just outside of Lahaina's town center. Most of the hotel's 200 spacious studio and one-bedroom units are worth your consideration, with towering ceilings, simple but comfortable furnishings, full kitchens, and wide lanais; many feature outstanding ocean views. Even the mountain vistas in the upper-floor units are lush and lovely. Although the outdoor pool is small and can get crowded, the ocean swimming is divine. You won't be living in the lap of luxury at the Lahaina Shores, but its relative privacy, affordability, and oceanfront location render it lipworthy.

THE PLANTATION INN, Lahaina
174 Lahainaluna Road
(808) 667-9225, (800) 433-6815
Inexpensive to Expensive

From Highway 30, turn west onto Lahainaluna Road.

This elegant, sparkling-clean, plantation-style bed and breakfast is an utterly refreshing place to stay. All 19 rooms have sensuous, plush furnishings and fabrics, hardwood floors, stained glass windows, bay and French windows, private verandas, canopy beds, VCRs, daily maid service, and central air-conditioning. Several rooms also have over-sized Jacuzzi tubs.

Attention to service is evident in the immaculate surroundings and in the care the staff takes to see to your every need. Outside you'll find a large lovely pool, an immaculate garden area, and a whimsical open-air common room where cookies and coffee are served all day. A generous full breakfast at either **LAHAINA COOLERS**, 183 Dickenson Street, Lahaina, (808) 661-7082, (Inexpensive), a nearby local favorite, or **ALOHA CANTINA**, Front Street, Lahaina, (808) 661-0830, (Inexpensive), on the waterfront, is included with your stay.

◆ **Romantic Suggestion:** You'll also want to plan at least one dinner at **GERARD'S** (reviewed in "Restaurant Kissing"), the hotel's lovely dining room. Special prices on meals are offered to guests.

WAI OLA, Lahaina
(808) 661-7901, (800) 492-4652
Inexpensive
Wedding facilities are available for a maximum of 70 people.

Call for reservations. Address and specific directions are provided upon confirmation.

Inexpensive *and* romantic accommodations are few and far between on the Hawaiian Islands, so we always get excited when we find a place we can enthusiastically recommend. Wai Ola is a private home, set in an unassuming residential neighborhood, just two blocks from Wahikuli Beach. Designed with privacy in mind, both available guest units have private entrances and are decorated with Peggy Hopper prints and pleasant furnishings. We preferred the larger one-bedroom apartment with a queen-size bed, TV/VCR, full kitchen and bathroom, and a sliding door that opens onto a common pool area enclosed by a colorful mural depicting orca whales. The studio apartment is considerably smaller and less expensive, though it too offers privacy, as well as a queen-size bed, TV/VCR, and a full kitchen. What a kissing bargain!

Pack insect repellent. Hawaii's trade winds tend to keep bugs on the move, but in the more tropical, jungle-like areas, mosquitoes are a problem.

Restaurant Kissing

AVALON, Lahaina
844 Front Street
(808) 667-5559
Moderate to Expensive
Wedding facilities are available for a maximum of 130 people.

From Highway 30 in the town of Lahaina, turn west onto Dickenson Street, drive until it dead-ends at Front Street, and turn right. The restaurant is at the back of a small courtyard of stores.

Set at the back of a small brick courtyard, somewhat away from the jam-packed main street of Lahaina, is this casual but charming oasis of Hawaiian and Asian cuisine. Actually, it isn't far enough away from the mainstream to be considered intimate, but the food and the setting are delightful and the savory offerings worth the culinary diversion from true romance. The noodles in ginger sauce or garlic–black bean sauce are delicious, the whole fresh opakapaka is beautifully presented, and the Szechwan cream pasta with scallops and sun-dried tomatoes is distinctive. For those who have a terrible time deciding which dessert to order, the decision has already been made. The only dessert is caramel Miranda, a plate of various tropical fruits baked atop a pool of caramel sauce, then topped with macadamia nut ice cream. Luscious!

DAVID PAUL'S LAHAINA GRILL, Lahaina
127 Lahainaluna Road
(808) 667-5117
Moderate for lunch, Expensive for dinner
Wedding facilities are available for a maximum of 100 people.

From Highway 30, turn west onto Lahainaluna Road.

Count on friendly, attentive service and superior, creative cooking at this sleek, bistro-style restaurant. The bold black-and-white-tiled floor, colorfully painted plates, and cozy tables draped in white linen fill the small dining room with drama. The varied menu includes a robust cioppino, a surprisingly authentic Caesar salad, and a light, fragrant vegetable paella they call *paellita*. Coffee lovers may want to try the unique but delicious roasted lamp chops marinated in Kona coffee and served with a hearty Kona coffee sauce.

GERARD'S, Lahaina
174 Lahainaluna Road, in the Plantation Inn
(808) 661-8939, (800) 433-6815
Expensive to Very Expensive
Wedding facilities are available for a maximum of 100 people.

From Highway 30, turn west onto Lahainaluna Road. The restaurant is located in the Plantation Inn.

Petite, quaint restaurants are hard to find in Hawaii: the large-scale hotels here like to emphasize affluence and grandeur. That is all fine and well, but Gerard's is a breath of fresh air. Relaxing in a gracious setting on an old-fashioned veranda, replete with white wicker furnishings, and enjoying a cornucopia of savory delights provides a perfect end to your perfect day on Maui. The menu is decidedly French, but the chef cleverly incorporates Hawaiian ingredients to create the freshest and most delicious meals possible. You won't be disappointed with any of the selections. The quails stuffed with truffles and foie gras, and the shiitake and oyster mushrooms in a light pastry shell were both absolutely wonderful. Prices are high, but you are encouraged to linger, enjoy soft guitar melodies, and savor every moment (and bite). Service is excellent, and reservations are a must.

KIMO'S, Lahaina
845 Front Street
(808) 661-4811
Inexpensive to Moderate

From Highway 30 in the town of Lahaina, turn west onto Dickenson Street, drive until it dead-ends at Front Street, and turn right.

Located in the heart of Front Street's commercial hustle and bustle, Kimo's lower dining room and bar resemble a crowded steak house—clearly not the most romantic of settings. Fortunately, crowds thin out in the upstairs open-air dining room, accented with beamed ceilings, Oriental carpets, high-backed Colonial-style chairs, and riveting views of the ocean and crashing surf. Kimo's casual menu features generous, well-prepared portions of steak and extremely fresh seafood. Try the fresh fish coated with Parmesan cheese and bread crumbs and topped with a lemon-caper butter—a real taste treat.

PACIFIC-O, Lahaina
505 Front Street
(808) 667-4341
Moderate to Expensive
Wedding facilities are available for a maximum of 150 people.

On the eastern end of Front Street, in the 505 Front Street Shopping Center.

Nothing compares to oceanfront dining (except maybe oceanfront kissing, but you have to eat sometime). The sound of the surf, the scent of the refreshing ocean air, and the sight of rolling turquoise waves remind you just how special the Hawaiian Islands are. You can appreciate all of these sensations from the casual outdoor deck of Pacific-O, along with inventive Pacific Rim cuisine and a relaxed tropical atmosphere. Inside, where there is open-air seating with green-and-white accents and pretty tiled floors, you can still experience the ocean.

Begin your meal with a tasty appetizer like shrimp wontons, whole shrimp wrapped in a basil leaf and a wonton wrapper, then served with a spicy sweet-and-sour sauce and Hawaiian salsa. For an entrée, consider trying the unique "Imu-style" catch of the day, grilled in a banana leaf and served with lemongrass pesto and vanilla bean sauce. The menu is truly imaginative, and the attentive staff can answer any questions you might have.

Lunchtime is extremely casual, with bikini-clad bodies wandering by as you dine, but at night, when the beach traffic slows down, Pacific-O turns exceedingly demure and romantic. Soft jazz accompanies your evening meal on Thursday, Friday, and Saturday nights from 9 P.M. until midnight.

◆ **Romantic Note:** The **OLD LAHAINA CAFE**, 505 Front Street, Lahaina, (808) 661-3303, (Moderate), next door hosts a clamorous nightly luau that you may want to see if you haven't experienced a luau yet. (For our thoughts on this matter, see "To Luau or Not To Luau" in the introduction). If you have a more amorous agenda, you can avoid the hubbub of this event by making sure your reservations at Pacific-O don't fall between 8 P.M. to 9 P.M.

> *Brochures that boast of ocean views from the rooms may mean a peekaboo glimpse of the water if you lean out the bathroom window. Be sure to get specifics about what kind of view you can really expect, and get it in writing.*

◆ **Romantic Warning:** Don't let the sexy sounds of a Spanish guitar entice you into **CASA DE MATEO**, right upstairs from Pacific-O. The so-called "Mexican" food is embarrassingly bad, with salsa that's more like spaghetti sauce and "nachos" made of flour tortillas filled with beans and squirted with sour cream. Don't say we didn't warn you.

Kihei

What can happen to paradise when you pave it without consideration for the natural beauty of the area is vividly on display in Kihei. One high-rise condominium complex after another sprawls along a once-spectacular sweep of beach. The beach is actually still magnificent, but the landscape has been indelibly changed and the traffic through town can be a nightmare. Most of the properties in Kihei are standard condo units—some with views, many directly on the beach, all with pools, and most without air-conditioning. Some of the best bargains around are located in this part of the island, and as long as you stick to our recommendations a romantic Hawaiian respite is possible in this busy neighborhood.

◆ **Romantic Note:** Kihei marks the border of the dry section between north and south on the island. In a typical year, only 10 to 15 inches of water fall in this region. The arid conditions contribute to the barren landscape, but mean fewer days spent indoors during the rainy season.

Hotel/Bed and Breakfast Kissing

MANA KAI-MAUI, Kihei   ◆
2960 South Kihei Road
(808) 879-1561, (800) 525-2025 (mainland)
Inexpensive to Expensive (rates include rental car)

Call for directions.

At the southernmost end of Kihei, looking out to the idyllic beaches of Wailea and Makena, this high-rise condominium building is an inexpensive place to enjoy great views and a sweeping sandy beach. Although the hotel on the whole is in pressing need of renovation, an upgrade is in progress that will hopefully spruce up the dated, sometimes downright drab one- and two-bedroom condominiums. In the meanwhile, what's the draw? For incredibly low prices, this hotel provides the basics for a romantic tropical interlude, including full kitchens and small but functional lanais with stellar views of the water and Haleakala.

◆ **Romantic Suggestion:** Resting just above water's edge, the **FIVE PALMS BEACH GRILL**, (Inexpensive to Moderate), the hotel's casual beachfront restaurant, offers terrace seating with beautiful ocean views. Service is friendly and laid-back, as is the kitchen, which serves up standard, hearty breakfasts, salads and sandwiches for lunch, and steak and fish for dinner.

◆ **Romantic Warning:** The bar at the entrance to the restaurant has a rather loud television and is filled with smoke. Hold your breath as you walk by; the atmosphere inside the dining room is totally unrelated.

SUGAR BEACH RESORT, Kihei
145 North Kihei Road
Reservations through Condominium Rentals Hawaii
(808) 879-2778
(800) 367-5242 (mainland U.S.), (800) 663-2101 (Canada)
Inexpensive to Expensive
Wedding facilities are available for a maximum of 200 people.

Off Highway 350, about three miles north of downtown Kihei.

Located between a high-rise hotel and a small strip mall with a Mexican restaurant and a convenience store, this mustard-colored low-rise condominium complex feels a bit cramped. The saving grace here is the five-mile stretch of soft sandy beach, which is directly in front of the building, just over a gentle grassy knoll. Soothing sounds of the waves help drown out the less soothing sounds of nearby traffic and the many children playing in the pool area, which is set between the two sections of the condominiums.

Sugar Beach is a good, affordable place to stay right on the beach (all oceanfront rooms have stunning views of the tranquil Pacific). Every unit is air-conditioned and has a full kitchen and standard bathroom, but the lack of affectionate ambience is disappointing. Decor in the privately owned condos can vary considerably from unit to unit.

Some have a rustic homey feel, with personal knickknacks and old hide-a-beds that could use reupholstering. Others have more of a hotel feel, with matching white wicker furniture, pale green carpet, and attractive floral linens. With these interiors, you may have to keep reminding yourself that you really are in the Hawaiian tropics, and not just in Southern California on a sunny day. We suggest that you wander on the beach, smell the fresh air, and wet your toes in the warm water to help refresh your memory.

◆ **Romantic Suggestion:** Units above the first floor that end with the number "35" have incredible views of both the ocean and the West Maui mountains. These rooms are also the furthest from the commotion around the pool area.

Restaurant Kissing

A PACIFIC CAFE, Kihei
1279 South Kihei Road, Suite B-201
(808) 879-0069
Moderate to Expensive
Wedding facilities are available for a maximum of 200 people.

Just off the main road in central Kihei, in the Azeka Place 2 Shopping Center.

Many island restaurants rely on oceanfront settings and tropical splendor to keep their patrons happy, but not A Pacific Cafe, which is located in a nondescript shopping center. You may decide the destination is not Hawaiian enough to meet your tropical expectations. Be patient: the expansive dining room is striking and truly complements the chef's culinary skill. Creative architectural touches, colorful artwork, vaulted ceilings, and warm terra-cotta-colored walls give distinction to the two separate dining rooms. Bamboo chairs with muted floral cushions and tables without tablecloths contribute to the casual but upbeat atmosphere.

Food is where A Pacific Cafe gets serious. The tiger-eye ahi sushi tempura (lightly coated with batter and quickly fried) with Chinese mustard sauce practically melts in your mouth, and the mahimahi with a garlic-sesame crust and creamy lime-ginger sauce is unforgettable. Each dish is beautifully presented and perfectly prepared. Our only complaint is that service is informative to the point of being intrusive and annoying. No one needs that much detail before they eat.

Wailea

In many ways, Wailea is the premier destination on Maui. Unlike the developments at Kaanapali, which are squished together with very little breathing room, Wailea's series of prestige hotel and condominium developments are quite spread out. You couldn't say that it isn't crowded here, and the shore is indeed obscured by these super resorts, but it isn't anywhere near as dense as Kaanapali. Plus, the resorts are absolutely some of the sexiest places to stay on the island, and the beaches are simply awesome. The major hotels in this area line up along a mile of premier beachfront like five sisters posing for a picture: Kea Lani, Stouffer Beach Resort Wailea, Four Seasons Resort Wailea, Maui Inter-Continental Wailea, and the prettiest sibling, Grand Wailea. It is hard to imagine being disappointed with any of them.

Those who have golf clubs or tennis racquets along can try to reserve time at the famous **WAILEA GOLF COURSE**, (808) 879-2966, or the 14-court **WAILEA TENNIS CLUB**, (808) 879-1958. But no matter where you stay, the entire area is one big playground for those who can afford to play.

♦ **Romantic Note:** The beaches here are among the most beautiful on Hawaii. They are somewhat difficult to reach around the massive hotels, but they are accessible. Remember, all beaches in Hawaii are available for use by the public.

Hotel/Bed and Breakfast Kissing

FOUR SEASONS RESORT, Wailea
3900 Wailea Alanui Drive
(808) 874-8000, (800) 334-6284
Very Expensive to Unbelievably Expensive
Wedding facilities and services are available for a maximum of 500 people; call for details.

Just off Highway 31, in the town of Wailea.

In this upscale resort neighborhood, one grandiose place begins to look like another, with the same stellar amenities and superior services. However, the Four Seasons Resort stands out for its fine assortment of 380 guest rooms decorated in refined shades of pale green or peach and appointed with spacious marble baths, soaking tubs, and separate glass showers. As you'd expect, the oceanfront rooms are prime, but since the property is set away from the water's edge, the views aren't exactly up close and personal. Still, the surroundings are gilt-edged and worth your wholehearted consideration. A fabulously elegant pool area with private cabanas lining the edge is undeniably one of the best places to kiss, and the Four Seasons' restaurants, particularly **SEASONS** (reviewed in "Restaurant Kissing"), burst with romantic flair. The **PACIFIC GRILL**, (Very Expensive), serving a bountiful breakfast buffet and casual fare, is also first-rate.

Romantic Suggestion: The various romance/honeymoon packages offered by the Four Seasons Resort are worth asking about. Any romantic detail you may have forgotten, they take care of.

GRAND WAILEA RESORT, Wailea
3850 Wailea Alanui Drive
(808) 875-1234, (800) 888-6100
Unbelievably Expensive and Beyond
Wedding facilities are available for a maximum of 2,000 people.

Just off Highway 31, in the town of Wailea.

There is little argument that the Grand Wailea is the ultimate resort spa in Hawaii—and possibly the world. This might sound like an exaggeration, but in fact it may be an understatement. Six hundred million dollars' worth of sheer opulence and grandeur dazzle you at every turn.

Flowers, water, trees, sounds, lights, and art have been utilized as design elements in 40 acres of sumptuous, tropical surroundings that will exceed your wildest fantasies. The 2,000-foot-long activity pool, better known as the Wailea Canyon, features water slides, waterfalls, caves, rapids, a Jacuzzi, and a sauna; it even has a water elevator that lifts you back to the top once you've completed the journey. A second, more formal pool features a spouting water fountain and a stunning hibiscus mosaic on the bottom. You can also take advantage of the scuba-diving pool (lessons are available), racquetball courts, aerobics room, game room, and weight-training room. Thoroughly exhausted? Pamper yourselves at the Grand Wailea's world-class **SPA GRANDE** (reviewed in "Miscellaneous Kissing"), which offers every conceivable therapy for the body.

When you first arrive, be sure to get specific directions to your room; it's all too easy to get lost on the way through the Grand Wailea's maze of six independent guest-room wings. Sumptuously appointed in up-scale hotel style, all of the rooms are lovely and chock-full of amenities (like ocean-view soaking tubs), although some rooms still retain a basic hotel feel. Ocean-view rooms look out over the pool, and are the most coveted and expensive in the resort. Actually, the Grand Wailea holds two of the most expensive suites in the world. For $10,000 a night, you too can live in the lap of luxury, but only if a sultan or celebrity hasn't beaten you to the punch. As if this weren't enough, each floor has its own butler on call. And for a real splurge, you can even order an extremely private multicourse dinner served by your own personal waiter on your lanai. Now that's romantic.

Appropriately, there's also an utterly quaint wedding chapel, set in the middle of a tropical garden and a freshwater pond. Its stained glass windows, depicting handsome Polynesians in repose, radiate golden light with the movement of the sun. As many as 60 weddings a month take place here. If this is where you'd like to exchange your vows, the Grand Wailea's wedding director can help create the wedding of your dreams, and maybe even beyond.

As you might expect, dining at this palace is a lavish experience. A near-legendary Japanese restaurant called **KINCHA** (Unbelievably Expensive) has incorporated more than 800 tons of rock from Mount Fuji in its foundation and surrounding gardens. With its soaring ceilings, open-air dining, and 40-foot-high murals, the **GRAND DINING ROOM,** (Expensive), is literally sublime (dinners are being served buffet-style for $29 per person until further notice). The thatched roofed **HUMUHUMUNUKUNUKUAPUA'A**, (Expensive to Very Expensive), (don't ask us to pronounce it; it's hard enough to spell) floats in a massive saltwater lagoon where tropical fish thrive. And there's more, but you should see it for yourselves.

◆ **Romantic Note:** Children in tow rarely make for a romantic escape, but if you happen to have the little darlings along, the Grand Wailea offers a 20,000-square-foot wonderland of day care. A computer room, theater, soda shop, arts-and-crafts room with pottery wheels, video-game room, infant care center, and a wonderful outdoor playground provide supervised fun for the younger set. The price for one child is $40 for a half-day, or $65 for a full day ($10 additional if you are not a hotel guest).

JASMINE HOUSE, Wailea   Unrated
883 Kupulau Drive
(808) 875-0400, (800) 604-4233 (mainland)
Inexpensive to Expensive
Wedding facilities are available for a maximum of 70 people.

Call for reservations and directions.

Still under construction when this book went to print, Jasmine House is a bed and breakfast that shows telltale signs of being a truly lip-worthy destination. Situated in an upscale residential neighborhood, the Spanish-style white stucco home enjoys views of the ocean, volcanic mountains, and other Hawaiian islands. Of the five available suites, the upstairs master suite promises to be the most spacious and impressive, with black lacquered Oriental furnishings, a private Jacuzzi tub, and French doors that swing open to a private lanai with delicious ocean views. All of the guest rooms have use of the kitchen and living areas in the main house, as well as access to the quiet Spanish courtyard overflowing with date palm, macadamia nut, orange, grapefruit, lichee, mango, and guava trees.

KEA LANI HOTEL, Wailea
4100 Wailea Alanui Drive
(808) 875-4100, (800) 882-4100
Very Expensive to Unbelievably Expensive and Beyond
Wedding facilities are available for a maximum of 600 people.

Just off Highway 31, in the town of Wailea.

Twenty-two acres of palm trees, turquoise lagoons, and tropical landscaping encompass this Mediterranean-style white stucco hotel. You will feel as if you have been transported to Greece, where scintillating white archways, alcoves, balconies, and footbridges contrast with the azure ocean.

All of the Kea Lani's 413 ocean-view rooms are impressive one-bedroom suites, beautifully designed with curved doorways, plush white fabrics and linens, and lovely wood antiques. Oversized marble bathrooms with deep soaking tubs and double lanais enhance the feeling of spaciousness. Amenities include full entertainment centers (two televisions, stereo, VCR, and a CD player), plus a microwave, refrigerator, and coffee-maker. For an extra splurge, reserve an even larger, more extravagant beachfront villa, replete with a full kitchen, two full bathrooms, laundry facilities, home entertainment center, and a private oceanfront plunge pool.

With its splendid multilevel pool area, 140-foot water slide, private poolside cabanas, wonderfully silky sand beach, excellent outdoor dining, and superior service, the Kea Lani competes effortlessly with Wailea's other premier properties. What makes this property stand out is the fact that its base prices are almost $100 less than any of its nearby competitors'. Although it's still expensive by most standards, it's worth every last penny.

◆ **Romantic Suggestion:** You don't have to walk far to find excellent cuisine at the Kea Lani Hotel. Breakfast, lunch, and dinner are served in the exquisite open-air dining room called **KEA LANI—THE RESTAURANT** (reviewed in "Restaurant Kissing").

MAKENA SURF, Wailea
3750 Wailea Alanui Drive
Reservations through Destination Resorts
(808) 879-1595, (800) 367-5246 (mainland)
Very Expensive to Unbelievably Expensive

Call for reservations and directions.

These four sprawling, private townhouse condominiums scattered around the Wailea beachfront aren't grand, but the attractive array of units provides an alternative to the excesses of Wailea's huge hotels. Each one-, two-, or three-bedroom unit is decorated differently, but you will find all the comforts of home plus central air-conditioning, a spacious lanai with partial or full ocean views, and a full kitchen. The only drawbacks are a somewhat cramped feeling, with front doors or lanais facing one another, and the rather small pool areas. Still, the homey surroundings make this a quiet and relaxing place to stay.

MAUI INTER-CONTINENTAL RESORT, Wailea
3700 Wailea Alanui Drive
(808) 879-1922, (800) 367-2960
Very Expensive to Unbelievably Expensive
Wedding facilities are available for a maximum of 900 people.

Just off Highway 31, in the town of Wailea.

The 22-acre Maui Inter-Continental Resort was the first hotel property built on the Wailea beach strip and it is also the most recently renovated, not to mention the closest to the water's edge. These last two factors, along with comparatively moderate prices and the widespread distribution of its 516 rooms, make it an ideal find. Although the $37 million restoration was primarily focused on improving the meeting rooms and banquet facilities, the oceanfront and ocean-view rooms were also generously upgraded. In addition to their great views, these rooms now sport Berber rugs, neutral beach tones, and attractive wicker furniture. As for the remaining rooms, though more affordable, they are sorely in need of renovation and cannot be romantically recommended until major improvements are made.

All of the amenities are here: an expansive pool area, sandy beach, rather good restaurants, and attentive service. The Maui Inter-Continental may not be as elegant as its ritzy neighbors, but it is still worth your affectionate consideration.

MAUI PRINCE HOTEL, Wailea
5400 Makena Alanui Drive
(808) 874-1111, (800) 321-6284
Expensive to Unbelievably Expensive
Wedding facilities and services are available for a maximum of 500 people; call for details.

Just off Highway 31, in the town of Wailea.

One of the last properties on the road through Wailea, the Maui Prince is surprisingly modest compared to its competition. An expansive, nondescript lobby encircles a small open-air courtyard with miniature waterfalls and an overstocked koi pond (we've never seen so many koi in one pond!). Although the hallways are somewhat sterile and even dated, all of the hotel's 310 rooms are attractive and comfortable, appointed with Peggy Hopper Hawaiian prints, white linens and Hawaiian-quilted pillows, and spacious lanais that face the ocean and the swimming pools. If outdoor activities are high on your agenda (second, of course, to kissing), you won't be disappointed with the Maui Prince's options: golf, snorkeling, tennis, swimming, scuba diving, boogie boarding, volleyball, and sailing, to name a few. While the Maui Prince lacks the upscale feel of its neighbors down the way, it can still provide you with all of the ingredients for a blissful tropical getaway—at a much better price.

♦ **Romantic Suggestion:** Although dining options are vast at the Maui Prince, they aren't necessarily romantic. **HAKONE,** (Expensive), serves excellent Japanese cuisine in a somewhat stark atmosphere, while the **PRINCE COURT,** (Expensive to Very Expensive), focuses on Pacific Rim delicacies.

STOUFFER RENAISSANCE WAILEA BEACH RESORT, Wailea
3550 Wailea Alanui Drive
(808) 879-4900, (800) 992-4532
Very Expensive to Unbelievably Expensive
Wedding facilities are available for a maximum of 100 people.

Just off Highway 31, in the town of Wailea.

A multimillion-dollar renovation has turned this Stouffer into a showcase of refinement and elegance. Water fountains flank the grand open-air lobby, set overlooking the ocean and appointed with cozy love seats and exotic flower arrangements. Winding pathways dotted with intriguing statues and lush gardens meander through more than 15 tropical acres, leading down to the lovely pool and pristine Mokapu Beach.

Guests are welcomed with a traditional lei greeting and ushered to their stately, sizable room, attractively decorated in soft tones of beige and taupe, and appointed with wicker love seats, cane coffee tables, TV/VCRs, large lanais with cushioned wrought-iron chairs and tables, and pretty tiled baths. Unfortunately, because of the way the property is situated, the ocean-view rooms have poor visibility out to the magical waters of the Pacific. This is one of the few places where a water-oriented room may not be the prize of the resort. Most of the other rooms have rather rich tropical vistas.

♦ **Romantic Note:** It can be tough to decide between the Stouffer's two distinguished restaurants, **RAFFLES** (reviewed in "Restaurant Kissing") and the **PALM COURT,** (Moderate to Expensive). Both are excellent, and the surroundings are superb. So forget deciding: dine at the casual, open-air Palm Court for lunch and the slightly more formal and refined Raffles for dinner. Your taste buds and hearts will be eternally grateful.

Restaurant Kissing

KEA LANI—THE RESTAURANT, Wailea
4100 Wailea Alanui Drive, in the Kea Lani Hotel
(808) 875-4100, (800) 659-4100
Moderate to Very Expensive
Wedding facilities are available for a maximum of 100 people.

Just off Highway 31, in the town of Wailea.

Ensconced in a grand hall with towering arched windows and a cathedral ceiling, the Kea Lani's namesake restaurant is a stunning place to dine. Oversized tropical bouquets and lush greenery add color to the stark white decor, providing an elegant ambience. The menu lists an interesting mix of Mediterranean and continental cuisine, most of it quite good. The fresh fish is always moist and tender, and the home-made desserts are stupendous.

◆ **Romantic Suggestion: CIAO**, (Moderate), the Kea Lani's less expensive dining option, is a delightful casual eatery with elegant Corinthian columns, marble floors, and a small handful of wrought-iron tables. Excellent cappuccinos and Maui's best pastries are served here at almost any time of the day. What a shame it is located in such a hard-to-find section of the Kea Lani.

RAFFLES, Wailea
3550 Wailea Alanui Drive,
in the Stouffer Renaissance Wailea Beach Resort
(808) 879-4900, (800) 992-4532
Moderate to Unbelievably Expensive and Beyond
Wedding facilities are available for a maximum of 12 people.

Just off Highway 31, in the town of Wailea.

Enormous picture windows showcase lush tropical scenery and ocean views at this regal, refined restaurant. Crisp white linens and dimly lit table lamps contribute to the room's understated elegance, perfectly designed for a dreamy, romantic dinner for two. Service is exceptional, and the talented kitchen consistently creates impressive Pacific Rim cuisine. After your meal has concluded, walk hand-in-hand through the Stouffer's meandering oceanfront property to the water's edge for a moonlit kiss. (Raffles' desserts are good, but this is even better.)

THE SEA WATCH RESTAURANT AT WAILEA,
Wailea
1 Wailea Golf Club Drive
(808) 875-8080
Moderate to Expensive
Wedding facilities are available for a maximum of 250 people.

Call for directions.

Because of the advantageous hillside setting, every table at the casually elegant Sea Watch Restaurant boasts views of Molokini Crater, Kahoolawe Island, and the sparkling blue Pacific Ocean. However, there is more than just sea watching to appreciate at this golf-course dining room. Superior Pacific Rim cuisine, featuring the freshest ingredients, is the specialty of the house, and each dish is presented with polished finesse. The grilled chicken breast in a guava-sesame crust is as delectable as it sounds, and the fresh fish options are equally savory. The chef will wok-sear your fish Thai-style with spicy lemongrass and black bean sauce; sauté it with shiitake mushrooms, capers, and lime beurre blanc; or grill it with fresh basil, tomatoes, and lemon butter sauce. (Not an easy choice, but you make the call.) Dessert decisions are a little easier: you simply can't go wrong with the ginger crème brûlée or the lilikoi cheesecake. Service is prompt and attentive.

SEASONS, Wailea
3900 Wailea Alanui Drive, at the Four Seasons Resort
(808) 874-8000
Expensive to Very Expensive
Wedding facilities are available for a maximum of 50 people.

The Four Seasons Resort is just off Highway 31, in the town of Wailea; the restaurant is in the hotel.

Fine food, soft music, low lighting, and a dance floor—with romance in mind, what more could you ask for? Not much. The Four Seasons' signature restaurant offers extraordinary cuisine, elegant ambience, and exemplary service. Varying shades of taupe and pale wood accents fill the dramatic dining room. Outdoor seating, surrounded by glowing torches, is slightly more casual, but every detail here is polished and refined. The cuisine, which they call "New American," incorporates locally grown produce and fresh Hawaiian ingredients into savory dishes like herb-roasted veal medallions with wild mushroom-onion tart in a pinot noir sauce, or grilled beef tenderloin served with Gorgonzola-potato fritters. Fresh-from-the-ocean fish entrées are always available and always excellent.

◆ **Romantic Option:** For $500, you can prearrange an **ULTIMATE ROMANTIC DINNER**. The price tag includes a private table on the grassy lawn overlooking the ocean. Tiki torches are lit all around, and your table for two is set with fine china, crystal, silver, crisp white linens, and fresh flowers. Iced champagne and an exquisite dinner (individually designed for your tastes and preferences) is served by your own personal waiter. This indulgence goes way off our cost rating chart, but for a special occasion, it just may be worth it. Let your credit limit be your guide.

Outdoor Kissing

WAILEA BEACH/POLO BEACH WALK

These beaches are in front of the Grand Wailea, Four Seasons, and Kea Lani hotels. Look for signs to either beach.

Can a beach walk be romantic if there isn't soft sand to dig your toes into? After wandering down the rocky stretch of shoreline between Wailea and Polo beaches, you will not only be convinced that romance is absolutely possible on a sandless beach, but you will also discover that it doesn't involve gritty sand particles in your shoes.

Exotic native plants line the partially paved walking path, and there are numerous places to stop, sit, smooch, and just savor the beauty around you. One of the most striking sites is **WAILEA POINT**, where furious waves crash into the island's volcanic edge (a Kodak moment if we've ever seen one).

Don't make the mistake of thinking this beach walk is reserved only for paying guests at the neighboring exclusive hotels. We've said it before, but it's worth saying again: one of the beauties of Hawaii is that there is no such thing as a private beach. The only trick is finding the public right-of-way path.

Miscellaneous Kissing

SPA GRANDE, Wailea
3858 Wailea Alanui Drive
(808) 875-1234, (800) 888-6100
Fees start at $50 a day for guests and $100 a day for nonguests.

Just off Highway 31, in the town of Wailea.

Imagine having two massage therapists working on your weary, appreciative body at the same time. Or being massaged side-by-side with your beloved, followed by a relaxing private herbal bath *à deux*. Body facials, all forms of hydra therapy, and total beauty treatments are performed in an amazing marble-ensconced forum. Here you can try the extraordinary "Terme Wailea" (women and men have their own separate areas for this one). You start with a Japanese-style bath or a loofah scrub, proceed to a plunge into a hot mineral tub, then a cool one, followed by steam, sauna, a waterfall shower, a unique herbal bath, and then a seemingly jet-powered shower. Combinations can total into the hundreds of dollars, depending on what indulgences you choose. You won't have the energy to kiss after this experience, but holding each other close for hours afterwards will be sheer bliss.

Upcountry

On the northeastern slopes of Haleakala, a different facet of island life is on display for those who can bear to leave the beach. Upcountry is where you'll find the last remnants of true "local" life on the islands.

As you drive farther away from the crowds, you climb up undulating hills covered with emerald green fields and dotted with patches of chaparral. Horses, cattle, and farm crops thrive here. At the end of the road is **TEDESCHI VINEYARDS,** Highway 37 on Ulupalakua Ranch, Ulupalakua, (808) 878-6058, the only commercial winery in Hawaii. Tours and wine tastings are available (the pineapple wine is better than it sounds), and the setting is lovely.

Upcountry weather is entirely different from the coast's. In the winter, evening temperatures can drop into the 40s and rain can be persistent. But the views are spellbinding, and the country calm is superlative. No high-rise or condominium developments exist for miles around. If Maui's over-developed beaches feel like paradise lost, this may just be paradise found.

Haliimaile

Restaurant Kissing

HALIIMAILE GENERAL STORE, Haliimaile
900 Haliimaile Road
(808) 572-2666
Very Inexpensive to Inexpensive
Wedding facilities are available for a maximum of 150 people.

Five miles up Highway 37 (Haleakala Highway), turn left at the Haliimaile cut-off sign. Continue one and a half miles to the Haliimaile General Store on the right.

Don't miss Haliimaile's old-fashioned general-store-turned-restaurant on your way through Upcountry. Recently renovated, this historic landmark has been tastefully transformed into a very casual, slightly earthy restaurant and cafe. Colorfully painted tropical fish hang from the high ceilings, and upbeat modern art graces the peach-colored walls. Light floods into the front dining room through large windows that look out onto the wraparound veranda, where you can sit outside and enjoy the Upcountry breezes. Interesting menu items like the Brie and grape quesadillas served with sweet pea guacamole, the Szechwan barbecued salmon, or the delicious homemade cakes and pies will keep your taste buds busy and your mind off the traffic whizzing past on nearby Highway 37.

Makawao

Little Makawao has slowly (and reluctantly) made the transition from 1968 to the 1990s. An eclectic assortment of restaurants and country shops line the small Western-style main street. Some are strictly bohemian (but still interesting), while others are urbane enough to sell lattes and designer ceramics. **ISLAND GLASS BLOWERS STUDIO AND GALLERY**, 3620 Baldwin Ave, Suite 101-A, Makawao, (808) 572-4527, is a favorite stop for hand-blown glass.

Hotel/Bed and Breakfast Kissing

OLINDA COUNTRY COTTAGE, Makawao
Reservations through Hawaii's Best Bed and Breakfasts
(808) 885-4550, (800) 262-9912 (mainland)
Inexpensive

Call for reservations. Address and specific directions are provided upon confirmation.

Breezes are nice and cool at 4,000 feet, which is where you will find this modest country cottage, far from the hustle and bustle of any town (not that Upcountry villages are really hectic). The lone one-bedroom cottage sits on a hillside with amazing views of the clouds floating over the island, casting shadows on the ocean and the cane fields. Inside, you'll find a queen-size bed with a down comforter, a cozy living room with a brick hearth and fireplace, and a full kitchen. Country-style floral wallpaper, curtains, and linens, and antique trinkets lend a homey touch.

Breakfast is provided the first morning, but you're on your own after that. The place isn't at all fancy, but it is very private, and extremely cozy when you snuggle up by the fireplace. (Hard to believe, but it really gets cool enough up here to enjoy a warm fire at night.)

♦ **Romantic Note:** The required minimum stay is two nights.

Restaurant Kissing

CASANOVA, Makawao
1188 Makawao Avenue
(808) 572-0220
Inexpensive
Wedding facilities are available for a maximum of 199 people.

At the intersection of Highway 365 (Makawao Avenue) and Highway 390 (Baldwin Avenue).

It's not easy to accommodate many tastes and styles without appearing confused and awkward, but somehow this attractive Italian eatery pulls it off. The front half of the restaurant is a somewhat smoke-filled nightspot where locals hang out while waiting for the music to begin. Anything from traditional folk music to reggae may be the special entertainment for the evening; sets start at 9:00 P.M. and continue into the wee hours. The back half of the restaurant holds a series of snugly grouped tables where you can indulge in appetizing Italian cuisine. Fresh bread, hearty portions, and efficient service are all standard at Casanova. Although the real Casanova had the reputation of being fickle, this namesake is always reliable.

Kula

Hotel/Bed and Breakfast Kissing

BLOOM COTTAGE, Kula
229 Kula Highway
(808) 878-1425
Inexpensive

Call for reservations. Specific directions are provided upon confirmation.

Named for the blooming herb and flower gardens that surround it, this charming white cottage with green shutters is straight out of a storybook. Those in search of quiet solitude will appreciate the cottage's semi-remote Upcountry location at 3,000 feet on the hushed slopes of Mount Haleakala. Because it is set behind the owner's home just off the Kula Highway, the only potential distraction is the sound of afternoon traffic.

Quaint antiques and knickknacks add touches of country charm to the two-bedroom cottage's lovely interior, fashioned with hardwood floors and high peaked white ceilings. When the cool fog rolls down the mountain, you can take refuge by the warm, wood-stocked fireplace or watch classic movies on the TV and VCR that are provided. Breakfast is your own private affair; the fully equipped kitchen is stocked with coffee, tea, island fruit and juice, granola, muffins, and breads.

♦ **Romantic Alternative:** Another overnight option in Kula is the **SILVER CLOUD UPCOUNTRY GUEST RANCH**, RR 2, Box 201, Kula, (808) 878-6101, (Inexpensive). Also known for its glorious pastoral views and relaxed setting, this quiet nine-acre property once was part of a working cattle ranch. Guests can stay in one of the 12 homey, modestly appointed guest rooms. A full, home-cooked country breakfast served family-style in the garden sun room the following morning is included in price. The Silver Cloud is a nice option for those who want to get away from it all and soak up the Upcountry's carefree, secluded beauty.

Restaurant Kissing

KULA LODGE RESTAURANT, Kula
RR 1, Box 475
(808) 878-2517
Inexpensive
Wedding facilities are available for a maximum of 120 people.

On the Haleakala Highway (Highway 377), near Crater Road.

As you begin the ascent to Haleakala Crater, you'll stumble across Kula Lodge Restaurant, renowned for its sensational views. Perched high in the mountains, the rustic dining room surveys panoramic vistas of gardens, forests, sloping hillsides, and the ocean in the distance. Two-person tables set alongside the windows enable you to relish the spectacular views first-hand. Modest and relaxed (no linens, no tablecloths), the casual dining room features open wood-beamed ceilings, wood sculptures, and leafy plants. Service is friendly and efficient, and the kitchen does a fair job with its standard seafood menu. We especially enjoyed the homemade salmon ravioli and sliced, roasted eggplant. After you've eaten your fill, wander through the restaurant's expansive herb and vegetable garden, where the chef hand-picks garnishes for every meal.

◆ **Romantic Suggestion:** Kula Lodge also has five rustic overnight accommodations that are worth mentioning. Not intended to be fancy, these modestly appointed chalets have private porches (some share the restaurant's magnificent view) and queen-size beds; one even has a fireplace.

High season is from mid-December through the end of March. Low season runs approximately from April to mid-December. Not only are rates lower in low season, but business hours may be more limited too.

Outdoor Kissing

HALEAKALA NATIONAL PARK
(808) 572-9306 for general park information
$4 admission fee per carload

Call for directions and additional informaiton.

Extending from the summit of Mount Haleakala eastward to the southern coast, Haleakala National Park links Haleakala Crater and the Kipahulu Coast near Hana. Although no roads connect these two areas, both can be reached by car from the town of Kahului. The park was originally created to preserve the spectacular beauty of Haleakala Crater, but recent additions have helped to protect the surrounding delicate ecosystems of Kipahulu Valley, the scenic pools along 'Ohe'o Gulch, and the splendid coastline.

Nothing is more spectacular than witnessing sunrise at 10,000 feet from the top of Haleakala Crater. Unfortunately, this is no secret, and everyone else on the island has the same idea (including those on the downhill bicycle excursions). The never-ending line of buses and cars on this windy, fog-shrouded road at 4 A.M. in the morning is nothing short of astonishing. This extinct volcanic crater is definitely worth the drive, but there are other, less crowded times to view Haleakala's splendor. Sunset, when the weather is more apt to be clear and the views are endless, is exceptional. Don't forgo a trip to Haleakala if the weather looks stormy—this can be the best and most thrilling time of all to see the crater, mainly because nobody else is on the road and the cloud formations hovering above the crater are hauntingly ominous.

◆ **Romantic Warning:** Take your time and drive cautiously up the long, winding road that leads to Haleakala Crater; local ranchers let their cattle graze and roam freely on the mountain's steep, grassy slopes. Cows cross the road at their leisure and don't bother to look both ways before crossing. Also, it can get very cold up here at sunrise or at dusk; expect (and prepare for) 30-degree temperatures. It does warm up during the day, so wear layers of clothing you can shed as the sun heats the mountain air.

East Maui

Haiku

Hotel/Bed and Breakfast Kissing

ANUE NUE, Haiku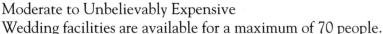
110 Kane Road
(808) 572-7586
Moderate to Unbelievably Expensive
Wedding facilities are available for a maximum of 70 people.

Call for reservations. Specific directions are provided upon confirmation.

You'll be amazed (and thoroughly impressed) with the quality and radiance of what has been created at Anue Nue (the Rainbow House). The sprawling U-shaped cedar structure, which comprises two self-contained pavilions (one at each end) and a main house at the center, sits on six acres of beautifully landscaped grounds with distant views of the Pacific. The house frames a tropical courtyard with Japanese gardens and a koi pond. Although each unit has its own entrance and is extremely private, long covered walkways between the pavilions and the main house make it possible to rent and share the entire building (perfect for a wedding party or if you are traveling in a group).

The two intimate pavilion units each have a queen-size bed, fully equipped kitchen, washer and dryer, charming terra-cotta-tiled bath, and designer decor with vivid French art, crisp linens, and hardwood floors. The main house boasts a similarly bold but plush interior and comfortable amenities, but it has much more space and can be rented as either a two- or three-bedroom unit. Champagne, a fruit basket, and tropical flowers welcome you to your room, and a breakfast basket is left in your refrigerator to prepare at your own morning pace.

Calling Anue Nue a vacation rental doesn't seem appropriate, but it really isn't a resort or a bed and breakfast either. Instead, it offers the best of both: resort-like amenities (a pool, tennis courts, and spa services), along with the coziness and individuality of an exclusive bed and breakfast. Whatever you call it, this unique retreat is just the kind of tropical therapy the doctor ordered.

◆ **Romantic Option:** There is also a lower-floor apartment available in the innkeepers' separate home. It is a little too mismatched and funky to be the preferred romantic suite, but it does have character and is the only unit that falls into the Inexpensive category.

GOLDEN BAMBOO RANCH, Haiku
Reservations through Hawaii's Best Bed and Breakfasts
(808) 885-4550, (800) 262-9912 (mainland)
Inexpensive

Call for reservations. Address and specific directions are provided upon confirmation.

Wind blowing through the trees, birds chirping, and the occasional whinny of a horse are about the only sounds you'll hear at this quiet little ranch. A wide variety of tropical fruit trees, flowers, and plants share the property with the friendly innkeepers and four resident horses. Needless to say, the pace at Golden Bamboo Ranch is relaxed and the atmosphere unpretentious. Three private little apartment-like units are available in one building, with an individual cottage right next door. The cottage is the most spacious and homey of the options, but each one has a certain amount of country charm. Simple breakfast fixings are left in your fridge to enjoy in your own sweet time.

HAIKULEANA, Haiku
Reservations through Hawaii's Best Bed and Breakfasts
(808) 885-4550, (800) 262-9912 (mainland)
Inexpensive

Call for reservations. Address and specific directions are provided upon confirmation.

Finally, a traditional bed and breakfast. The Haikuleana is a historic plantation home located in the small neighborhood setting of Haiku. Each of the four cozy guest rooms has the warmth and charm you expect at a B&B, with country-style wallpaper or cedar-paneled walls, pinstriped comforters, floral pillows, hardwood floors, and wicker furnishings. A comfortable living room with floral curtains and cushioned rattan furniture provides a sunny spot to relax or visit with other guests. Generous gourmet breakfasts are served family-style every morning. Such close proximity to other guests isn't for everyone, but those who have come to know and appreciate what B&Bs are all about will love the Haikuleana.

PILIALOHA, Haiku
(808) 572-1440
Inexpensive

Call for reservations. Address and specific directions are provided upon confirmation.

A lone cottage adjacent to the owners' home crowns an acre of green lawn surrounded by a thick evergreen and eucalyptus forest. Everything is immaculate, totally private, and affectionately decorated, with modest yet comfortable furnishings and a beautifully stocked kitchen filled with breakfast goodies. Beach chairs, picnic coolers, floats, snorkeling equipment, and blankets are available to make any outing hassle-free. It may not be the beach, but this is every inch an intimate romantic getaway.

Huelo

Hotel/Bed and Breakfast Kissing

HUELO POINT LOOKOUT BED AND BREAKFAST,
Huelo
Door of Faith Church Road
(808) 573-0914
Inexpensive
Wedding facilities are available for a maximum of 30 people.

Call for reservations. Specific directions are provided upon confirmation.

If you think the road to Hana is tricky, just wait until you drive the mildly adventurous dirt road to this bed and breakfast. Don't worry, though, because detailed directions are provided in advance, and if you get lost the innkeepers are so sweet they will come find you. The rewards for reaching Huelo Point Lookout are the truly charming accommodations and the very reasonable rates (not always an easy combination to find in Hawaii).

Nestled on two soft green acres, not far from the ocean cliffs of Waipio Bay, this property enjoys views of the distant ocean, fertile surrounding fields, and Haleakala when the clouds cooperate. Weather is nothing less than epic here. In a matter of minutes it can go from sunny and silent to windy and violent to cool and rainy, then back to sunny again. At some point in this tropical drama, rainbows usually pass right overhead. (An outdoor Jacuzzi set in the front lawn is a wonderful place to witness this all first-hand while soaking in swirling, steamy waters, or you could be cooling off in the new pool.)

Three units are available now, with renovations underway to add a fourth that should be just as private and lovely as the others. The Lookout House Suite makes up the lower half of the main house. It has a small kitchennette, full wraparound deck, and walls of windows that allow you to look out to swaying palms and the ocean from a king-size bed. The large bath with two pedestal sinks holds a bright blue tiled tub-for-two set beside a window full of lush greenery. Star Cottage is set far enough away from the main house to be totally private and is small enough to be entirely intimate. Upstairs is a bedroom and study area, and downstairs is a full-size kitchen and an alluring sitting room with skylights and expansive windows. Other features include a private outdoor shower and decks facing nature's surrounding grandeur. Finally, a tropical garden surrounds the petite Haleakala Cottage, a simple but sweet studio unit with a king-size bed, kitchenette, and view of the famous crater (weather permitting). Vivid colors and striking floral prints tastefully abound in every unit. A Maui-style continental breakfast with fresh tropical fruits, muffins, and Kona coffee is left in your fridge to enjoy at your leisure.

Hana

The road to heavenly Hana has saved this remote section of Maui from becoming overdeveloped, or indeed developed at all. More than any other area of the major islands, this is the way Hawaii used to be. The best way to describe the excursion to Hana by car is "death by driving." There are over 600 hairpin turns in what most people would call an unpassable road. The unpredictable road repairs, which cause unbelievable backups and delays, are another hazard. Despite these conditions, almost 2,000 people in hundreds of cars arrive daily, including sightseeing vans by the dozens.

What could be enthralling enough to attract such a caravan? The main highlight is the **SEVEN POOLS** (Oheo Gulch), a freshwater swimming hole with a cascading waterfall and the endless Pacific beyond. (This is the kind of scenery most of us see only in the movies.) Also, the drive itself is a wondrous journey through a rain forest, replete with remarkable panoramas (see "Outdoor Kissing").

Is Hana worth the trip? This pristine town of only a few hundred people, with tropical surroundings and staggering views of the countryside and the ocean, makes an enchanting backdrop for a heart-stirring getaway. If you come early enough (allow two hours for the drive from most points on the island) or late enough in the day and stay at least a night or two, it is more than worth the drive, and there are many other spots to discover besides the Seven Pools. **HAMOA BEACH** is a lovely gray sand beach in the town center; **WAILUA FALLS**, seven miles outside of town, is a cascading waterfall that ends in a clear blue pool. **WAI'ANAPANAPA STATE PARK** has a black sand beach and camping. An ancient footpath winds along the rugged coastline, passing blow holes and sea caves. From all perspectives, Hana is probably the most romantic part of Maui.

◆ **Romantic Note:** Hana doesn't offer much in the way of dining or shopping; the outdoors is the attraction here and little else. The only restaurant and the major accommodations in town are at the beautiful **HOTEL HANA-MAUI** (reviewed in "Hotel/Bed and Breakfast Kissing"). Other lodgings include home and condominium rentals, and a couple of bed and breakfasts. Bring a picnic with you, as well as towels and swimwear, so you can take a plunge in the waters, both fresh and salt, when the mood seems right.

◆ **Romantic Suggestion:** On your way to and from Hana, consider stopping at **MAMA'S FISH HOUSE**, 799 Poho, Paia, (808) 579-8488, (Moderate to Expensive), for lunch or dinner. The casual wood interior is filled with exuberance, and the kitchen has consistently served great fresh fish dishes for more than 30 years. The view of the water and a nearby rocky beach is dazzling.

Sandals may not provide enough traction for the various hikes on each island. Be sure to pack comfortable walking shoes.

Hotel/Bed and Breakfast Kissing

EKENA, Hana
(808) 248-7047
Inexpensive to Moderate

Call for reservations. Specific address and directions are provided upon confirmation.

Exotic yellow flowers trim the entrance gates of this spectacular contemporary home perched high on a hillside. Nine acres of verdant tropical landscaping enfold the spacious two-story guest home, which surveys panoramic 360-degree views of the emerald hills below and the Pacific Ocean beyond. Although Ekena can accommodate up to ten people, its first priority is privacy; the house is rented out to only one party at a time, even if there are only two of you.

Sunshine cascades through skylights in the 2,600-square-foot upper unit, which is slightly more spacious and appropriately more expensive than the smaller lower unit. Aside from space, the units are almost identical: both have wraparound decks that allow you to take full advantage of the breathtaking views; both have been embellished with an abundance of tropical bouquets, plush white carpeting, and plain but comfortable furnishings. A full kitchen, TV and VCR, plus a washer and dryer make both units enviable places to stay and relish heavenly Hana.

HAMOA BAY BUNGALOW, Hana
Hana Highway
(808) 248-7884
Moderate

Approximately 2.2 miles past the Hasegawa General Store on the Hana Highway. Look for the red reflectors and Balinese statues with umbrellas at the entrance of this property.

Funky best describes this Balinese-inspired studio cottage, elevated among palm fronds in a thick jungle garden dotted with Balinese statues and artifacts. Built on the site of an ancient Hawaiian village, Hamoa Bay Bungalow retains a "spirit of place" and exudes a meditative ambience. A king-size bamboo bed fits comfortably in the papaya-scented 600-square-foot cottage, which also offers a full kitchen, private bath,

TV/VCR, and a discerning collection of movies to choose from. French doors open onto a screened porch and a double Jacuzzi that overlooks enormous Java plum trees, guava trees, lau'wae ferns, papaya and banana trees, and glimpses of the ocean. (Hamoa Beach is a mere five-minute walk through a grove of African tulip trees.) A breakfast basket containing fruit and muffins is left outside your doorstep for you to gather in the morning at your leisure.

HANA ALII HOLIDAYS, Hana
(808) 248-7742, (800) 548-0478 (mainland)
Inexpensive to Very Expensive

Call for reservations. Directions to the individual rentals are provided upon confirmaiton.

A handful of tropical vacation rentals that include cottages and homes in a range of sizes and conditions are available through the Hana Alii Holidays rental service. Be specific about what you're looking for when you book your reservation, because each of these properties is romantic for different reasons: some have stunning ocean views; others are secluded among palm trees; several even have the luxury of Jacuzzi tubs, kitchenettes, TVs, and washer/dryers. Set up housekeeping in the property of your choice and soak up Hana's tropical bliss.

One of our favorites is **KA HALE KEA**, which rests on ten acres of quiet country, complete with panoramic ocean views, soaking tub (also with views), sun room with wet bar, fully equipped kitchen, and two bedroom/bath suites—ample space for you and one other romantic couple. We also loved **HONOKALANI COTTAGE**, a charming wood-frame bungalow with a wraparound deck that takes full advantage of the ocean view and the lush tropical setting. We found the open one-room layout delightful. Another standout is **HALE HANA BAY**, a petite oceanfront cottage with imposing views from the deck and living room. Comfort abounds, and all the amenities are here, including privacy and lush surroundings.

◆ **Romantic Note:** Minimum stays can vary from three days to a week.

---

*Sunscreen (at least SPF 15) is essential and must be applied
20 minutes before you go outside.*

HANA HALE MALAMALAMA, Hana
Reservations through Hawaii's Best Bed and Breakfasts
(800) 262-9912, (800) 262-9912 (mainland)
Inexpensive

Call for reservations. Specific directions are provided upon confirmation.

Well-known author Tom Robbins spoke from experience when he described Hana Hale Malamalama as "somewhere between Eden and Paradise." (He's a regular here.) Nestled beside a recently restored ancient Hawaiian fishpond teeming with awa, mullet, and koi, Hana Hale Malamalama offers a truly unique experience. Two of the property's three guest rooms (the Garden Suite and the Royal Suite) are situated in a lovely, circular duplex cottage, originally built and designed out of nara wood in the Philippines and painstakingly transported and rebuilt in Hana. Surrounded by lush tropical foliage, both units have wood detailing, comfortable furnishings, private decks, and complete kitchens. The Garden Suite, on the lower floor, is the property's least expensive and funkiest unit; its bathroom shower overlooks a natural lava tube.

Sheltered by a kamani tree and coconut palms, the Treehouse Cottage has lovely views of the fishpond and Hana Bay. Pyramid-shaped skylights allow lots of radiant sun into the bedroom and living areas, and a large whirlpool tub designed for two is perfect for couples looking for unrivaled privacy.

♦ **Romantic Note:** Breakfast is not provided with your stay, but the private, fully equipped kitchens in every unit make it convenient for you to take turns serving breakfast in bed to each other.

HANA PLANTATION HOUSES, Hana
(808) 248-7049, (800) 228-4262
Inexpensive to Very Expensive
Wedding facilities are available for a maximum of 40 people.

Call for directions and a specific description of individual rentals.

Known for its exceptionally discriminating selection of fabulous cottages and homes, Hana Plantation Houses is a reliable rental agency in the Hana area. You can't go wrong with any of their properties, all of which are distinctive and unique. Many of these homes are spacious, with grand views and tropical settings. Fully equipped kitchens, TV/

VCRs, outdoor Jacuzzis, cozy living rooms, full baths, and private lanais are some of the amenities available. They even offer a solar-powered cottage near Hana Bay.

◆ **Romantic Note:** Minimum stays can vary from three days to a week.

HOTEL HANA-MAUI, Hana
(808) 248-8211, (800) 321-4262
Very Expensive to Unbelievably Expensive
Wedding facilities are available for a maximum of 50 people.

Take the road to Hana and follow the signs to the hotel.

For all intents and purposes, this is literally the only game in town when it comes to anything in the way of hotel accommodations and restaurants, and it has been like that forever. Inaccessibility is the main, if not only, reason for the lack of competition, because everything else about this area is spectacular.

Coming up on its 50th anniversary, the Hotel Hana-Maui was once owned by millionairess Carolyn Hunt. Her exquisite taste and style is still apparent in the 93 sumptuous bungalows and cottages scattered over 66 acres of lush Hana hillside. Plush oversized furnishings, comfy beds, roomy baths with walk-in tile showers and soaking tubs, and floor-to-ceiling sliding glass doors that open to your own private patio make this a perfect getaway. Who would have expected such polish and sophistication in remote little Hana? Many of the units also have handsome lawn furniture, views, and hot tubs. Don't search for a television or radio in your room: you have really been removed from technology here (there is a phone, but at least some of the potentially intrusive technology is absent). A wonderful large pool area overlooks rolling lawns and the ocean in the distance.

Isolation, serenity, and unrivaled luxury are what make this place so captivating. You'd be hard put to find anything quite like the Hotel Hana-Maui anywhere else in Hawaii (or anywhere else in the world).

◆ **Romantic Warning:** The hotel's only drawback is its dining room, which serves bland, overcooked food at unreasonably high prices. It wouldn't be such a big deal if there were other restaurants to choose from, but this is it. With room rates starting at $325 a night, the Hotel Hana-Maui should try to provide an on-site restaurant that complements the outstanding accommodations.

◆ **Romantic Suggestion:** The beaches aren't easily accessible, but the hotel provides a shuttle to a stretch of gray sand about a mile away. A short, tricky walk away from the hotel is a small, secluded red sand beach. Lava rocks at the opening of this bay keep the waters calm, while the surging ocean crashes against the large boulders. Go early in the morning and you are likely to be the only ones here; later in the day some of the locals and other guests often find their way down here.

Outdoor Kissing

THE ROAD TO HANA

Starting at the town of Paia, the Hana Highway (Highway 360) winds 44 miles to the town of Hana.

During your vacation on Maui, you may wonder where all the untouched, lush, tropical landscapes are—the ones that *always* pop into your mind when you think of the Hawaiian Islands. Wonder no more. Travel on winding Highway 360 (better known as the Hana Highway), on the northern side of the island, and you'll find them.

The road to Hana is one area on Maui where the natural beauty of the landscape rules and commercial development has not yet bulldozed its way through. Depending on the amount of traffic heading to paradise with you (or depending on your desire to stop and get to know the scenery more intimately), the trip can take between two and five hours. There are over 100 one-lane bridges and 617 hairpin turns curling over and around 200-foot drop-offs. Abundant foliage lines the road in a rainbow of greens. Below, the thunderous surf crashes against jet black lava rock. Picturesque waterfalls, freshwater pools (swim at your own risk), and dirt trails that wind under overgrown branches are some of the heavenly sights along the way.

However, be forewarned. The big, and we mean *big*, drawback of this daylong excursion is the bumper-to-bumper procession of tour vans and rental cars. With everyone traveling the same road to paradise that you are, the trip can take a lot longer than it should. Also, the actual *town* of Hana is a bit of a disappointment, and you may feel let down by the lack of sights, restaurants, and accommodations. We suggest you not bother to stop, but instead continue on for about 30 more minutes to the stunning **SEVEN POOLS** (Oheo Gulch).

These precious freshwater pools are all fed by connecting water-falls that begin high up in the hills of Maui. Each one gently cascades into the one below it, until the last one spills out into the awaiting open mouth of the Pacific. These natural beauties are your true reward for making it this far, and a definite must-see for anyone visiting Maui. Unfortunately, the Seven Pools are also on everyone else's list of sights, so this is not always the best place for undisturbed time together. Nonetheless, the pools are exquisite and undeniably refreshing after the long, hot drive.

*"There are swords about me to keep me safe:
They are the kisses of your lips."*
Mary Carolyn Davies

Kauai

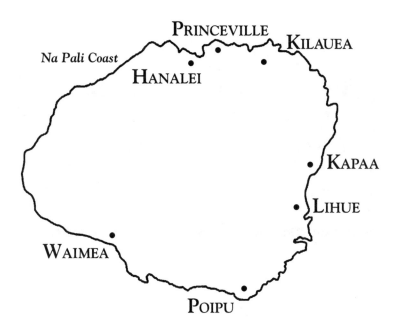

Na Pali Coast

PRINCEVILLE

KILAUEA

HANALEI

KAPAA

LIHUE

WAIMEA

POIPU

"I have found men who didn't know how to kiss. I've always found time to teach them."
Mae West

KAUAI

It's no wonder Kauai is called the "Garden Isle." Kauai's landscape is sheer poetry, with burgeoning fruit trees of every kind, brilliant tropical flowers, fertile valleys, extreme cliffs, breathtaking mountains and canyons, and pristine sandy beaches. Masses of colorful bougainvillea bloom along the roadside, palm fronds sway high atop coconut trees, and acres upon acres of sugarcane rustle in the trade winds.

Kauai is a friendly oasis for those seeking refuge from the hectic pace of the real world, yet there is still an abundance of things to see and do. Hikers, bikers, and outdoor enthusiasts of all types and ages fare especially well here. Lovers looking for quiet beauty can kayak through **HANALEI NATIONAL WILDLIFE REFUGE**, while those with more active intentions will appreciate **NA PALI COAST STATE PARK**, on the lush North Shore, and **WAIMEA CANYON STATE PARK** and **KOKEE STATE PARK**, on the dry, desert-like west side of the island. Treks through these magnificent parks vary in difficulty and range from one or two hours to several days. To obtain maps and information in advance, call **KAUAI STATE PARKS VISITOR INFORMATION**, (808) 241-3444, open Monday through Friday from 8 A.M. to 4 P.M., or write to the **DIVISION OF STATE PARKS**, 3060 Eiwa Street, Room 306, Lihue, HI 96766.

In September 1992, Kauai's tranquil island paradise was transformed by the most devastating natural disaster in Hawaii's recorded history: Hurricane Iniki. Although short-lived, Iniki's fury will never be forgotten, and few were spared from her reign of destruction. The island was literally defoliated in the storm and nearly 50 percent of the island's homes were damaged, if not altogether destroyed. Especially in the coastal areas, winds lifted roofs off houses, while beaches, roads, homes, hotels, and more were tossed, crushed, and ravaged by lethal winds and waves.

Fortunately, Mother Nature and the human spirit are resilient, and within months the flora and fauna, as well as tourists, began to return. Only seven months after the hurricane, Kauai's lush landscape revealed few traces of the hurricane's ruin. Extensive community efforts rebuilt homes and replaced roofs, but not all buildings were so easily replaced;

some of the largest hotels on the South Shore have still not reopened. Insurance nightmares plague many, and others have lost much of their land to the ocean.

If this relatively recent disaster leaves you wondering whether you should travel to Kauai for a tropical romantic interlude, the answer is absolutely, positively, most definitely YES! This is the island of choice for lovers who want a true taste of paradise. Debates continue over which Hawaiian island offers the most romantic opportunities, but in terms of peacefulness, privacy, and natural beauty, Kauai is number one.

West Shore

Kauai's dry West Shore harbors several nondescript towns tracing the coast and offers few options in terms of dining and lodging for tourists. Nevertheless, you'll want to make a day trip here (if not several) to view the West Shore's natural wonders, including breathtaking Waimea Canyon and the beautiful sandy beaches.

Waimea

Hotel/Bed and Breakfast Kissing

WAIMEA PLANTATION COTTAGES, Waimea
9600 Kaumualii Highway
(808) 338-1625, (800) 992-4632
Inexpensive to Expensive

From the Lihue Airport, follow Highway 50 west to Waimea. The cottages are on the left.

Dating back to the early 1900s, these picturesque former sugar plantation workers' cottages are now yours to rent. Forty-eight homes, in varying degrees of desirability, outline a property where very little has been changed since the days when farming was Kauai's primary enterprise. Some cottages feature an alluring black sand beach just yards from your lanai, while others, set on tall stilts, are packed tightly together along a dirt road with only a peekaboo view of the water. All of the homes have been affectionately restored, but still manage to retain the relaxing feel of old Hawaii. The best choices are the cottages set right on the beach, with shady ocean-view verandas and cozy wicker furniture on the porch. All of the cottages boast a full kitchen, hardwood floors, period furnishings made of koa and mahogany, cable television, stereo, and private bathroom with tub and shower. Tennis courts and a swimming pool are also available to guests.

◆ **Romantic Warning:** Many cottages are clustered on this property, and the fact that Waimea Plantation Cottages caters to groups and families could pose major privacy and noise problems. This is, however, the only romantic overnight option in Waimea, and it does offer a wide range of prices to fit most budgets. After a long day of exploring all the intriguing hiking trails and beaches in the area, you'll be happy to return to this affable place to rest your weary feet and warm hearts.

◆ **Additional Romantic Warning: KOKEE LODGE**, Waimea Canyon Drive, Waimea, (808) 335-6061, (Very Inexpensive), is the only other lodging option in Waimea. The lodge rents cabins at the top of Waimea Canyon Drive, but think twice before you book a stay in one of these musty, run-down units. Service is gruff, wild roosters roam (and crow) freely, and rats (big ones) are a problem. The only reason to stay overnight up here is if you want do a lot of hiking and would prefer not to drive up and down the hill each day, but the drive really isn't that bad. You'd be better off in a tent than in one of Kokee Lodge's cabins; information on campsites in **KOKEE STATE PARK** (reviewed in "Outdoor Kissing") can be obtained by calling the Division of State Parks, (808) 241-3444.

Restaurant Kissing

THE GROVE DINING ROOM, Waimea   ◆ ❤
9400 Kaumualii Highway, at the Waimea Plantation Cottages
(808) 338-2300
Inexpensive
Wedding facilities are available for a maximum of 300 people.

Before flying, make sure you are both signed up as frequent flyers.
Mileage to Hawaii adds up quickly.

From the Lihue Airport, follow Highway 50 west to Waimea. The dining room is at the Waimea Plantation Cottages, on the left.

The Grove Dining Room is just about the only dining option in Waimea, and thankfully it is quite charming. Seats on the pretty deck of this historic plantation-style building look out to the namesake grove of 765 coconut trees, quaint vacation cottages, and the ocean in the distance. Cooling breezes flow through the small, simple dining room, and the atmosphere is relaxed and comfortable. It isn't fancy, but service is courteous and you can get a filling meal at an affordable price. Standard options are available in the morning and early afternoon (eggs, pancakes, and waffles at breakfast; soups, salads, and sandwiches at lunch). At dinnertime, the kitchen gets a little bit more creative, offering a variety of seafood, steak, and chicken dishes. It isn't gourmet, and there are usually a lot of people around, but the Asian-style crab cakes with plum and chili sauce make a nice starter, the fresh catch of the day is reliably good, and the house dessert specialty, Kikiaola Sand Pie (coffee and vanilla ice cream in a macadamia nut crust), provides a sweet finish.

Outdoor Kissing

WAIMEA CANYON/KOKEE STATE PARK
(808) 241-3446

Heading westbound on Highway 50, turn right onto Waimea Canyon Drive (Highway 550) or travel another three miles to Kekaha and turn uphill on Kokee Road, which later joins Waimea Canyon Drive. Either way, it is about a 40-minute drive.

"The Grand Canyon of the Pacific," as Waimea Canyon has been dubbed, lives up to its noble nickname. A long, twisting road journeys up 4,000 feet to stunning vistas that will surprise anyone who thinks all of the Garden Isle's beauty lies in lush gardens. Make your first stop at the **WAIMEA CANYON LOOKOUT** to breathe in the fresh, cool air and admire the way the steep, verdant valleys contrast with bare volcanic rock and rich red soil. A spectacular kaleidoscope of colors surrounds you, ranging from lush green forest to glowing crimson earth laced with chaparral. As you continue up the hill, be sure to pause at the **PUU KA PELE** and **PUU HINAHINA** lookouts; each stop offers another magnificent perspective on the canyon.

Proceed next to **KOKEE STATE PARK**, where you can visit a small museum and lodge, but stop here only if you're ravenous or need a hiking trail map; otherwise you'll be frustrated by the shabby facilities. Continue on to the **KALALAU** and the **PUU O KILA** lookouts, which are perched above the Na Pali Coast, a vast green landscape facing the shimmering blue ocean. The scenery is so breathtaking, you may need mouth-to-mouth resuscitation. Hopefully you're with someone who can help.

◆ **Romantic Note:** Bring along comfortable shoes and a light jacket; the temperature at this altitude is cooler but still pleasant, and perfect for hiking. The many trails range from easy walks to rugged hikes, all with incredible scenery. For more information and trail maps, write in advance to the **STATE DEPARTMENT OF LAND AND NATU-RAL RESOURCES**, 3060 Eiwa Street, Room 306, Lihue, HI 96766, or call (808) 241-3444.

◆ **Romantic Suggestion:** The view from the Kalalau lookout can also be seen from the opposite perspective—from the ocean looking up. Invigorating boat cruises depart from the North Shore and offer remarkable access to the awesome **NA PALI COAST** (reviewed in "Outdoor Kissing" in the North Shore section).

Mana

Outdoor Kissing

POLIHALE STATE PARK, Mana

From Lihue Airport, follow Highway 50 south and then west, past the towns of Kekaha and Mana, until the highway ends. Turn onto the dirt road and follow signs to Polihale.

Our curiosity was instantly piqued when we surveyed our map of Kauai and discovered that the highway along the West Shore eventually turns into a dirt road, then ends altogether at Polihale State Park. Before we knew it, we found ourselves in search of this intriguing beach. Although the dirt road is well marked on the map, we couldn't help but wonder if we had taken the wrong turnoff as we wound our way several miles along the bumpy, potholed road with nothing but dry brush in sight. To our sheer delight, after 15 minutes of dusty trying-to-be-patient driving, we finally came upon a velvety, sandy beach set beside the sheer cliffs of the Na Pali Coast. As the sun sank below the horizon, weaving a tapestry of colors across the sky, we were held captive in the beauty of the moment (and in each other's arms).

◆ **Romantic Warning:** Polihale Beach has long been celebrated as one of Kauai's most beautiful beaches, which (much to our chagrin) means it isn't really as much of a secret as the lengthy dirt road might lead you to believe. The potholes deter many tourists, but those with four-wheel-drive vehicles aren't deterred at all—they actually drive right onto the beach. It isn't exactly picturesque to have the shore dotted with trucks, but once the sun starts to set you'll focus on the horizon instead.

South Shore

Before Hurricane Iniki, Kauai's South Shore was famous for its extraordinary sand beaches and luxury resort hotels. It is hard to imagine, but the sheer force of Iniki swallowed up and literally erased many of those beaches with violent winds and turbulent waves. Many homes were essentially blown off their foundations, and some of the largest hotels were gutted by the wind. Now, three years later, most of the properties that are going to reopen have and South Shore business is picking up again. A few large resorts remain in a state of total disrepair, but there are plenty of condominium complexes and hotels to choose from, and the restaurant selection gets better by the day.

◆ **Romantic Note:** Despite the toll that Iniki took here, you can still count on the South Shore to be Kauai's "sunny side." Kauai is the wettest of all the Hawaiian Islands, so you may get some sprinkles here, but not nearly as many as on the North Shore.

Please send us your feedback on places we have written about,
or let us know if there are new places that we did not include (but should).
A "Kiss and Tell" form is provided at the end of this book.

Poipu

Hotel/Bed and Breakfast Kissing

EMBASSY VACATION RESORT—POIPU POINT,
Poipu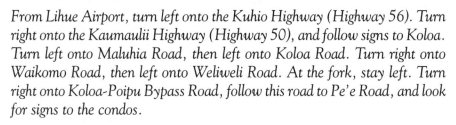
1613 Pe'e Road
(808) 742-1888, (800) 426-3350 (mainland)
Very Expensive to Unbelievably Expensive

From Lihue Airport, turn left onto the Kuhio Highway (Highway 56). Turn right onto the Kaumaulii Highway (Highway 50), and follow signs to Koloa. Turn left onto Maluhia Road, then left onto Koloa Road. Turn right onto Waikomo Road, then left onto Weliweli Road. At the fork, stay left. Turn right onto Koloa-Poipu Bypass Road, follow this road to Pe'e Road, and look for signs to the condos.

Open for just under a year and located on Kauai's sunnier side, these 217 luxury condo units are, for the most part, run like a hotel. Currently, half of the units are on a time-share plan, with the goal being to eventually make them all time-shares. This shouldn't be a problem; the management promises that the time-share sales department won't try to find you during your stay to get you to buy—that is, unless you want them to.

Every unit has plush carpets in cream and beige tones, comfy sofas in cool greens and blues, extra-large master bedrooms with down comforters in classic prints, a spacious bathroom with marble accents, and a full kitchen with marble countertops. As an added comfort, each unit also has air-conditioning, which is rare in many condos. Choose a one- or two-bedroom garden-view, partial ocean-view, ocean-view, or oceanfront room, depending on your budget, although even the garden-view rooms are in the Very Expensive price range.

Obviously, attractive and comfortable rooms are a major requirement for inclusion in this book, but in this case they're a must, because the rest of the property isn't quite up to par. The landscaping (or lack thereof) looks as though the groundskeeper went on an extended vacation. Also, the pool area and other guest facilities seem curiously empty. As yet, there are no restaurants on the property, but a complimentary continental breakfast is served poolside each morning.

GLORIA'S SPOUTING HORN BED AND BREAKFAST, Poipu ◆ ◆ ◆
4464 Lawai Beach Road
(808) 742-6995
Moderate
Wedding facilities are available for a maximum of 25 people.

This bed and breakfast is located on Lawai Beach Road, just east of the Spouting Horn, which is clearly marked on every map of the island.

After having been completely demolished by Hurricane Iniki, Gloria's Spouting Horn Bed and Breakfast is back in business and better than ever. A stunning, newly built cedar home stands proudly at the water's edge, as if challenging Mother Nature to blow a furious storm this way again. (Hopefully, the "hurricane proofness" of this building, and the rest of those on the island, won't be tested anytime soon.)

Hammocks sway between tall palms in the nicely landscaped front yard, and waves collide with the black rock shoreline. All three guest rooms enjoy this magnificent ocean scene. The cozy first-floor suite (appropriately nicknamed the Love Nest) has a grand bent-willow canopy bed and intricate bent-willow furniture. The two suites upstairs have vaulted ceilings and a more traditional flair, with brass headboards and floral linens. Spacious lanais, private baths with deep, Japanese-style soaking tubs, wet bars, microwaves, and little refrigerators in every suite add to the comfort and convenience of your stay. An extended continental breakfast is served in the main living/dining room, and trays are provided so you can take it back to your room if the two of you, like most lovebirds, prefer to visit only with each other in the morning.

GRANTHAM RESORTS, Poipu
2721 Poipu Road
(808) 742-7220, (800) 325-5701 (mainland)
Moderate to Very Expensive

From the Lihue Airport, travel southwest on Highway 50 and turn left at the junction of Highways 50 and 520. Follow Highway 520 south to Poipu, where it turns into Poipu Road; the rental office is on the right, in the Waikomo Stream Villas parking lot.

Grantham Resorts is one of the many vacation rental companies on Kauai that offer a varied selection of luxury condominiums and private homes. The casually adorned **WAIKOMO STREAM VILLAS**, the more plush **NIHI KAI VILLAS**, and the elegant **MAKAHUENA**, among other condominium complexes managed by Grantham Resorts, are spacious and pleasant, providing one-, two-, and three-bedroom suites, full kitchens, view lanais, swimming pools, tennis courts, and nearby golf courses—in fact, almost everything but air-conditioning. Of the three properties mentioned above, our favorite units are those at the Makahueana, with all-new interiors, striking decor, and a fabulous oceanside location. The more specific you are about requesting a suite with ocean views and attractive decor, the happier you will be once you get there. With prices topping out at $230 for oceanfront accommodations in high season, this is one of the better deals on the island.

◆ **Romantic Alternative:** If you're in the mood for ultimate waterfront seclusion, consider one of Grantham's vacation homes. **HALE HOKU**, located at the water's edge, is a two-bedroom apartment on the lower floor of a private home, facing the dramatic Pacific surf. Prices range from Moderate to Very Expensive, depending on the style, amenities, and location. Many of these homes are simply spectacular and couldn't be more ideal for your enamored encounter on Kauai.

HYATT REGENCY KAUAI, Poipu
1571 Poipu Road
(808) 742-1234, (800) 233-1234
Very Expensive to Unbelievably Expensive
Wedding facilities are available for a maximum of 1,000 people.

From the Lihue Airport, travel southwest on Highway 50 and turn left at the junction of Highways 50 and 520. Follow Highway 520 south to Poipu, where it turns into Poipu Road; the hotel is near the end of the road, on the right.

A testament to resilience, the Hyatt Regency Kauai was the first major South Shore resort to reopen after the hurricane. Although it hasn't had many competitors over the past few years, neighboring properties are now up and running. Still, the Hyatt is one of the only resorts to sport such grandiose style on the entire island, and if your budget allows, the Hyatt should be a primary consideration. Enveloped by 50 acres of jungle-like landscape and fronting the ocean and a sandy beach, this palatial resort is designed to be reminiscent of Hawaii in the 1920s, with green tiled roofs and white stucco walls. The Hyatt claims to get the most sunshine of all the hotels in Kauai, which is a truism for the entire South Shore. Guests who want to take full advantage of the weather can do so in style: the Hyatt offers a five-acre saltwater lagoon, three pools (one winds through the tropical garden landscape, while another has slides, waterfalls, and Jacuzzis), a full-service health and fitness spa, a nearby golf course, tennis courts, and riding stables, plus an ocean-view lounge and restaurants where you can hold hands and watch the waves.

Yes, the Hyatt really is as extravagant as it sounds! You could actually plan a couple of days around the dining options here: you can enjoy the extravagant breakfast buffet at the **ILIMA TERRACE**, have lunch there too, then after a day of sunning and swimming, savor sunset and cocktails at the **SEAVIEW TERRACE** and have a relaxed dinner at **TIDEPOOLS** or the more formal **DONDERO'S** (all are reviewed in "Restaurant Kissing").

Six hundred air-conditioned guest suites provide a luxurious retreat from all of the other hotel guests, with tasteful plantation-style furnishings, attractive tiled baths, and muted floral linens. Rooms without ocean views are less costly and face the majestic Haupu Mountain Range, while ocean-view rooms survey the sprawling tropical grounds and overlook the sparkling waters of Kenoneloa Bay. Rooms start in the Very Expensive category (even those with no ocean view), but without a doubt the Hyatt is one of Kauai's few full-scale resorts, and the staff is prepared to make many of your romantic whims come true.

KIAHUNA PLANTATION, Poipu   ❥ ❥ ❥
2253 Poipu Road
(808) 742-6411, (800) 367-7052
Moderate to Unbelievably Expensive
Wedding facilities and services are available; call for details.

On Poipu Road, across from the Poipu Shopping Village.

A hidden blessing of Hurricane Iniki (at least for people who visit Kauai now) is that the restoration of many properties meant practically everything had to be replaced. Such was the case at the sprawling

Kiahuna Plantation. The carpet and furnishings in each of the 333 condominium units are all brand spanking new. Every comfortably sized one- or two-bedroom unit is decorated differently, but most are simply adorned with rattan furniture and pale tropical prints, and all feature full kitchens, dining and living rooms facing a garden or ocean view, private lanais, and ceiling fans (but no air-conditioning).

Besides the lack of air-conditioning, the only other disadvantage is that the pool area is across the street, beside a parking lot and tennis courts, far enough away to be a hassle. Fortunately, you can choose instead to visit the great stretch of sandy beach that fronts the property (a much more romantic option, regardless of where the pool is).

◆ Romantic Alternative: COLONY'S POIPU KAI RESORT, 1941 Poipu Road, Poipu, (808) 742-6464, (800) 777-1700, (Moderate to Very Expensive), was one of the first condominium properties to reopen after Hurricane Iniki hit, which helps explain why the units here are more timeworn than others in the area. The five condominium subdivisions here are scattered across 70 acres of well-manicured tropical grounds, close to the ocean (but not close enough to have unobstructed views). None of the units are air-conditioned, and each one is individually owned and decorated, meaning that amenities and decor can vary significantly from one to the next.

POIPU SHORES OCEANFRONT CONDOMINIUMS, Poipu
1775 Pe'e Road
(808) 742-7700, (800) 367-5004
Moderate to Very Expensive

Call for reservations and directions.

From its vantage point on a black lava rock cliff, this relatively small condominium complex offers incredible ocean views. The 31 units include one-, two-, or three-bedroom suites, with only two categories available: oceanfront and deluxe oceanfront. All have full kitchens and, yes, superb ocean views. As is the case with so many individually owned condos, each one is decorated in a different way and some are more stylish than others. Hawaiian-style rattan furnishings with pastel print linens in the bedroom fill some, while others have a more homey feel, with the owners' personal belongings and touches throughout. There is no direct beach access from the complex, but a lovely pool area overlooking the ocean almost makes up for it. Poipu Shores is a great alternative to the pricier options in the area, and if you are specific about what you want your room to look like, you won't be disappointed.

SUNSET MAKAI HALE, Poipu
(808) 742-1161
Unbelievably Expensive and Beyond
Wedding facilities are available for a maximum of 30 people.

Call for reservations. Address and specific directions are provided upon confirmation.

You will be engulfed by a sense of utter peacefulness and evocative beauty even before you walk through the front door of this creatively designed, Asian-style home. Architecturally, this place is a true work of art, with every angle and detail poised strictly for the benefit of guests who want to view the outdoor surroundings. Cedar ceilings and walls are accented with rough ocean-rock columns, and dark brick floors covered by Oriental rugs lead you through each exquisite room. Tall floor-to-ceiling windows with breathtaking views of the Pacific surround you as you meander through the formal dining room, full kitchen, living room, and two bedrooms on the main floor. Each window is strategically placed so that the water and sky are always in view. Both bedrooms are appointed with plush ivory carpeting, minimalist decor, Oriental-style antiques pleasantly mixed with contemporary furnishings, king-size beds, cable television, and a stereo.

The upstairs bedroom is the most desirable and private of the three, with exposed beams, cathedral ceilings, a king-size bed, towering windows on each side of the room, and a bathroom with even *more* windows that let you feel as though you're bathing in the raging ocean itself. Outside at the rear of the home, next to the foamy white waves, is a narrow lap pool just off a spacious lanai that is just as alluring as the inside of the home, and surrounded by lush green shrubbery, rustling palm trees, and soft grass.

◆ **Romantic Note:** There is certainly enough space to share this home with one or two other couples, or even the whole family. Without splitting the cost this way, the price really becomes unbearable.

VICTORIAN GARDEN COTTAGE, Poipu
Reservations through Rosewood Bed and Breakfast
(808) 822-5216
Inexpensive

Call for reservations. Address and specific directions are provided upon confirmation.

Although this rental property is neither Victorian nor a cottage, it is still exceedingly charming and romantic. Myriad flowers generously and immaculately embrace the semiprivate brick patio entrance and every inch of the contemporary one-story home. Simply entering and exiting this adorable location is an eye-pleasing experience.

Dark gray slate floors, crisp white paneled walls, exposed beam ceilings, and country furnishings fill the spacious interior. Two bedrooms are available, with the master bedroom being the best choice. A king-size four-poster bed with floral linens, a large white tiled bathroom, and windows viewing the backyard's lush grass and colorful flowers make the room thoroughly inviting. Next to the entryway is the second bedroom; it holds twin beds, but unless you have children in tow, it is attractive but not romantic. A second full white tiled bathroom is located in the hallway.

On the other side of the entry is a sitting area with cozy couches and cable television, and just beyond that lies a full, open, white tiled kitchen, carrying a fresh look throughout the entire house. Bright colors peek at you through every window here, making this home a highly alluring find.

WHALER'S COVE, Poipu
2640 Puuholo Road
(808) 742-7571, (800) 225-2683
Very Expensive
Wedding facilities are available for a maximum of 40 people.

From Poipu Road, turn onto Lawai Road (marked by signs for Spouting Horn), and watch for Puuholo Road on the left. Whaler's Cove is straight down this road.

When brochures make much of "oceanfront luxury," we get suspicious. Advertising execs tend to throw this term around rather indiscriminately, and more often than not the property they are describing is neither oceanfront nor luxurious. The Whaler's Cove brochure not only boasts of oceanfront luxury, it also claims to be romantic, unpretentious, and breathtaking (some pretty big britches to fill, in our opinion). Much to our romantically inclined amazement, these stunning two-bedroom condominiums offer all that, along with being tranquil, private, and absolutely gorgeous!

Just to give you an idea of the outstanding quality here, $14 million was spent on renovating and refurbishing the two fairly small buildings that hold 38 condominiums units (25 of which are available to rent). Many rooms look as if they dropped directly off a page in *House Beautiful* or *Architectural Digest*, with marble floors, high ceilings, sumptuous decorator furnishings, Jacuzzi tubs, and eclectic art. Others are more simply adorned, but everything is still stylish and sophisticated, from the koa wood-trimmed kitchen cabinets to the spacious upstairs master bedroom with private tiled lanai. Just as the brochure promises, every unit truly is oceanfront, so you can enjoy the sight and sound of the sea hitting the black rock beach below all day and all night. Outside, an attractive pool and Jacuzzi area, surrounded by slate rockery and pretty landscaping, also faces the ocean.

Now for a reality check. All of this loveliness doesn't come cheap (rooms are $275 a night). But compared to what other nearby resorts and condominium properties charge for accommodations that are a lot less elegant, the price is relatively reasonable. Whaler's Cove is a truly romantic getaway on this magical isle.

◆ **Romantic Note:** When booking your reservation, try to describe what type of decor you prefer. Specific units can't be held in advance, but if they can get an idea of your taste and style, the gracious staff should be able to place you in a room that will make you and yours very happy.

Restaurant Kissing

DONDERO'S, Poipu
1571 Poipu Road, in the Hyatt Regency Kauai
(808) 742-1234
Expensive

From the Lihue Airport, travel southwest on Highway 50 and turn left at the junction of Highways 50 and 520. Follow Highway 520 south to Poipu, where it turns into Poipu Road; the restaurant is in the Hyatt, near the end of the road, on the right.

It's no surprise that Dondero's is full of intricate marble flooring, lovely green tilework with inlaid seashells, and colorful murals of the Mediterranean countryside. This level of opulence is typical of the incredible Hyatt Regency Kauai. Although prices are steep, the service is efficient, and you'll savor Kauai's finest Italian cuisine. Start off your meal with a delicious Gorgonzola, walnut, and apple salad, then move on to the sautéed shrimp with lemon over spinach pasta, or the sautéed chicken breast with Marsala and grapes. Top it all off with one of Dondero's scrumptious desserts and you'll have a meal made in heaven.

◆ **Romantic Alternatives:** All of the Hyatt's other dining options have something romantic to offer, from the casually intimate grass huts at **TIDEPOOLS** to the open-air **ILIMA TERRACE** to the **SEAVIEW TERRACE** lounge with its amazing ocean view (all are reviewed elsewhere in this section).

THE HOUSE OF SEAFOOD, Poipu
1941 Poipu Road
(808) 742-6433
Expensive
Wedding facilities are available for a maximum of 40 people.

On Poipu Road, between Hoowili and Pe'e roads, beside the Poipu Kai condominium complex.

As the waiter rattled off the ten different types of fish, prepared ten different ways, indecision drove us to try the most exotic-sounding entrées—which turned out not to be the best choice. Creativity is good, but the delicate flavor of the fish can get overwhelmed in the confusion of too many ingredients.

Service at The House of Seafood is casual, and the softly lit room, with open beams draped in plants, and tables set beside open windows, is lovely. (The view of the neighboring tennis court, however, is not so lovely.) If you want to experiment with the vast assortment of Hawaiian fish, this is the place to do it. Their selection and variety is unrivaled on the island, and if you stick to simple preparations you will leave satisfied.

ILIMA TERRACE, Poipu
1571 Poipu Road, in the Hyatt Regency Kauai
(808) 742-1234
Moderate

From the Lihue Airport, travel southwest on Highway 50 and turn left at the junction of Highways 50 and 520. Follow Highway 520 south to Poipu, where it turns into Poipu Road; the restaurant is in the Hyatt, near the end of the road, on the right.

Treat yourselves to a bountiful breakfast or relaxed lunch accompanied by spectacular ocean views in this breezy, open-air restaurant. High ceilings, weathered brass chandeliers, floral tablecloths, and wicker chairs set the mood for fresh, casual dining. The breakfast buffet is a cornucopia of tropical delights, and the lunch menu offers unusual island treats including papaya and smoked tuna salad, and salmon broiled and simmered in sake and soy sauce. Top off your meal with a cup of steaming Kona coffee, then wander through the Hyatt's lovely garden landscape for a kiss on the beach.

ROY'S POIPU BAR AND GRILL, Poipu
2360 Kiahuna Plantation Drive, in the Poipu Shopping Village
(808) 742-5000
Moderate to Expensive
Wedding facilities are available for a maximum of 130 people.

Just off Poipu Road, in the Poipu Shopping Village, across from Kiahuna Plantation.

Roy's restaurants have spread like wildfire over the Pacific Islands and beyond, with one on Oahu, two on Maui, one each in Guam and Tokyo, and now this one on Kauai. Like all the others, this one features a lively, casual atmosphere, enhanced by marble-topped tables, shiny dark brown rattan chairs, track lighting, and bright artwork. Although the location in an outdoor shopping mall is less than amorous, once you have experienced the excellent service and the delectable cuisine, you will see why Roy's restaurants have gained such popularity.

The only problem with dining at Roy's is that it can get expensive. Everything on the menu looks so good that you'll want to order at least two appetizers, an entrée for each of you, and, of course, two desserts. Ordering just one item and sharing it can be fun at some restaurants, but when you're talking about Roy's lemongrass-crusted fish satay served with a Thai peanut sauce, spinach and shiitake ravioli in a sun-dried tomato and garlic cream sauce, and rich chocolate soufflé, dividing them exactly in half might be difficult, and a conflict could arise. Play it safe: just share bites with each other, order more if need be, and enjoy!

SEAVIEW TERRACE, Poipu
1571 Poipu Road, in the Hyatt Regency Kauai
(808) 742-1234
Expensive

From the Lihue Airport, travel southwest on Highway 50 and turn left at the junction of Highways 50 and 520. Follow Highway 520 south to Poipu, where it turns into Poipu Road; the lounge is in the Hyatt, near the end of the road, on the right.

You'll be impressed by the Hyatt's prodigious grounds, and one of the best places to behold them (and the vast Pacific) is from the deck of the Seaview Terrace. The view from up here truly is spectacular, and the atmosphere is relaxed enough that you can take your time absorbing it all as you indulge in drinks and appetizers. As the sun sets, watch the pounding surf roll in and admire the palms silhouetted against the ocean; then, after dark, witness a whole new tropical world emerge as tiki torches light up the landscape. Hawaiian music is played from 6 P.M. to 9 P.M. nightly, amplifying the already romantic mood.

TIDEPOOLS, Poipu
1571 Poipu Road, in the Hyatt Regency Kauai
(808) 742-1234
Expensive

From the Lihue Airport, travel southwest on Highway 50 and turn left at the junction of Highways 50 and 520. Follow Highway 520 south to Poipu, where it turns into Poipu Road; the restaurant is in the Hyatt, near the end of the road, on the right.

Tidepools is the Hyatt's casual (but still intimate) dining alternative for those who want superior views of the sun setting over the ocean but don't want to spend a fortune. Guests dine in romantic grass-thatched Polynesian huts surrounded by peaceful lagoons. Stone floors, rattan chairs, and little glowing lamps at every table enhance the warm Hawaiian mood. The unique surroundings (and relatively moderate prices) make dishes such as charred ahi, fresh lobster, and mud pie seem that much more delicious.

Outdoor Kissing

MAHAULEPU BEACH, Poipu

From the Lihue Airport, travel southwest on Highway 50 and turn left at the junction of Highways 50 and 520. Follow Highway 520 south to Poipu, where it turns into Poipu Road; follow this road beyond the Hyatt's golf courses and continue toward the ocean.

Adventure can usually ignite romantic feelings. Finding this beach isn't an overly challenging quest, but you do drive down unmarked, bumpy sugarcane plantation roads to a run-down shack, surrounded by chickens, where you sign in and continue to the beach. Sound interesting? Well, it is. The only problem is that you may feel like you're trespassing. (Fortunately, Hawaii's beaches are not private property, so you aren't anywhere you aren't supposed to be; you just have to pass through private sugarcane fields to get to this particular beach.)

Since it takes some effort to get here, Mahaulepu Beach offers more solitude than the Hyatt's beach area, just on the other side of Shipwreck Point. You still won't be totally alone, but this soft, sandy stretch of beach does offer a peaceful place to wade through the waves that lap against the shore, and there is enough privacy that you'll feel comfortable sneaking a kiss when you feel so inspired.

◆ **Romantic Alternative:** At the edge of the Hyatt's property you'll find somewhat more accessible **SHIPWRECK POINT**, a dramatic lookout where the ocean meets a steep rocky ledge. Cliff diving is said to be popular here, but we didn't see any brave souls trying it. A more romantic pastime is witnessing a glorious sunset from here.

East Shore

Believe it or not, even Kauai has traffic, and you're most likely to get caught in it on the East Shore. The highway here runs along an overdeveloped coast that is crowded with hotels, gas stations, restaurants, houses, and even more hotels. The advantage of this area is its extremely affordable accommodations and restaurants, but, unfortunately, only a few of these are worth recommending for an intimate rendezvous. But don't give up the East Shore altogether. We discovered some wonderful places for kissing purposes, despite the traffic.

Anahola

Hotel/Bed and Breakfast Kissing

THE FOGELSTROM HOUSE
Reservations through Anini Beach Vacation Rentals
(808) 826-4000, (800) 448-6333
Unbelievably Expensive

Call for reservations. Specific directions are provided upon confirmation.

Have you ever dreamed of paradise? Your dream can come true at this plantation-style Hawaiian home embracing the stunning expanse of Anahola Bay. Every nuance of this 5,167-square-foot residence brings pleasure to the beholder. Long winding corridors lead to four well-spaced bedrooms, each with its own sheltered-from-view outdoor shower and patio. Getting clean in this setting can provide as much (or more) fun as getting dirty. The bedrooms and bathrooms are ample throughout, with floor-to-ceiling windows and incredible detailing, but the two master suites located at opposite ends of the home are especially enormous and comfortable.

You enter this island mansion through large koa wood double doors. Abundant large windows and skylights fill the house with radiant sunshine and provide nearby but protected partial views of the heavenly blue waters of the Pacific. The stunningly large and airy living room and dining area are flanked by 40 feet of sliding glass doors that open to a large, lushly green backyard encircled by towering palm trees. The interior holds a comfortable amalgam of rattan and white furnishings (surprisingly sparse, given the home's grandiose architectural design), plus hardwood floors, a marble fireplace, and an enviable designer kitchen. All the amenities are here, including a TV/VCR and stereo system.

Just a few feet beyond the backyard is the crashing surf of Anahola Bay. Upon waking, brew a fresh pot of Kona coffee, then take cup in hand and stroll out to the beach for a leisurely morning constitutional. Later in the day, be sure to take a walk around this huge stretch of astonishingly empty beach. One area is laden with tide pools, another boasts prime snorkeling conditions, and still another has rocky lava-encrusted terrain that makes hiking some of the shoreline a challenge.

♦ **Romantic Note:** There is a four-night minimum here. The rental company that tends this property also has an interesting (and sufficiently prestigious) assortment of other rental properties at varying prices. Ask for their brochure; it will prove enlightening.

Kapaa

Hotel/Bed and Breakfast Kissing

HALE O' WAILELE, Kapaa   ◆ ◆ ◆ ◆
7084 Kahuna Road
(808) 822-7911, (800) 775-2824
Inexpensive to Moderate
Wedding facilities are available for a maximum of 300 people.

From the Lihue Airport, head north on Highway 51, which turns into Highway 56. At the end of the town of Kapaa, turn left onto Kawaihau Road. At the wooden bridge, turn left onto Kahuna Road. Take the first long driveway on your right, with a white sign that reads "KUPONO FARMS TROPICAL FLOWERS," to Hale O' Wailele.

What do you get when you combine eight sprawling acres with over 100 different species of fragrant tropical flowers and palm trees, sparkling ponds with colorful koi, views of mountain waterfalls, and two homes with ultra-comfortable and elegant accommodations? Well, in this amorous travel guide you get a four-lip rating.

The name of this bed and breakfast, Hale O' Wailele, means "House of Leaping Waterfalls," reflecting its prime position at the base of the Makaleha Mountains. (Depending on the season, you can see anywhere from two to 12 waterfalls flowing down the rocky cliff-side.) To us, Hale O' Wailele also means true hospitality in one of the most opulent outdoor settings on the island.

As you enter the first home, you pass through an inviting common room appointed with leather couches, an attractive entertainment center with stereo and TV/VCR, and windows that showcase the Eden-like surroundings. Hawaiian family heirlooms and stylish contemporary furnishings prove to be pleasing complements.

The three bedrooms in this home surround the common area; the best one is an exquisite master bedroom equipped with Persian rugs set atop hardwood floors, a comfy king-size bed, a television and VCR, a marble bathroom, and a private Jacuzzi on an adjacent outdoor deck. The two other rooms share a bathroom, which isn't all that romantic, but the shared bathroom is remarkably spacious and lovely, with marble accents. One room holds a king-size bed and the other has two double beds, but both rooms are equipped with beautiful linens in handsome colors, cable television and VCR, a small refrigerator, and views of the alluring landscape.

Newly built on the expansive property is the house named Waonahele, which means "House at the Edge of the Forest," and it features the same meticulous attention to detail. The three bedrooms here are furnished with cream and beige linens, gray slate floors, private marble bathrooms, and a television and VCR. A common area with Victorian-style furnishings is lined with gigantic picture windows that take advantage of the stunning surroundings.

Regardless of which house your room is in, every morning you can enjoy a full Hawaiian-style breakfast buffet at the large table in the common area or (the passionately preferable option) in your room. Breakfast may consist of piping hot omelets, French toast, fresh island fruit, and sweet breads. Traditional Hawaiian delights such as rice pudding or haupia (a coconut concoction) may also be enjoyed. If you can muster the will to leave your room, you will be pleased with all the recreational options available, including a full weight room, golf carts (so you can explore the property), and flower gardens where you can gather blossoms to make a personalized lei. Snorkeling equipment and mountain bikes can be rented for a nominal fee. Hale O' Wailele defines the true meaning of hospitality in one of the most opulent outdoor settings on the island.

KAPAA SANDS, Kapaa
380 Papaloa Road
(808) 822-4901, (800) 222-4901
Inexpensive

From Highway 56, driving through Kapaa, turn toward the water onto Papaloa Road. The condos are on the right.

Sandwiched between the road and the ocean, these condominium units offer a clean and inexpensive place to relax and enjoy the fragrant Hawaiian breezes, and should not be overlooked. All of the units are decorated differently, which means some of the units are very nice but some are pretty run-down. Be persistent in giving exact details of the kind of decor you want when making reservations. The units are either studios or two-bedroom condos, and are classified as ocean-view (which is somewhat misleading, because all you can really see is the unit in front of yours and a partial view of the ocean) and oceanfront (which, thankfully, truly do look right out to the churning sea). All units have full kitchens, a snug sitting area, and a private bathroom.

The best choices are the two-bedroom units; all of the studios are furnished with old Murphy beds that can be very uncomfortable. Also, the pool area borders the parking lot, which is a letdown. Due to heavy undertow, the ocean here is not safe for swimming, but a soft grassy knoll and a sandy beach area await just steps from your unit, and they are great spots for taking it easy on warm Hawaiian afternoons.

LANIKAI, Kapaa
390 Papaloa Road
(808) 822-7700, (800) 755-2824
Very Expensive

From Highway 56, driving through Kapaa, turn toward the water on Papaloa Road. These condos are on the right.

We would have liked these condo units to offer much more luxury and comfort for the steep prices they command. The outdated decor, lack of air-conditioning, and the location on a busy street make them hard to recommend. What these condos *do* offer are spacious view suites with either one or two bedrooms (the master bedroom is on the ocean side in the odd-numbered rooms, on the parking lot side in the even-numbered rooms), full kitchens, large soaking tubs and separate standing showers, king- or queen-size beds, and private laundry facilities. The pool area, which is directly on the beach, is the most attractive part of the property and a great place to soak away the afternoon.

---

*In Hawaii, presenting a lei is the customary way to express
love and respect. When in Rome . . .*

MAKANA INN, Kapaa
Reservations through Hawaii's Best Bed and Breakfasts
(808) 885-4550, (800) 262-9912 (mainland)
Inexpensive

Call for reservations; specific directions are provided upon confirmation.

At the end of a sleepy cul de sac surrounded by mountain views and rolling green pastures, and just three miles from the beach, lies this charming bed and breakfast with a special added attraction. Magnificent Arabian and show horses are the owner's passion, and these beautiful creatures live on the property just steps from the two rental options available to you.

The first option, a private and spacious guest cottage, sits next to the host's home. Its hardwood floors, cozy sitting area with hidden television and VCR, and kitchenette arrayed nicely for light cooking are all you need to feel at home. The bedroom, set at the back of the cottage, has a king-size bed bedecked with Hawaiian-print linens, an adjacent bathroom with tub and shower, and an outdoor lanai open to views of Mount Waialeale and the spirited horses.

The second option, the Garden Apartment, is located in the basement level of the host's home. Guest can enjoy a small kitchenette, library area, king-size bed with bright linens, private bathroom (with a shower only), and lots of sunny windows that allow full views of the lush green pastures. Whether you choose the apartment or the cottage, you will be greeted with an "Aloha breakfast basket" containing fresh fruit, juices, coffee, tea, milk, and muffins.

WAILUA BAY VIEW CONDOMINIUMS, Kapaa
320 Papaloa Road
Reservations through Prosser Realty
(808) 245-4711, (800) 767-4707 (mainland)
Inexpensive

Follow the Kuhio Highway north into Kapaa. The condominium complex is on the right.

Once you've experienced the affordable privacy and comfort of these units, you'll wonder why the nearby hotels get any business at all. If it weren't for the ceaseless roar of the cars on the busy highway behind this condominium complex, it would be an even better find. These individually owned and decorated one-bedroom, one-bath apartments front the beach and offer exquisite ocean views from private lanais. Fishermen work the shore, surfers frequent the waves, and in winter and early spring you're likely to sight whales swimming in the distance or sea turtles closer in.

Each beautifully restored unit offers tasteful Hawaiian furnishings, pastel decor (a lot of pink) embellished with the owners' personal touches, a spacious full kitchen, washer and dryer, and a splendid ocean view. Ceiling fans and louvered windows help compensate for the lack of air-conditioning in many of the units.

The parking lot side of the building isn't the most attractive setting for a pool, but at these prices, you probably won't be too concerned. Especially since the beach next door provides ample swimming and sunning space.

♦ **Romantic Note:** Rooms that are a little bit farther from the road are just $10 more per night—money well spent, in our opinion. If you stay for a full week, the eighth night is free.

Restaurant Kissing

A PACIFIC CAFE, Kapaa
4831 Kuhio Highway (Highway 56), Suite 220
(808) 822-0013
Moderate to Expensive
Wedding facilities are available for a maximum of 30 people.

Follow Kuhio Highway north into Kapaa. The restaurant is in the Kauai Village Shopping Center, on the left.

Although A Pacific Cafe is one of the best restaurants in all of Hawaii, we were somewhat reluctant to try it when we discovered this "cafe" is nestled in the middle of a shopping mall, next to a shoe store. Not surprisingly, we didn't find intimate candlelight dining. Instead, we discovered a brightly lit, stylish room, filled with black lacquered rattan chairs and red wood tables, that was way too lively for quiet conversation.

Yet the hustle and bustle seemed to disappear after our first divine bite of scallop ravioli covered in a light lime cream sauce, sprinkled with fish eggs, and garnished with a beautiful array of indigenous vegetables. As the extravaganza of Hawaiian regional cuisine continued, we marveled over angel hair pasta with Chinese pesto and grilled Hawaiian fish skewers; lobster and asparagus risotto with shrimp-tomato broth; blackened ono with papaya-basil sauce and papaya-ginger salsa; and a white chocolate terrine with strawberry sauce. Forget the candles! With food like this, who needs dim lighting? A spotlight (and a standing ovation) would not be out of place.

Hanamaulu

Restaurant Kissing

HANAMAULU CAFE, Hanamaulu   ❤ ❤ ❤
3-4253 Kuhio Highway (Highway 56)
(808) 245-3225
Moderate
Wedding facilities are available for a maximum of 200 people.

From the Lihue Airport, head north on Highway 570, then follow Highway 56 north to Hanamaulu. The restaurant is on the right.

You may wonder if we are serious about recommending this place when you first enter. However, once you venture beyond the front dining area, which looks like a typical Chinese restaurant, with old carpeting and vinyl-covered chairs, you'll be pleasantly surprised by the five shoji-screened tea rooms that surround a lush Japanese garden and koi pond. Slip off your shoes, pull up a cushion, and sit Japanese-style (or stretch out your legs; there's plenty of room under the table) while you enjoy this lovely scene.

Order a nine-course Chinese or Japanese meal to experience dishes such as crispy-fried ginger chicken, sweet-and-sour spareribs, and chop suey with noodles, or sample tasty delicacies from the authentic sushi bar. The food is fresh and nicely presented, and the service is gracious and friendly (although it can get slow once the dining room fills up for dinner). This place is extremely popular, so reservations are a must—make sure you ask to be seated in the back garden area.

◆ **Romantic Warning:** If you aren't lucky enough to be the only couple seated in one of the tea rooms, seating is far too close for comfort (up to 12 people can be seated at one long table). An earlier dinner offers a bit more privacy, so that by the time things are becoming hectic, you are opening your fortune cookies and getting ready to leave.

Lihue

Hotel/Bed and Breakfast Kissing

ASTON KAUAI BEACH VILLAS, Lihue ◆◆
4330 Kauai Beach Drive
(808) 245-7711
(800) 922-7866 (mainland), (800) 321-2558 (inter-island)
Inexpensive to Expensive

Follow Highway 56 four miles north from the airport and turn right onto Kauai Beach Drive, where you'll see a sign for the Outrigger Hotel. The Aston Kauai Beach Villas are down the same driveway, on the left.

Affordable luxury is hard to come by on the East Shore, where low-priced, cockroach-ridden (no kidding) hotels are in abundance. At the Aston's beachfront condominiums, however, affordability and comfort go hand in hand. The ocean is just steps away from your spacious lanai, and the prices are so low you have to wonder what the catch is. Luckily, there isn't one. The Aston isn't what you would call a luxury resort, but when it comes to basic, clean accommodations (and more), the Aston has it all: simple rattan furnishings, pastel blue decor, spacious one- and two-bedroom suites, tennis courts, outdoor swimming pool and Jacuzzi, and a luscious white sand beach out front. Why can't life always be like this?

◆ **Romantic Warning:** Don't be fooled by the stately appearance and waterfront setting of the **OUTRIGGER BEACH HOTEL,** 4331 Kauai Beach Drive, Lihue, (808) 245-1955, (Moderate to Unbelievably Expensive), next door. Yes, the manicured lawns, waterfalls, swimming pool, and plethora of palm trees are impressive, but the very standard hotel rooms make the Outrigger seem outrageously overpriced. Cement lanais provide pleasing beach views, but this and the fact that you've left Lihue's traffic behind are the rooms' only redeeming qualities.

Restaurant Kissing

GAYLORD'S AT KILOHANA, Lihue

3-2087 Kuamualii Highway
(808) 245-5608
Moderate to Expensive
Wedding facilities are available for a maximum of 650 people.

Travel east along Route 50 (Kaumualii Highway). Look for the Kilohana sign on the left, just before the town of Lihue. The restaurant is in the Kilohana Building.

A noble Clydesdale harnessed to a white carriage stands patiently in the circular brick driveway of the beautifully restored Tudor-style mansion that houses Gaylord's. A U-shaped covered courtyard at the back of the home holds the elegant dining room, which features brick pillars, charming wrought-iron tables, and white linens. The absence of walls allows everyone to have a lovely view of the manicured lawn.

The chicken and rosemary fettuccine with sautéed mushrooms, Thai basil, artichoke hearts, and coconut milk was delightful, as was the Seafood Rhapsody with sautéed prawns, broiled lobster tail, and grilled mahimahi served with herbed drawn butter. Unfortunately, the sauces can be too rich, and the lack of vegetarian choices can be frustrating if one or both of you are so inclined. Still, the efficient service and friendly setting make dinner here a tranquil pleasure.

Wailua

Outdoor Kissing

FERN GROTTO, Wailua

Follow Kuhio Highway north into Wailua. Watch for signs to the Fern Grotto on your left, just past the Wailua River.

The quiet Wailua River meanders through a lush tropical jungle, past tumbling waterfalls, and into the naturally formed amphitheater called the Fern Grotto. To fully experience the extraordinary beauty and serenity of this place, we suggest that you decline a tour with hundreds of other travelers on the Wailua River Cruise (it won't be hard to resist). Instead, rent kayaks from **KAYAK KAUAI OUTFITTERS**, 1340 Kuhio Highway, Kapaa, (808) 822-9179, (800) 437-3507, ($25 to $35 per person), and survey this gorgeous river at your own romantic pace.

Wailua Homesteads

Hotel/Bed and Breakfast Kissing

INN PARADISE, Wailua Homesteads
6381 Makana Road
(808) 822-2542
Inexpensive

Follow Highway 56 north and turn left onto Highway 580. Drive three miles, turn right onto Highway 581, go less than a mile, and turn right onto Opaekka Road. Take the second right onto Makana Road. The inn is the first house on the left.

You can best appreciate the beauty of Kapaa by staying in a bed and breakfast like Inn Paradise, a modern home that overlooks three acres of a lush valley in a residential area far from the madding crowds. The inn's wraparound lanai provides ideal vantage points for viewing the surrounding countryside and the waterfalls that sometimes emerge through the mist on the distant hillside.

Although the three available guest suites share the lanai, all provide plenty of seclusion, along with private entrances, king-size beds, ceiling fans, and attractive wicker and rattan furnishings. The main difference between the rooms is size. The Prince Kuhio Suite, a studio-type unit with a tiny kitchenette area, is the smallest; the Queen Kapule Suite has a separate bedroom, living room, and small kitchen; and the King Kaumualii Suite has two bedrooms, a full kitchen, and separate living and dining rooms. Whichever one you choose, you will receive a complimentary welcome basket filled with fruit, juice, coffee, muffins, honey, and fresh jam for breakfast in bed. Linger as long as you want. There's no rush to get to the beach; it's just a quick three miles away.

KEALOHA RISE, Wailua Homesteads
Reservations through Rosewood Bed and Breakfast
(808) 822-5216
Inexpensive

Call for reservations. Address and specific directions are provided upon confirmation.

Kealoa Rise is a contemporary home with modern touches, ample space, and a supreme amount of privacy. The neighborhood setting is somewhat nondescript but peaceful, and views of nearby ridges and Sleeping Giant (a verdant mountain with a distinctive profile) help make up for the lack of an ocean vista. (So does the reasonable price tag.)

A vaulted ceiling in the living room, dining room, and kitchen adds to the feeling of spaciousness in this vacation rental. Bamboo furnishings with pastel floral cushions add tropical flair, and a free-standing gas fireplace all but begs to set the mood for a romantic evening. Two large bedrooms are set at opposite ends of the house and each has its own bathroom, so even if you bring the kids or travel with another couple, privacy is assured. Breakfast items are not included with your stay, so at some point you'll have to make a trip to the nearby grocery store. After that, do what the brochure suggests and make yourselves at home.

◆ **Romantic Note:** Renovations of a cottage unit in the backyard are underway. This little cottage has a separate bedroom, fully equipped small kitchen, and living room area. Furnishings will include the traditional rattan and floral print linens that are so appropriate in Hawaii. All in all, it promises to be a cozy vacation spot for two.

◆ **Romantic Alternative:** Another affordable option is **OPAEKAA FALLS HALE**, Wailua Homesteads, reservations through Rosewood Bed and Breakfast, (808) 822-5216, (Inexpensive), an apartment-like unit in a nearby home. A mint green spiral staircase leads up to a deck and private accommodations that include a full kitchen, a carpeted living room with contemporary decor, a small bedroom with a queen-size bed, a standard tiled bath, and a washer and dryer. The deck overlooks a pretty pool area (sorry, it's only for looking; guests are not allowed to swim in it) and the tranquil Wailua River valley. Breakfast items are left for you in the kitchen and replenished as needed.

ROSEWOOD BED AND BREAKFAST,
Wailua Homesteads   ❖ ❖ ❖
872 Kamalu Road
(808) 822-5216
Inexpensive to Moderate
Wedding facilities are available for a maximum of 125 people.

Call for reservations. Directions are provided upon confirmation.

You'll breathe sighs of relief (and contentment) as you leave the busy town of Kapaa behind and wind your way up into Wailua Homesteads' lush countryside to this picturesque farmhouse framed by flowers and a white picket fence. You might yearn for the ocean (it's nowhere in sight), but only for a moment—the solitude and peacefulness here more than compensate for the lack of nearby water. (Besides, the beach is a mere ten minutes away.)

Although the main house holds two guest suites, you'll want to stay in one of the two self-contained cottages in the backyard. Directly behind the main house lies the Thatched Cottage, which has eclectic antique furnishings, a full kitchen, thatched roof, and private outdoor shower (popular with free spirits). We prefer the newer, and very sweet, Victorian Cottage, with its hardwood floors, full white tiled kitchen and eating area, sun room with white wicker couches, bright bedroom with Laura Ashley linens, white tiled bathroom, and upstairs loft bedroom. The two guest suites in the main house are homey and spacious, but much less private and appropriately less expensive.

Discerning touches such as chocolates on your pillows and champagne for special occasions make any stay here a pleasure. Not to mention breakfast: fresh papaya and other tropical fruits, organic granola with macadamia nuts, and Kona coffee, stocked in your refrigerator if you stay in a cottage or served in the main house if you're staying there. After just one peaceful night, you'll be refreshed and ready for another blissful day in the sun.

North Shore

The increased rainfall on this side of the island may be a deterrent to some, but the resulting landscape makes it a blessing in disguise. We found the showers invigorating, and they make everything here extra green and fresh. The North Shore is also home to some incredible beaches (made famous in movies such as *South Pacific*) and the **HANALEI NATIONAL WILDLIFE RESERVE**, a fertile valley set aside for a variety of rare birds.

Haena

Outdoor Kissing

KUHIO HIGHWAY (HIGHWAY 56)

Venture past the surprisingly busy town of Kapaa and the Kuhio Highway will take you through phenomenal landscapes and quint-essential island scenery. Much of the drive is waterside, but even when the ocean isn't in sight, lush foliage and dramatic rocky peaks usher you toward the North Shore. The descent into the verdant **HANALEI NATIONAL WILDLIFE RESERVE** and the roadside lookouts there-after are the crowning glories of the drive. A narrow road, with many one-lane bridges, crosses calm rivers; passes popular snorkeling spots like **TUNNELS BEACH**, as well as the impressive **WAIKAPALA'E** and **WAIKANALOA** wet caves; and ends at **KEE BEACH**, where various trails to the Na Pali Coast and lush rain forests begin.

◆ **Romantic Suggestions:** At first glance, the end of the Kuhio Highway looks like nothing more than a busy parking lot and a small, crowded beach area. Although Kee Beach is usually pretty packed, snorkeling among its coral reefs is a cooling option. We also strongly recommend heading away from the beach (and most of the beach-goers) on the pathway that follows the left side of the shore. This easy trail leads to a hillside terraced with volcanic rocks, where you can sit and behold the exhilarating arrival of dusk. It's a different painting every night, as the setting sun brushes glorious colors onto the canvas where the ocean meets the sky. Look at the sun long enough and you might even catch a glimpse of the infamous "green flash" (a phenomenon that occurs when the the last rays of sunlight hit a par-ticular species of phosphorescent plankton near the water's surface, causing a brief flash of green light). Don't count on a "green flash" every night—conditions have to be just right—but it is best seen from a boat or the West Shore.

Another very special place is nearby. Just look up the side of the mountain (which is Bali Hai) for a grove of palm trees, then search for the path that leads there. This grove is a sacred *heiau* (Hawaiian temple), the birthplace of the hula and one of the last sites where human sacrifices were made. Don't worry; these days, small lava rocks wrapped in ti leaves are the only offerings left for the Hawaiian gods.

NA PALI COAST STATE PARK
(808) 241-3444, Division of State Parks
Overnight permit (free) required for backpackers.

At the end of Highway 56 in Hanalei, look for signs for Na Pali Coast State Park.

One of the largest state parks in the United States, Na Pali Coast State Park covers 6,175 spectacular acres. Heaven and earth merge at the exquisitely beautiful Na Pali coastline, a 14-mile-long rocky shoreline that is virtually inaccessible by car or foot. At the base of these formidable cliffs are some of the most remote, unspoiled beaches in the world. Verdant tropical rain forest and deep valleys cover the inhabitable land, making it tricky for even the most accomplished hikers and backpackers. The combination of such beauty with such difficult access is, perhaps, what keeps this domain more like heaven than earth.

Most of the area is more easily (although not intimately) seen via boat; try **HANALEI SEA TOURS**, (808) 826-7254, or **LIKO KAUAI CRUISES**, (808) 338-0333. The sea caves, lush rolling hills, mammoth cliffs, and staggering waterfalls are all breathtakingly awesome. During many boat excursions (particularly early in the day), spinner dolphins, whales, and sea turtles cavort in the waves, providing lively aquatic entertainment. Helicopter tours are also available, and give you an overview of this landscape unparalleled in enchantment and beauty; try **OHANA HELICOPTER TOURS**, (808) 245-3996, or **ISLAND HELICOPTERS**, (808) 245-8588. (Prices for boat tours start at about $55 per person. Prices for helicopter tours start at about $130 per person. Helicopter tours often include a souvenir video, and they usually take a more in-depth look at the island than just the Na Pali coastline.)

With the right shoes (it can get wet), athletic prowess (some of the ascents are fairly steep), and provisions (such as drinking water and snacks), you can also hike into the region. For an arduous single-day trek, follow the four-mile round-trip trail starting at **HAENA BEACH PARK** and ending at **HANAKAPIAI BEACH**. Branching off from this path is a four-mile round-trip approach to stunning **HANAKAPIAI FALLS**. Although it takes a relatively healthy body to consummate this journey, the glimpse of Eden is phenomenal. For those who can kiss and backpack at the same time, the 11-mile (one-way) **KALALAU TRAIL** overflows with scenic wonder. (Mid-May through mid-September, **CAPTAIN ZODIAK TOURS**, (808) 826-9371, offers drop-off and pickup service for backpackers with legal permits.) Depending on your level of expertise, the hike can take two to three days.

◆ **Romantic Warning:** The waters here can be rough and rollicking, making even the most stalwart seasick. Estimate your tolerance level before you head out on a cruise, or what you thought was going to be a romantic excursion could turn into a nightmare.

Hanalei

Hotel/Bed and Breakfast Kissing

HALE MAKAI BEACH COTTAGES, Hanalei   ◆ ◆ ◖
Reservations through Hanalei Aloha Rental Management, Inc.
(808) 826-7288, (800) 487-9833 (mainland)
Inexpensive to Moderate

Call for reservations. Address and specific directions are provided upon confirmation.

Besides vacation rental homes, there aren't many romantic lodging options in Hanalei, so Hale Makai is a real find. The four one- and two-bedroom cottages here, nicely spaced from each other, share a beachfront acre. Two units sit right at the edge of the sandy beach, facing the crystal blue water and sometimes turbulent surf. The other two are behind the oceanfront units, but they still partake in the stunning view.

Hawaiian-style rattan and bamboo furniture with pastel cushions adorns each cottage's living room, and the bedrooms have queen-size beds with tropical-print linens. Staying in for meals is a money-saving option, since the fully equipped kitchens come with everything except food. Some of the kitchen appliances show wear and tear, but this isn't a problem (yet). Once you look out the window and remember how close you are to the ocean, all will be forgiven. In fact, you may not ever want to leave.

◆ **Romantic Alternative: TUTU'S COUNTRY COTTAGE,** Hanalei, (808) 826-6111, (Inexpensive), isn't beachfront (it is in a residential area close to other homes), but the comfortable country-style furnishings are quite appealing, and you have ample space to yourselves. Also, the beach is only a few minutes' walk away.

Outdoor Kissing

KAYAK KAUAI OUTFITTERS, Hanalei
Kuhio Highway
(808) 826-9844, (800) 437-3507
$25 to $35 per person

The rental office is the third building on the right, coming into the village of Hanalei, just off the Kuhio Highway.

Unlike other modes of transportation, kayaks can carry couples to an isolated section of paradise. At Kayak Kauai Outfitters, the carefree staff will strap a couple of kayaks on your car and send you on your merry way. We felt a bit unprepared at this apparent independence, but it truly was as easy as we had been told, and the tranquillity we found on the Hanalei River was sublime. We wouldn't have believed the brilliant orange hau tree flowers floating on the water and fish jumping repeatedly if we hadn't seen them for ourselves.

Kissing might be difficult between kayaks, but be daring—the water is shallow in most places and warm. If you can both swim, the worst that can happen is that you'll be in the water together. Doesn't sound so bad, does it? Chances are, especially if you're beginners like us, you'll get pretty wet anyhow, so dress accordingly.

A word to the wise: unless you've done this together before, we highly recommend that you rent one kayak each rather than sharing a double. Two beginners could spend all day zigzagging up the river, each person blaming the other for the lack of steering ability. It might be funny at first, but trust us—once your arms are sore, it could get ugly.

◆ **Romantic Note:** On this particular river, the first half of the journey is close to the road and breezy, but hang in there—once you go under the bridge, the waters are calmer and the scenery only gets better.

◆ **Romantic Suggestion:** Bring a sack lunch and picnic at the grassy pasture you'll find at the end of the river. **THE HANALEI GOURMET**, 5-5161 Kuhio Highway, Hanalei, (808) 826-2524, (Inexpensive), is close by and offers the best lunches in the area, with a nice variety of sandwiches. French rolls seem to keep the best, and ask them to go light on the mayo and mustard (you'll be carrying your picnic around for a while, so you don't want them to get soggy).

◆ **Romantic Option:** Kayak Kauai Outfitters has another office in Kapaa, and both branches offer guided kayak excursions that include hiking, camping, mountain biking, and snorkeling (prices range from $45 to $175 per person). Triathlete types might be interested in the journeys described as "rigorous" or "workouts" in the brochure, but there are also "relaxing and safe" outings to choose from.

Kilauea

Hotel/Bed and Breakfast Kissing

KAI MANA, Kilauea   ❖ ❖ ❖
Reservations through Hawaii's Best Bed and Breakfasts
(808) 885-4550, (800) 262-9912 (mainland)
Inexpensive to Moderate

Call for reservations. Specific directions are provided upon confirmation.

Although three rooms in the main house are available at Kai Mana, the private dome-shaped cottage set on a grassy hill is the most inviting choice. The inside is quaint and cozy, with a full, tiled kitchen at the center; a spacious living room that boasts television, VCR, and an ample redwood couch; a bedroom arrayed in bright tropical prints on a queen-size bed; and a tiny bathroom with shower. Wraparound windows offer views of the water and the stunning sunsets. Use of the Jacuzzi on the deck of the main house and beach access are included. With respect to your privacy, the managers stay well away, even for breakfast, so you'll have to get your own provisions for morning meals or a midnight snack.

The three bedrooms in the main house, which is closer to the beach and views of the cliff and distant lighthouse, offer you a choice between a king-, queen-, or two double-size beds; all have bold tropical print linens and dark carpeting. Each of the rooms has a private bathroom, a private entrance from the lanai, and use of the Jacuzzi, which is not at all private, but does have a nice view of the Pacific and the coastline. The decor in these rooms is a bit dreary, but the prices are excitingly low, and therefore hard to pass up.

Kai Mana offers some additional services that may intrigue you, including massage and body work (arranged by appointment), and counseling sessions with Shakti Gawain, the owner of the home and best-selling author of many spiritual books. All are designed to give you a healing and relaxing experience.

PAVILIONS AT SEACLIFF, Kilauea   ◆ ◆ ◆ (
Reservations through Bali Hai Realty
(808) 828-6615, (800) 292-6615
Unbelievably Expensive and Beyond
Wedding facilities are available for a maxium of 50 people; call for details.

Call for reservations. Address and specific directions are provided upon confirmation.

When you drive through the stately weathered brass gates and see this property, you'll wonder, "Is this really all for me?" Your significant other may remind you that it's for "us," but relax and get ready for the "complete retreat," as it has been appropriately dubbed. We hate to risk sounding like the glossy brochure, but this home, perched atop seven manicured acres, has everything: three ocean-view master suites, blue tiled pool and Jacuzzi, tennis court and sand volleyball court, charming gazebo, landscaped putting green, exercise room, full kitchen, and spacious living and dining rooms—all for your own private use! The Euro-style decor in cream and granite is tastefully elegant, and you won't believe the unobstructed vista of rolling surf and majestic mountains seen from almost every inch of the property.

Office facilities are available, but if you can, leave work behind and devote your stay to the rare indulgences found here. The full maid, butler, and catering services available are much more conducive to romance than the business center.

Our only complaint about Pavilions at Seacliff is that the rates are prohibitive for most mortals (a three-day minimum stay is required). However, with all the amenities and space, sharing this home with one or two other couples could still be romantic and would place this exceptional property in the Expensive to Very Expensive price range—not a bargain, but a lot less devastating.

SECRET BEACH COTTAGE, Kilauea
Reservations through Hawaii's Best Bed and Breakfasts
(808) 885-4550, (800) 262-9912 (mainland)
Expensive to Very Expensive

Call for reservations. Address and specific directions are provided upon confirmation.

Private and exquisite, Secret Beach Cottage is perfect for couples who want the sophistication and luxury of a hotel but prefer the privacy and comfort of a home. A gate at the entryway ensures that you will have this little oasis all to yourselves—all five and a half acres of lovely landscaped tropical gardens and a small cottage that really is a romantic's dream come true.

Sumptuous, plush furnishings fill the one-bedroom bungalow, along with high ceilings, an indoor/outdoor shower, and a separate kitchen and living room area. Everything is top of the line, from the marble countertops to the double-headed shower to the fine linens and soft towels. The cottage is on the small side, but the owner has managed to fit in everything beautifully (including a stereo system, cable television with a VCR, and a washer and dryer discreetly tucked away in cabinets).

If you can bring yourselves to leave this incredible interior, go for a short (albeit steep) walk down to **KAUAPEA (SECRET) BEACH** (reviewed in "Outdoor Kissing"). Banana and papaya trees, haleconias, ginger, and more tropical beauties line the terraced garden path to the beach. After your trip to the grocery store (Secret Beach Cottage is a vacation rental, so the food is up to you), you won't want to leave your hideaway again.

♦ **Romantic Note:** There is a three-night minimum.

If conditions are just right for a rainbow but it is nighttime, watch for a moonbow, a pale glowing arch lit by the moon.

Restaurant Kissing

CASA DI AMICI, Kilauea
2484 Keneke Street
(808) 828-1555
Moderate to Expensive
Wedding facilities are available for a maximum of 25 people.

Head north on Highway 56, turn right into Kilauea Town, and follow signs for the lighthouse. Turn left onto Lighthouse Road; the restaurant is on the right, in the Kong Lung Center.

This charming restaurant serves absolutely delicious Italian food. A white, lattice-framed entrance invites you into the small open-air dining room filled with hanging plants, rattan chairs, and footed pedestal tables covered with crisp white linens. Soft melodies from the piano in the center of the room waft through the air, along with the savory aroma of traditional Italian dishes.

Start your meal with a fresh salad or uncommon appetizer, such as the roasted red peppers served hot with quartered tomatoes and anchovies in olive oil. For the main course, seafood dishes are especially good; try the flavorful Scampi Di Amici—jumbo prawns, garlic, capers, fresh tomatoes, basil, and olive oil served on a generous bed of linguine. Or be creative and combine your favorite pasta with one of five rich sauces. Arrabiatta, a distinctive roma tomato sauce with sautéed pancetta and crushed chili peppers, is sure to spice up your palate. Top off your meal with a foamy cappuccino and dessert; all of them are superb.

Romantic Note: If service had been faster and more attentive, this place would have earned four lips. Since this is practically the only fine dining option in the neighborhood, they are usually busy, and reservations are a must.

Outdoor Kissing

KAUAPEA BEACH (SECRET BEACH)

Between Kilauea Point and Kalihiwai Bay. Ask for directions from your host or from someone once you are in Kilauea.

Even though Kauapea Beach isn't really a secret any more, most people still call it Secret Beach. That could be because it is not all that easy to find, not particularly easy to get to, and certainly not easy to hike back from. A long, steep descent on a rather precarious path takes you to at least a mile of sandy shore set at the edge of the Kilauea cliffs. Although swimming isn't recommended because of a strong undertow, you can usually sight playful dolphins in the surf. Beachcombing and wading are also enjoyable options.

♦ **Romantic Note:** Secret Beach is also a well-known nude beach. Some may consider this worthy of a Romantic Warning instead of just a Note, but if you were hoping to do something daring on your vacation that you could never get away with in your hometown, this might be the place to do it. Just don't forget the SPF 15 sunscreen.

Princeville

Hotel/Bed and Breakfast Kissing

HALE 'AHA, Princeville
3875 Kamehameha Road
(808) 826-6733, (800) 826-6733
Inexpensive to Expensive

Head north on Highway 56 and turn right into the Princeville Resort. Follow the main road (Ka Haku), then turn right onto Kamehameha Road; the house is on the right.

You'll find this affectionate bed and breakfast nestled in the otherwise impersonal Princeville Resort. While the mix of vacation rentals and private estates in this sprawling development can make a tourist feel a bit like an intruder, Hale 'Aha is an intimate alternative.

Covering the entire upper level is the Penthouse Suite, with a king-size bed, large sitting area with couches, an open-beamed ceiling, small kitchenette, washer and dryer, and private lanai facing the ocean. A Jacuzzi tub big enough for two awaits in the bathroom. On the main level is the Honeymoon Suite, which also has a two-person Jacuzzi, plus a king-size bed, kitchenette, small sitting area with views of the golf course, and a peekaboo view of the ocean. Both the Bali Hai Mountain and On the Golf Course rooms are much smaller, and the views are primarily of the golf course and surrounding gardens, but their lower prices may tempt you. The contemporary decor throughout Hale 'Aha relies a bit too much on ultra-cheery pastels, from the whitewashed beams and floral curtains to the peach carpeting, but everything is sparkling clean, and guests have ample privacy.

In the morning, breakfast awaits at a large table in the living room, and you can look forward to fruit smoothies, cereals, homemade bread with guava butter, and Kona coffee.

HANALEI BAY RESORT AND SUITES, Princeville
5380 Honoiki Road
(808) 826-6522
(800) 827-4427 (mainland), (800) 221-6061 (inter-island)
Moderate to Unbelievably Expensive
Wedding facilities are available for a maximum of 150 people.

Head north on Highway 56 and turn right into the Princeville Resort; follow signs to the hotel.

Much more modest than the neighboring Princeville Hotel, the Hanalei Bay just might fit your style. Most assuredly it will fit your budget. Spread out on 22 acres, this 230-room complex is housed in a series of wood-paneled contemporary buildings. Walking from one end to the other could be a nightmare in the heat of the afternoon, but a 24-hour shuttle service is available to take you to and fro.

Choices for accommodations are limitless, with the least expensive being the "hotel room with refrigerator" (their classification, not ours). The next level in price is the "studio with kitchenette," then a "one-, two-, or three- bedroom with full kitchen," and, finally, a "two- or three-bedroom prestige suite with kitchen," at the tip-top of the price range. No matter which unit you end up with, you can look forward to soft carpeting, rattan furnishings, a king- or queen-size bed, air-conditioning, telephone, color television, lanai, and private bathroom. Many also have views of the absolutely awe-inspiring mountains and cliffs of Bali Hai, which jut into the deep blue Pacific.

If you plan to island hop, visit Oahu first. It can be a jarring place to end your vacation after spending time on the comparatively more tranquil islands.

◆ **Romantic Suggestion:** Hanalei Bay's **BALI HAI** restaurant, (Moderate to Expensive), features an open-air setting and is an amazing spot to watch the sunset and share a cocktail or fruit smoothie. The Pacific Rim cuisine rates just a hair above average, and service is friendly but inexperienced.

HANALEI NORTH SHORE PROPERTIES, Princeville
(808) 826-9622, (800) 488-3336
Expensive to Unbelievably Expensive

Call for reservations and detailed descriptions of the various vacations rentals this company manages.

Although the office is in Princeville, the incredible homes managed by this company are scattered along the North Shore, from Haena to Moloaa Bay. These homes range from one to four bedrooms, and most have views; some are even beachfront. Without a doubt, a private home can be a nice alternative to a busy resort or standard-issue condo. Special indulgences can include cook or maid service, even personal massages. Just be specific and define your romantic needs (as far as lodging goes, that is), and this friendly office will accommodate you.

◆ **Romantic Note:** A one-week minimum stay is required, but once you see the North Shore and all it has to offer, you'll be thankful for this rule.

KALANI AINA, Princeville
4620 Kuawa Road
(808) 828-1123
Inexpensive

Call for reservations. Directions are provided upon confirmation.

Kalani Aina has something unique to offer, but only for true animal lovers: puppies! The friendly owners of this homey bed and breakfast raise golden retrievers on the side, and even if your timing isn't right to see puppies, the grownup dogs and resident horse and cats are just as lovable. Located several miles from the beach, at the end of a road in a cozy neighborhood, this home offers one room with a king-size bed draped in floral linens, a small sitting area, television and VCR, and a double-headed shower in the bathroom. Just outside your door a hammock swings in the breeze, perfect for lazy afternoons, and the tiled hot tub sitting under a gazebo can be a very romantic spot on moonlit nights.

A continental breakfast of fresh coffee and juices, fresh fruit, a variety of cereals, toast, jellies, and fresh pastries is served on the lanai. Watching your honey get kisses from a fuzzy little puppy could melt your heart and easily inspire more kissing of your own.

PRINCEVILLE HOTEL, Princeville
5520 Ka Haku Road
(808) 826-9644, (800) 826-4400
Very Expensive to Unbelievably Expensive
Wedding facilities are available for a maximum of 500 people.

Head north on Highway 56 and turn right into the Princeville Resort; follow signs to the hotel.

Even the most worldly travelers who think they've seen it all will be wowed upon entering the ornate lobby of this polished, simply gorgeous hotel. Deep green, rust, black, and white marble tiles grace the floor and partially cover the walls. Resplendent, lofty red and gold tapestries serve as the primary artwork, plush sofas and chairs invite dallying, and immense crystal and wrought-iron chandeliers hang majestically overhead. Grandiose windows embrace two sides of the lobby, so views of the ocean and the magnificent Na Pali Coast are always within sight. The effect is stunningly aristocratic and grand.

An adjacent living room with the same decor provides space for high tea and evening entertainment, while the windswept wraparound terrace holds the **CAFE HANALEI**. From this vantage point you can revel in the rapturous, unimaginably beautiful paradise surrounding you. Informal dining here, whether for breakfast, lunch, or dinner, is truly a feast for all of your senses, as well as your souls and hearts.

Fortunately, unlike many other prominent local hotels with impressive lobbies, the accommodations surpass their buildup. The soft cream carpeting, classic wood furnishings, separate sitting area with oversized sofa, and king-size bed layered with generous pillows create a wonderful environment. Each unit has a large picture window (but unfortunately no lanai) that looks out to the mesmerizing Pacific, Hanalei Bay, and the pool area, or to the surrounding mountains, depending on what you're willing to pay. Spacious, utterly sensual bathrooms done in the hotel's signature dark green marble seem to have enough room to host a small cocktail party (they are undoubtedly attractive enough). A final distinctive feature is the soaking tub with a huge privacy window that looks out through the room to the dazzling view beyond.

The hotel's **LA CASCATA** (reviewed in "Restaurant Kissing") serves delicious Mediterranean Italian cuisine.

Restaurant Kissing

LA CASCATA, Princeville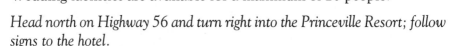
5520 Ka Haku Road, in the Princeville Hotel
(808) 826-9644, (800) 826-4400
Moderate to Expensive
Wedding facilities are available for a maximum of 20 people.

Head north on Highway 56 and turn right into the Princeville Resort; follow signs to the hotel.

As you dine in this seductive restaurant with soft candlelight and rustic flourishes, you might have to remind yourselves that you are on a tropical Polynesian island, not the Italian Riviera. The terra-cotta tiled floors, high-backed upholstered chairs, wrought-iron wall sconces, and bouquet on every table combine Mediterranean warmth with continental elegance. But you only need to glance through the tall windows at the azure Pacific Ocean and the misty Hanalei hillside to know exactly where you are. Delicate spices enhance the flavor of every dish, and interesting pastas with rich, creamy sauces leave your palate begging for more. We highly recommend the splendidly prepared prawn and asparagus risotto, with all flavors present and accounted for.

Unfortunately, service can be unpredictable and a wee bit absent-minded. Tables are too large to foster much intimacy, but the acoustic guitar is pleasantly soft and melodious, and could easily inspire some between-course kisses.

Outdoor Kissing

KAWEONUI POINT BEACH (SEALODGE BEACH) ❤ ❤ ❤

Take Highway 56 northbound and turn right into the Princeville Resort. Turn right on Kamehameha Road and follow it to its end, the parking lot for the Sealodge Condos. The trail to the beach begins at the oceanfront corner of the Sealodge, between two units.

Bring your sense of adventure—finding this romantic spot is half the thrill. A bumpy overgrown dirt trail wanders down to a little stream you can easily hop over on rocks. Farther along your trek is an imposing mass of black lava rock jutting over the water's edge. Many travelers stop here, thinking they've reached the end of the journey, but those poor souls don't have our book. The secret to finding Kaweonu Beach is to not be deceived by the water on both sides of you. Continue to the left on what's left of the crumbly dirt path, and be careful as you edge around the corner. When you finally (and joyfully) behold the strip of sandy beach tucked into this hidden cove, walk just a little more and give each other a pat on the back (or more if you like)—you worked hard to find this special spot.

As hard as it is to find, this beach is not as private as you may hope. It certainly wasn't crowded the day we discovered it, but we would have preferred to have it all to ourselves. Who wouldn't?

◆ **Romantic Warning:** The hike isn't lengthy, but the trail is a bit steep, narrow, and difficult at times. A healthy heart and shoes with good traction are a must.

Wainiha

Hotel/Bed and Breakfast Kissing

TASSA HANALEI, Wainiha
5121 Wainiha Powerhouse Road
(808) 826-7298
Inexpensive
Wedding facilities are available for a maximum of 25 people.

Call for reservations. Specific directions are provided upon confirmation.

New Age California meets laid-back Hawaii in this funky but endearing bed and breakfast modeled after a Zen Buddhist retreat and situated deep in the residential foothills outside of Hanalei. Notice the shells embedded in stepping stones as you enter, and the Healing Temple, an all-white, open-air bungalow set aside for massages and aromatherapy. Four hundred crystals, strategically placed around the property, enhance the "spiritual energy" here. Tassa Hanalei may not be for everyone, but it is unique.

Of the three lodging options, the King Kamehameha Suite offers the most space and privacy, with it own bathroom and a small deck that surveys the lush property. The Queen Liliuokalani and Princess Kaiulani suites are also nice, but they share a bathroom (just a short walk across the lawn). Both have French doors that open out to a river just yards away. The beautiful furnishings, queen-size beds, richly colored carpets, stained glass windows, and lovely Royal Hawaiian portraits in every unit are all artistic and tastefully executed.

Guests are encouraged to take a swim in the cooling waters of the Waineha River, which gently flows through the grounds, and eat fruit from the various tropical trees. To ensure your privacy, a scrumptious and creative breakfast is left on your doorstep in the morning. Sample home-baked sweet breads or macaroon crêpes filled with mangos and topped with yogurt.

> "A kiss is the anatomical juxtaposition of two orbicular muscles in a state of contraction."
> Cary Grant

Hawaii

"THE BIG ISLAND"

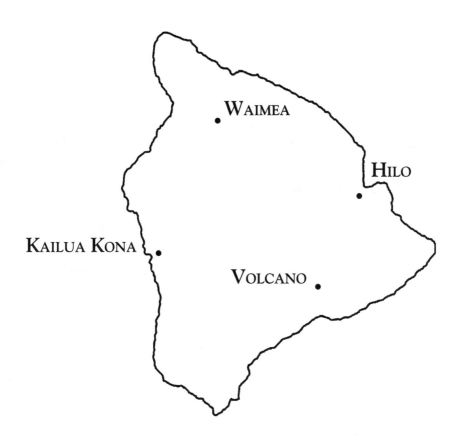

WAIMEA

HILO

KAILUA KONA

VOLCANO

*"You are always new. The last of your kisses
was ever the sweetest..."*
John Keats

HAWAII — THE BIG ISLAND

Without exaggeration, when they say big here, they mean big! Hawaii, the largest island in the Hawaiian archipelago, encompasses over 4,000 square miles of astounding and unique scenery. And thanks to continuing eruptions from Kilauea, the magma-spewing volcano, it is still growing. Topographically speaking, the Big Island has a stunning assortment of features: snow-dabbed mountaintops in winter; endless acres of barren black lava beds as sterile and haunting as the moon; verdant tropical rain forests; and some of the tallest peaks in the United States.

From a tourist's perspective, Hawaii is unlike any of the other Hawaiian Islands. Beaches here are few and far between, and most feature lava rock or black sand. Although you can swim to your hearts' content in these distinctive waters (the snorkeling and the sunsets here are extraordinary), the shoreline is more conducive to scenic viewing than swimming or sunbathing. But this apparent shortcoming has been an asset for the Big Island. The lack of sandy swimming beaches and the vast beds of encrusted lava have prevented developers from taking hold as they have on the other islands. Also, there are plenty of wide open spaces—enough so that you never really feel the impact of civilization. The whole island has a population of 120,000, which is sparse in proportion to its size. (Oahu, at one-third the size, has just under 1 million people, and Maui, only slightly larger than Oahu, has 100,000.)

To fully appreciate all that the Big Island has to offer, a rental car is a must. Driving around this island makes for a wondrous, but extremely long, excursion (driving the perimeter takes at least eight hours); set aside a couple of days to see all of it. Every mile reveals a new panorama of the island's dramatically disparate landscapes. On the dry northwest side, at the base of Mauna Kea and Mauna Lani, which rise an imperious 13,000 feet and 11,000 feet respectively, the rolling acres of chaparral abruptly turn into a desolate expanse of lava field. Just beyond this fascinatingly bleak landscape is the breathtaking **KOHALA COAST**, with its magnificent but hard-to-reach shoreline. Although most of the beaches along this stretch of coast are too dangerous for swimming, they offer gorgeous vantage points where you can share a scintillating sunset.

Farther south lies the **KONA DISTRICT. NORTH KONA** consists primarily of the venerable Hawaiian fishing village of **KAILUA
KONA**, which has become increasingly commercialized over the last
five years and is the largest tourist attraction on the Big Island. Fortunately, this is really the only place you'll find crowds. **SOUTH KONA**
offers exquisite snorkeling (some of the best to be found anywhere) in
many of its undersea parks. Finally, to the east is the tiny two-store
town (no kidding) of Volcano, as well as **HAWAII VOLCANOES
NATIONAL PARK**, where you can study and witness first-hand the
awesome history of the earth's creation.

Truly, this is an island of natural wonders and romantic seclusion.
Thankfully, most of the island's accommodations (with the exception
of those in Kailua Kona and Hilo) are separated from each other by
many miles, offering relatively undisturbed retreats into the surrounding natural beauty for those seeking sanctuary from life in the fast lane.

◆ **Romantic Note:** Pure Kona coffee is considered the most flavorful
in the world. Coffee lovers should by all means try this magic brew to see
why, according to legend, the gods still choose the Big Island as a place
to indulge their eccentricities. But be cautious; not everyone serves pure
Kona coffee. Some places use a blend of beans containing as little as 10
to 20 percent Kona, and with nowhere near the same taste as true Kona.

Kona District

Kailua Kona

Just south of the Keahole-Kona Airport is the Big Island's major
metropolis and largest tourist stopover: the town of Kailua Kona. Its
shores, nearby streets, and highways are bursting at the seams with
hotels, restaurants, cafes, gift stores, gas stations, and local residences.
This scene is a bit startling once you have explored the rest of the
island, because you can go for miles and never see development like
this again. Although the crowds in Kailua Kona hardly compare to
those in Waikiki on the island of Oahu, be forewarned that this is not
the place to come for quiet refuge on great beaches. Kailua Kona wel-
comes you in warm Hawaiian style, offering many options for tourists

who seek easily accessible lodging, dining, and entertainment, but this is not the area where you will find anything resembling paradise.

Hotel/Bed and Breakfast Kissing

ASTON ROYAL SEA CLIFF RESORT, Kailua Kona
75-6040 Alii Drive
(808) 329-8021, (800) 922-7866
Moderate to Unbelievably Expensive

The resort is several miles south of downtown Kailua Kona, on Alii Drive.

Although the white stucco exterior could use some touching up, the Aston's sprawling design is a welcome change from the repetitious, nondescript, and very run-down hotels found throughout Kailua Kona. Stroll through spacious open-air hallways to your one- or two-bedroom suite. The 149 rental units here are condominiums, but the property is run (and looks) more like a hotel. Each room has the same plain decor, a view lanai, cushioned wicker furnishings, soothing pastels, a full kitchen, large tiled bathroom, and tropical floral bedspread. They aren't fancy, but they also aren't exorbitantly priced. In fact, this is one of the few places where we do not recommend the most expensive rooms, even if you are willing to splurge, because the Very Expensive oceanfront villas are sadly in need of refurbishment. During value season (April through mid-December), you can get a one- or two-bedroom unit with spectacular ocean views for less than $200. Not bad in this neighborhood.

Last but not least, the two outdoor pools have unobstructed ocean views and are surrounded by a well-groomed landscape with colorful flower beds, a small waterfall, palm trees, and an expansive lush lawn. When dusk's cool breezes arrive, refresh yourselves in the surf and then warm yourselves in the Jacuzzi. Comfort should always be this affordable on Hawaii!

HALE MALIA BED AND BREAKFAST,
Kailua Kona
(808) 326-1641
Inexpensive to Moderate

Call for reservations. Address and directions are provided upon confirmation.

This contemporary oceanfront home, distinguished by a wraparound lanai that is only a few yards away from the crashing Pacific surf, is a real find. Take in the lava rock beach and dazzling ocean views from a window seat in the capacious common room, which is graced with square white pillars, whitewashed beams, a cathedral ceiling, and casual decor. Outdoors, whale watch from a hammock on the small private beach (filled with more volcanic debris and not accessible for swimming) in the front yard.

Awash in sunlight, the three guest rooms exude homespun country charm while providing modern comforts. Each has a private bath, but our favorites are the two rooms with full, spectacular ocean views. Forest green tones adorn the large master suite, which features a queen-size bed, massive antique headboard, matching vanity, and jetted bathtub. The smaller, but equally attractive, full ocean-view room has a striking black-and-white handmade quilt. Both of these rooms have direct access to the lanai and face the brilliant ocean beyond, making it hard to recommend the partial ocean-view room, which is on the back of the house and looks out to the ocean through only one window.

In the morning, a continental breakfast of fruits, fresh-baked muffins, and Kona coffee is served on the lanai as a prelude to an active day of snorkeling, fishing, kayaking, scuba diving, or sightseeing, all just minutes from this comfortable retreat.

KAILUA PLANTATION HOUSE, Kailua Kona
75-5948 Alii Drive
(808) 329-3727
Inexpensive to Expensive
Wedding facilities are available for a maximum of 50 people.

The inn is south of downtown Kailua Kona, on the ocean side of Alii Drive.

Ah, sweet sanctuary at last. Many of the Big Island's bed and breakfasts are private homes that have been converted to accommodate guests; more often than not they are too casual for comfort and too homey for romance. The Plantation House is a welcome exception to this rule. Built and designed to serve exclusively as a bed and breakfast, this inn offers its guests the intimacy and seclusion of a small property with the luxury of a superior hotel. A rare combination, especially in the Hawaiian Islands.

Set on the edge of a black lava beach, this impressive two-story plantation-style mansion offers exquisite views of the turbulent Pacific surf from every angle. Busy Alii Drive, right behind the house, is the only potential drawback, but as long as you don't stay in either of the two rooms facing the noisy street, the inn's design is such that you won't even know the traffic is there once you're inside. You can relish the ocean breezes undisturbed from the spacious and stylish common room, wraparound lanai, outdoor Jacuzzi, or small triangular dipping pool. And you've only just begun.

Each of the three non-streetside guest rooms has a spectacular ocean view, private bath, private lanai, and enticing details. The deluxe first-floor Pilialoha Suite offers plush linens and a platform Jacuzzi tub for two, accentuated by an overhead skylight. The Kai o Lani ("Heavenly Waters") Room is appointed with a bamboo-and-rattan queen-size canopy bed and a spacious bathroom with Jacuzzi tub. Even the smaller, African-inspired Hale Apelika room is beguiling, with its zebra prints, burgundy tones, and rattan-and-bamboo furnishings. You will feel pampered from the moment you arrive, and the morning's full buffet breakfast of fresh-baked muffins, breads, baked dishes, local fruits, and Kona coffee will make your departure that much more difficult. In that case, you just might want to book another night or two.

KALAHIKI COTTAGE, Kailua Kona
Reservations through Hawaii's Best Bed and Breakfasts
(808) 885-4550, (800) 262-9912 (mainland)
Inexpensive

Call for reservations. Address and specific directions are provided upon confirmation.

Set high in the hills of McCandless Ranch (with only a peekaboo view of the ocean), this rambler-style cottage is surrounded by indigenous tropical fruit trees, large spice plants, shrubs, a 68-foot swimming pool, and a bubbling Jacuzzi. The layout of the home is disappointingly cramped, with one narrow hallway connecting all the rooms. However, the beautifully preserved antique furnishings in the bedroom (they have been in the owner's family for years) and the sleek black and white tiles in the full kitchen and bathroom make up for the poor use of space. Each morning, an extended continental breakfast is brought to you by the innkeeper (who lives in a house beyond the cottage). Enjoy your morning meal outside on the spacious covered porch, which moonlights as an outdoor living room with an abundance of wicker chairs and tables.

PUANANI, Kailua Kona ♦♦♦
Reservations through Hawaii's Best Bed and Breakfasts
(808) 885-4550, (800) 262-9912 (mainland)
Inexpensive

Call for reservations. Specific directions are provided upon confirmation.

Puanani means "beautiful flower," and this property in a quiet residential area is embellished with a multitude of them. Gorgeous foliage surrounds the striking new two-story cedar home capped with a blue tile roof. Sounds of a flowing fountain and swaying palms set a peaceful mood as you enter, and a waterfall trickles into a 40-foot lap pool in the lush backyard. All of this tropical splendor was created by the gracious hosts themselves, and they have done an incredible job.

Guests can rent one of two units—a studio or a one-bedroom with a separate sitting area—placed on opposite ends of the first floor. Both are quite spacious and wonderfully secluded; both have a tiled private bath, kitchenette, queen-size bed, handmade Hawaiian quilt, attractive antique furnishings, and a private entrance. A distant ocean view can be had from both rooms, but the verdant grounds will more than satisfy your senses. A simple but filling continental-style breakfast is left in your room every morning.

Peace and quiet, plus privacy and affordability, are never easy to find under one roof, especially in Hawaii, but they are just what you will find here. Cherish it.

ROYAL KONA RESORT, Kailua Kona
75-5852 Alii Drive
(808) 329-3111, (800) 774-5662
Moderate to Expensive
Wedding facilities are available for a maximum of 250 people.

Follow Alii Drive south from Kailua Kona. The Royal Kona is several miles down on the right.

The three colossal white terraced buildings of the Royal Kona Resort seem out of place on Kailua Kona's rugged tropical beachfront. It is hard to believe there are only 454 rooms here, because it feels more like 1,000. This is no place for quiet moments, although the brochure leads you to think otherwise, boasting of tourist delights such as a private lagoon, freshwater swimming pool, coconut grove, and lovely ocean views. If the hotel were more secluded and had a better floor plan, romantics undoubtedly *would* be delighted by these tropical amenities. However, because of its vast size and busy location (directly off highly trafficked Alii Drive), the Royal Kona is not for everybody.

So who is this property for and why are we including it? It just might be right for you, because this overwhelming hotel complex offers tennis courts, nearby golf courses, shopping, an exciting luau three nights a week, budget oceanfront restaurants, plain but clean hotel rooms with cement lanais that have decent views, and proximity to Kailua Kona's various tourist activities. It has everything but peace and quiet. If activity and convenience are paramount, the one-lip rating may be enough for you. The surroundings may not whisper romance, but you can count on affordable essentials. The rest is up to you.

◆ **Romantic Suggestion:** Ask about the Royal Kona's specially priced packages, which include an oceanfront room, daily breakfast buffet, and an economy rental car. You can explore the rest of the island and save money at the same time.

SEA VILLAGE, Kailua Kona
75-6002 Alii Drive
Reservations through Paradise Management Corporation
(808) 538-7145
(800) 367-5205 (mainland), (800) 272-5252 (inter-island)
Inexpensive to Moderate

Head south on Alii Drive from downtown Kailua Kona. The Sea Village condominium complex is several miles down on the right.

Condominium rental can be an affordable alternative for budget-minded lovers who seek romantic asylum on the Big Island. Of course, with condominiums you run the risk of ending up with interiors that don't suit your style. Such is the case at Sea Village, where most units have somewhat dated tropical decor. On the other hand, Sea Village does provide large one- or two-bedroom, fully equipped apartments with a good amount of privacy at extremely reasonable rates. (It actually feels like a steal.) Rates decrease the longer you stay, so it is to your advantage to extend your Hawaiian vacation.

You can select from garden, ocean-view, or oceanfront suites (the better the view, the higher the price), each with a large kitchen, washer/dryer, view lanai, and weekly maid service. Lounge near the small oceanside pool and sip a drink from the convenient wet bar, or be daring and venture together from the lava rock beach into the frenzied Pacific surf, literally just yards away. And for those who like to be near the center of the action, Kailua Kona's restaurants, shopping, snorkeling, and tourist activities are only a five-minute drive away.

Restaurant Kissing

KONA INN RESTAURANT, Kailua Kona
75-5744 Alii Drive
(808) 329-4455
Inexpensive to Moderate
Wedding facilities are available for a maximum of 60 people.

In the heart of Kailua Kona at the center of the Kona Inn Shopping Center. Follow Alii Drive through Kailua Kona; the shopping center is on the ocean side.

Take refuge from the commotion of Kailua Kona at the Kona Inn, where you can sink into a high-backed wicker chair, a cool drink in hand, and gaze out over the Pacific Ocean. This cozy oceanfront restaurant nestled in the midst of a charming stretch of shops provides the perfect retreat for weary and hungry tourists. Walk through etched glass doors (past a potentially noisy open bar) into an open-air dining room overlaid with Oriental rugs and lined by antique-looking wood tables with ocean views. The seating is fairly tight, so request a table nearest the open side of the restaurant. If you don't get a table there, don't be dismayed. No matter where you sit, you will have a view of the ocean.

Don't expect too much from the mostly seafood menu, which offers a standard selection ranging from sautéed scampi to steak and lobster. Still, the wait staff is more than pleasant, prices are reasonable, and the hypnotic sounds of the surf serve as a lovely serenade.

◆ **Romantic Alternative: FISHERMAN'S LANDING,** 75-5744 Alii Drive, Kailua Kona, (808) 326-2555, (Inexpensive), is another option for tourists who want to put up their feet and drink in views of the ocean. Just a few steps down the wharf from the Kona Inn Restaurant, you can enjoy views of the waves breaking over black lava rocks in a more casual setting. Green linens and candles adorn tables on a wooden deck framed by wood pillars, while hanging plants and lanterns and mounted sharks provide a rustic ambience in the open-air dining room. Entrées here are less expensive and even more basic than at the Kona Inn Restaurant, but adequate.

MICHAELANGELO'S, Kailua Kona
Waterfront Row #2
(808) 329-4436
Moderate to Expensive
Wedding facilities are available for a maximum of 172 people.

Follow Alii Drive one mile south from the town of Kailua Kona to Waterfront Row, a wooden shopping center and restaurant complex on the right. Michaelangelo's is on the second floor.

Romantic inclinations will be well tended to in the eclectic interior of this Italian restaurant set on the second floor of a waterfront shopping center. Open beams and high ceilings with skylights soar above booths highlighted with swirls of rolled fabric, candles, green paisley linens, and faux marble–painted walls. The decor is more contemporary and intense than you would expect in Hawaii, but if you sit in the more casual deck area, the ocean views and palm trees remind you that you're still in the tropics, at least until your meal arrives. The ambrosial aromas will take you halfway around the world. The small menu offers mainly traditional Italian dishes with an emphasis on pasta and chicken, and everything is good. Try the excellent angel hair pasta with sundried tomato pesto or the chicken parmigiana. Service is warm but entirely professional.

---

*Feedback from readers is one of the ways we find out
if an establishment is living up to its lip rating. Please send us
your comments; a "Kiss and Tell" form is provided at the end of this book.*

PALM CAFE, Kailua Kona
75-5819 Alii Drive
(808) 329-7765
Moderate
Wedding facilities are available for a maximum of 120 people.

Drive south on Alii Drive from the town of Kailua Kona for about a half mile. The Palm Cafe is on the left, in a green two-story building.

Appropriately, palm trees encircle the plantation-style building that houses this lovely second-floor open-air cafe, which overlooks the street below and the ocean beyond. White French doors open into a commodious dining room filled with an abundance of plants, floral fabrics, handsome booths, colorful pillows, and wood and wicker furnishings. While sunsets framed by the silhouettes of swaying palms and sailboats are absolutely stunning from here, the never-ceasing traffic of Alii Drive below detracts from the cafe's charming ambience.

Even so, the Palm Cafe is Kailua Kona's most romantic and innovative dining option. The fresh Hawaiian fish grilled with ginger, green onion, shoyu, and hot peanut oil and the marinated mahimahi with smooth lobster sauce and coconut cream are nothing less than remarkable. It's also hard to pass up the sautéed ono in an outstanding spicy caramelized peanut crust, caressed by papaya-tomato relish. Service is exemplary, and the kitchen deftly handles the Pacific Rim cuisine with French-Asian accents.

◆ **Romantic Note:** The Palm Cafe is open evenings only.

◆ **Romantic Alternative:** For more casual dining and bistro-style fare, visit **UNDER THE PALM**, 75-5819 Alii Drive, Kailua Kona, (808) 329-7366, (Inexpensive), located, as the name suggests, under the Palm Cafe. Breakfast, lunch, or dinner can be enjoyed on a relaxed open-air patio or in the dining room. Fresh light salads, pizzas with interesting toppings, unusual sandwiches, and tasty grilled selections are just right in this warm climate. Drop by for dinner and drinks after 6 P.M., when the pace picks up and live contemporary Hawaiian music helps mask the nearby traffic noise.

Never take the ocean for granted. A calm-looking surface can be deceiving.
Strong undercurrents or large waves may be only moments or steps away.

Kealakekua

Hotel/Bed and Breakfast Kissing

KEALAKEKUA BAY BED AND BREAKFAST,
Kealakekua
82-6002 Napoopoo Road
(808) 328-8150, (800) 328-8150 (mainland)
Moderate
Wedding facilities are available for a maximum of 100 people.

From Keahole Airport, turn right onto Highway 11. Follow the highway south to Napoopoo Road and turn right (you'll see a sign for Kealakekua Bay). Go four miles downhill past the Coffee Mill, turn right at the new concrete driveway, and stay to the left.

Surrounded by a state historical park and verdant conservation land, the bed and breakfast and private rental home here truly feel like getaways. You arrive at the main house, which is the bed and breakfast, via a long gravel drive. Farther on is the Ohana House, which can be yours alone.

Kealakekua Bay Bed and Breakfast has two bright and cheery suites, each with Hawaiian print linens, a private bathroom, and a private entrance from tiled lanais. Breakfast is served at separate tables in an adjacent eating area. While both suites are comfortable and clean, we highly recommend the space and privacy of the Ohana House. Accented by dark koa wood floors and an open beamed ceiling, the Ohana House offers two and a half bathrooms, a full kitchen (which, for a fee, can be stocked with breakfast goodies), a spacious eating area, and a living room with comfy couches set in front of colossal windows that take full advantage of the natural surroundings. Unfortunately, you'll have to sleep on futon beds in the two bedrooms, but they are queen-size, which is ample for snuggling. This roomy home can sleep eight, but the affordable price makes it just right for two.

MERRYMAN'S BED AND BREAKFAST, Kealakekua
(808) 323-2276, (800) 545-4390 (mainland)
Inexpensive

Call for reservations. Address and directions are provided upon confirmation.

Witness all the tropics have to offer in this inviting two-story farmhouse set on a breezy hillside with distant, panoramic views of the Kona Coast. Knotty pine walls, exposed beams, a cathedral ceiling, and hardwood floor in the sizable upstairs living room contribute to the distinctive country atmosphere. Unwind in the cozy comfort of cushioned wicker furniture as you peer through sweeping bay windows that focus attention on the sparkling ocean beyond. And that's just the common area.

All four of the guest rooms are beautifully maintained. The homey Deluxe Master Suite has beautiful linens, a private all-wood bathroom, a lanai, and a limited ocean view. Downstairs, the Rose Room is augmented with floral linens, sparkling tiled bath, and private entrance; it's perfect for couples who desire more secluded accommodations. The remaining two upstairs guest rooms share a bath (which is large, but obviously not private), but still offer sufficient elbow room.

The engaging hosts offer you all the comforts of their sunny home, including a newly installed Jacuzzi tub set under palm trees in the front yard, a plentiful full breakfast, and complimentary beach and snorkeling gear if needed. If you want to lounge around the countryside or explore the Kona Gold Coast and don't need the beach out your front door (it's a ten-minute drive away), this is an ideal retreat.

◆ Romantic Suggestion: KEALAKEKUA BAY is ten minutes from Merryman's, and the drive is well worth every splendid moment. Wind down a lushly tropical residential hillside past coconut and papaya trees, exotic flowers, and warbling colorful birds. The mesmerizing blue Pacific seems to expand as you descend, beckoning you closer at every turn. Unfortunately, when you finally reach the water's edge, you're apt to find crowds of eager snorkelers preparing to enter the underwater park. Snorkeling is wonderful here, but you'll probably want to find a spot with fewer people around. One option is to rent a kayak (prices start at $20 per person) and paddle over to CAPTAIN COOK'S MONUMENT, where the water is crystal clear and calm, and the sea life is extraordinary.

Holualoa

Hotel/Bed and Breakfast Kissing

HOLUALOA INN, Holualoa
(808) 324-1121, (800) 392-1812 (mainland)
Inexpensive to Moderate

Call for reservations. Address and specific directions are provided upon confirmation.

The colorful melding of Eastern, Western, and Polynesian cultures, traditions, people, and cuisine is a hallmark of the Hawaiian Islands. Thoroughly honoring this ideal is the Holualoa Inn, which derives its bucolic elegance from sources around the world. The three-story cedar structure, reminiscent of the Pacific Northwest, rests gracefully atop the upper portion of a 40-acre working cattle ranch and coffee farm. Cedar walls, exposed beams, and cathedral ceilings blend harmoniously with polished eucalyptus floors that extend throughout the rambling house. You'll find ample space for two in the expansive upstairs and downstairs common areas, which are tastefully appointed with unusual, contemporary art pieces and a mixture of modern and antique furnishings. A grand piano and a billiard table provide options for entertainment (not that you'd need them for romance), and a small kitchenette stocked with complimentary snacks is available for guests at all hours. Borrow a book from the lending library and curl up in one of the many cozy corners. Better yet, luxuriate near the outdoor pool in a lounge chair and bask in the sunshine. Enfolded by fig, papaya, and plumeria trees, you can lose yourself in enchanting views of the surrounding countryside, Kailua Bay, and the Pacific beyond.

Choose from four alluring guest rooms (they really are amazing) with authentic Polynesian themes. All offer the utmost privacy, as they are scattered throughout the house. Unusual wooden beds, fascinating art, sizable baths (one room has a Jacuzzi tub), ocean views, and beautiful floral linens invite you to stay inside. But before you do, steal to the rooftop gazebo for the best ocean views and a starlight kiss. In the morning, awaken to streaming sunlight and the aromas of a home-cooked breakfast. Sample local fruits and relish the host's custard French toast, waffles, or breakfast casserole. We're not exaggerating—this one is as romantic as it gets.

ROSY'S REST, Holualoa   ❤ ❤ ❤
Reservations through Hawaii's Best Bed and Breakfasts
(808) 885-4550, (800) 262-9912 (mainland)
Inexpensive

Call for reservations. Address and specific directions are provided upon confirmation.

Come to Rosy's Rest for a healthy dose of country charm, warm (but not intrusive) hospitality, wonderfully sequestered accommodations, and very reasonable rates. All of this is waiting in Rosy's rustic two-story cottage, which is trimmed with hand-crafted ohia-wood railings. Impressive craftsmanship continues throughout the two units, one on the lower level with a full kitchen and separate bedroom, and the other a second-floor studio with a small refrigerator and microwave. Both have queen-size beds with handmade quilts and natural wood frames, stained glass windows, private tiled bathrooms, and country-inspired details. Although the studio is smaller, a vaulted ceiling gives it an open, spacious feeling. Distant views of Kailua Kona and the ocean can be seen from both units, but the second-floor studio has the better vantage point from its private tiled patio.

Each room also enjoys a pastoral view of the resident pony (Christina) in her corral out front. The only distraction from this otherwise peaceful scene is the road just beyond that. Traffic quiets down after dark, but this road is the main highway into the small village of Holualoa.

A Hawaiian/European-style continental breakfast of breads, cheeses, and fruit is left in your fridge every night so you can have an entirely intimate breakfast when the two of you so desire.

Brochures that boast of ocean views from the rooms may mean a peekaboo glimpse of the water if you lean out the bathroom window. Be sure to get specifics about what kind of view you can really expect, and get it in writing.

Waiohinu

Hotel/Bed and Breakfast Kissing

WHALING'S HOBBIT HOUSE, Waiohinu
Reservations through Hawaii's Best Bed and Breakfasts
(808) 885-4550, (800) 262-9912 (mainland)
Inexpensive

Call for reservations. Address and specific directions are provided upon confirmation.

Nestled high in the lush Hawaiian hills, with nothing else in sight but trees, grass, and the distant Pacific Ocean, this spacious and self-sufficient cottage is a truly special place to call home for as long as your hearts desire. Intricate stained glass and unique woodwork fill every corner. Everything you need and more is here for your convenience, including a large full kitchen with eating space, a living area with a comfy couch set in front of a picture window with stunning views of the rolling hills, and a quaint bedroom with antique furnishings and a dark wood queen-size bed. We were especially taken with the large tiled bathroom, the main attraction being a two-person soaking tub surrounded by tall stained glass windows set in redwood frames. The large tiled shower can also accommodate two nicely.

In the morning, a variety of cereals, French toast, muffins, fruit, juice, and coffee are brought to your room; you have the choice of eating inside or sitting outside on a picnic table that overlooks the Big Island's untouched beauty. If the two of you love being alone together, Whaling's Hobbit House is the destination you've both been looking for.

◆ **Romantic Note:** The Hobbit House is only accessible with a four-wheel-drive vehicle. If you don't have one, the owners will pick you up at a prearranged time and place.

Kohala Coast

Barren yet breathtaking, the seemingly eternal stretches of black lava end abruptly at the thundering Pacific surf in a strangely surrealistic landscape. The unrelenting beds of lava and the absence of sandy swimming beaches have deterred hotel development along the Kohala Coast (and elsewhere on the island), so relatively little of the land is marred by cement and steel. Consequently, the existing resorts here are few and far between—and exceedingly secluded. Plan to make yourselves at home in the resort of your choice, because there is little in terms of restaurants and shopping anywhere nearby. But who needs shopping? You will have everything you need, and more, in the confines of your hotel and in the surrounding splendor of nearby mountains and water. If you crave privacy more than you crave swimming and sand, the Kohala Coast will be your slice of paradise.

Hotel/Bed and Breakfast Kissing

HAPUNA BEACH PRINCE HOTEL, Kohala Coast
62-100 Kaunaoa Drive
(808) 880-1111, (800) 882-6060 (mainland)
Unbelievably Expensive and Beyond
Wedding facilities are available for a maximum of 650 people.

Just off Queen Kaahumanu Highway (Highway 19), on Kaunaoa Drive.

Simplicity is the watchword at the Hapuna Beach Prince Hotel, from the open-air slate-floored lobby with its towering stone pillars and Asian art pieces to the pale wood, wicker, and tan accents in the 350 guest rooms. But while these muted tones are preferable to bright obnoxious prints, the overabundance of gray and beige imparts a somewhat stark feeling. Every one of the guest rooms could use a considerable amount of warming up.

Despite the standard hotel look of the rooms and suites, all of the traditional amenities are available, and every unit either has an ocean view or faces the oceanfront, which may help explain the exorbitant prices. Or perhaps it is the proximity to the soft golden sands of Hapuna Beach, one of the best beaches on the island. Then again, it could simply be that the rooms here are overpriced (a problem not exactly unheard of in Hawaii). Nevertheless, if saving money isn't a top priority but staying in a quiet beachside retreat with friendly service and all of the offerings of a full-scale resort is, the Hapuna Beach Prince Hotel is a possibility.

◆ **Romantic Note:** Restaurant options here include the casually intimate **COAST GRILLE**, (Expensive), for Euro-Hawaiian cuisine accompanied by ocean views in an open-air setting, and the more formal **BISTRO**, (Expensive), for Mediterranean fare in an atmosphere of subdued elegance. Both restaurants have impressive menus, but we preferred by far the Coast Grille's relaxed tropical demeanor.

THE ISLANDS AT MAUNA LANI, Kohala Coast
2 Kaniku Drive
(808) 885-5022, (800) 642-6284
Very Expensive to Unbelievably Expensive

From the Keahole Airport, drive north on the Queen Kaahumanu Highway (Highway 19) and turn left into the Mauna Lani Resort. Follow signs to the Visitor Arrival Center, where you register at the Classic Resorts desk. A map with directions is provided upon check-in.

Five acres of man-made saltwater lagoons nearly surround The Islands at Mauna Lani, a property made up of brand-new luxury townhomes. The artificial ponds and waterfalls do not even begin to compare to an actual oceanside setting, but if the idea of having a place all to yourselves sounds appealing, consider staying here. The 41 two- or three-bedroom, split-level homes are all attractively decorated in varying styles. What they have in common are white oak floors and ceilings, a wet bar and gas barbecue outside, expansive windows, a huge full kitchen with pale wood cabinets, a laundry room, and central air-conditioning. The kitchen is stocked in advance with a complete assortment of groceries, and a full-size rental car is yours for the duration of your stay.

All this and they only deserve a two-and-a-half-lip rating? Well, despite beautiful furnishings in many of the homes, the units feel somewhat sterile and they are extremely close to one another, leaving little elbow or breathing room. Also, the ocean is nowhere in sight. Thankfully, there is a swimming pool at the center of the property, and beach access is just a short drive away.

◆ **Romantic Alternative: MAUNA LANI POINT**, 2 Kaniku Drive, Kohala Coast, (808) 885-5022, (800) 642-6284, (Expensive to Unbelievably Expensive), is yet another condominium resort. Roomy one-, two-, and three-bedroom suites feature ocean views beyond a golf course.

Unfortunately, the decor is different in each suite, and it ranges from casual contemporary to downright tacky. These units hardly compare to the elegance found at The Islands at Mauna Lani, but if oceanfront is a requirement for your romantic state of mind, this is an option.

KONA VILLAGE, Kailua Kona   ◆ ◆ ◆ ◆
Queen Kaahumanu Highway (Highway 19)
(808) 325-5555
(800) 367-5290 (mainland), (800) 432-5450 (inter-island)
Expensive to Very Expensive
Wedding facilities are available for a maximum of 300 people; call for details.

From the Keahole Airport, drive north six miles up the Queen Kaahumanu Highway (Highway 19). Kona Village is on the left (watch for a cluster of flagpoles and a small tollbooth with a thatched roof).

Picture a romantic island getaway with plenty of privacy and an abundance of sand, water, fragrant flowers, and palm trees around every corner, and you've pictured Kona Village. This is truly an escapist's dream, but those who can't live without modern conveniences (i.e. televisions, telephones, alarm clocks, radios) will be better off elsewhere. What will you find here? Blissful peace and isolation. Staying at Kona Village is like being transported to an ancient seaside Hawaiian fishing settlement: you sleep under a thatched roof in a private, self-contained *hale* (bungalow) designed exclusively for romantic exile. A total of 125 *hales* in a full range of sizes (and prices) dot the resort's 82 creatively landscaped acres; they are decorated in a variety of authentic and colorful Polynesian themes (Samoan, Fijian, Tahitian, and more).

Although furnishings in the *hales* are simple, they include all the required comforts: king-size beds, colorful linens, private baths, and refrigerators (well stocked with cool drinks). Dusty walking paths meander past cottages tucked under palm trees, nestled near a large lagoon teeming with birds, set atop jet black lava rock and black sand, or scattered along a stretch of soft white beach. It feels magical after dark as you walk beneath an arena of twinkling stars; sit at the water's edge and try to catch a glimpse of the mysterious manta ray; or listen to the gentle rush of the man-made waterfall from the spacious outdoor hot tub or small swimming pools (there are two on the property).

Civilization feels light-years away, and this illusion is enhanced by the fact that you don't have to worry about money (until you pay the tab, of course.) Experience a cashless society where three daily meals are provided (they are included in the room price). Alas, although Kona Village's weekly luau is truly one of the best on the Big Island (see the review in "Miscellaneous Kissing"), the food at both of the restaurants here is best described as mediocre. What a disappointment in an otherwise idyllic tropical paradise.

◆ **Romantic Note:** At Kona Village, children are welcomed with open arms, but with so many activities set up for them to do during the day, they are rarely ever in sight.

MAUNA KEA BEACH HOTEL, Kohala Coast   **Unrated**
62-100 Mauna Kea Beach Drive
(808) 800-1111, (800) 882-6060 (mainland)
Very Expensive to Unbelievably Expensive
Wedding facilities are available for a maximum of 500 people.

Just off Queen Kaahumanu Highway (Highway 19), on Mauna Kea Beach Drive.

Although it was impossible to get a look at the extensive renovations taking place at the Mauna Kea Beach Hotel, it gives every indication of reopening with splendor and grace. The romantic potential of the 300-plus rooms is promising. Still, we know how developers and advertising executives can exaggerate, so we will reserve final judgment until the construction is complete. What we can assure you of is the crescent-shaped stretch of soft sandy beach and the serene turquoise bay fronting the property. Regardless of the hotel's restoration, this beach will always be one of *the* best places to kiss in Hawaii (especially at sunset).

MAUNA LANI BAY HOTEL AND BUNGALOWS,
Kohala Coast   ❤ ❤
68-1400 Mauna Lani Drive
(808) 885-6622, (800) 367-2323
Moderate to Unbelievably Expensive and Beyond
Wedding facilities are available for a maximum of 600 people.

From the Keahole Airport, drive north on the Queen Kaahumanu Highway (Highway 19). Watch for signs; the entrance to the hotel is on the left.

When *Lifestyles of the Rich and Famous* rated the Mauna Lani Bay the number-one resort in the United States, they were probably referring to the five unique, ultra-luxurious bungalows (ten lips at least!) that only the rich and famous could possibly afford. Located right on the water's edge, with panoramic ocean views, each one has more space than most homes, along with a sumptuous marble bath, Jacuzzi, private pool, personal butler, and plush oversized furnishings, all for about $2,500 a night. If you can swallow that price, you already know about overindulging the senses.

The rest of us (the underpaid and the obscure) are consigned to a large, white plaster hotel, which, due to its rather dramatic architectural design, looks as if it's sliding into the sea. Set on the rugged and secluded Kohala Coast, the hotel is surrounded by lush foliage, manicured grounds, waterfalls and protected fishponds, and a premier waterfront golf course etched in black lava rock. A five-story open-air lobby hints of older construction, but renovations have added a fresh and welcoming grandeur. Guest rooms are attractive and exceedingly comfortable, though somewhat on the snug side. Most have lanais looking out to the spectacular ocean view, which creates a more spacious feeling inside (the Garden Rooms look out to the parking area).

Resort amenities abound; in addition to the aforementioned championship golf course (you've probably seen it on TV, with its unparalleled over-the-water par-three hole), the Mauna Lani offers tennis courts, a lovely swimming pool, three miles of private white sand beach, a health club, and six restaurants, including **THE CANOE HOUSE** (reviewed in "Restaurant Kissing").

RITZ-CARLTON MAUNA LANI, Kohala Coast
One North Kaniku Drive
(808) 885-2000, (800) 845-9905 (mainland)
Very Expensive to Unbelievably Expensive and Beyond
Wedding facilities are available for a maximum of 300 people.

From the Keahole Airport, drive north up the Queen Kaahumanu Highway (Highway 19) for approximately 15 miles. The hotel is located in the Mauna Lani Resort on the left; follow the signs.

Timeless elegance is what the Ritz-Carlton promises. It is a promise kept. Everything is appropriately grand, yet understated. Rooms are located off a winding maze of stately corridors graced with hand-painted vases, Oriental carpets, antique furnishings, classical art, and floral wall coverings. Even the elevators are replete with wood paneling, Oriental rugs, and overhead chandeliers. The guest suites are less ornate than the elevators, but do provide rich color schemes, plush linens, attractive marble baths with separate tubs and showers, and private lanais, most with rousing views of the surrounding grounds and ocean. For an extra charge, luxuriate in a Club Floor Suite, where you can awaken to a generous continental breakfast and douse your sweet tooth before bedtime with late-night chocolates and a cordial, served just down the hall in the elegant common room.

It only gets better from here. Thirty-two acres of verdant tropical gardens and golf course encompass the sprawling hotel. Rocky waterfalls, fishponds filled with trout, quaint footbridges, and lush vegetation surround you as you follow rambling paths past a large swimming pool with water-spitting stone frog fountains. One negative: the Ritz has only two hot tubs for 541 rooms—one is set near a waterfall and the other is just yards from the pounding surf—which means you will probably have to wait in line or sit shoulder-to-shoulder with strangers. If that's the case, wander farther away toward the white sandy beach and private lagoon, which are often entirely deserted after dark.

◆ **Romantic Note:** You don't have to leave the property for fine dining (which is lucky, because the nearest town is half an hour away). The casual, poolside **CAFE RESTAURANT AND LOUNGE** offers a variety of healthful Pacific Rim dishes and refreshments to enjoy during breaks from swimming or sunbathing. **THE DINING ROOM** and **THE GRILL** (both are reviewed in "Restaurant Kissing") will appease your appetites in first-class surroundings.

Restaurant Kissing

THE CANOE HOUSE, Kohala Coast
1 Mauna Lani Drive, in the Mauna Lani Resort
(808) 885-6622, (800) 367-2323
Very Expensive

From the Keahole Airport, follow the Queen Kaahumanu Highway (Highway 19) north. Watch for signs; the entrance to the Mauna Lani Resort is on the left.

Considered one of the best restaurants on the coast, The Canoe House comes awfully close to living up to its challenging reputation. The open-air room allows distant views of the gentle water and breathtaking sunsets through swaying palms and tiki torches, making the outside an integral part of your dining experience. Under a thatched roof with wood detailing, soft candlelight and comfortable seating fill the interior with a subtle elegance that blends perfectly with the energy of the waves and the warmth of the air. Unfortunately, the service can be rather aloof.

Like many of Hawaii's restaurants, The Canoe House serves Pacific Rim cuisine, with a few continental items thrown in to round out the menu. Seared ahi with pineapple salsa and curried sticky rice, and garlic chicken with wasabi "smashed" potatoes are two delicious examples. Presentation and fresh ingredients are emphasized here, but taste is the first consideration (portions could be more generous), and everything is more than delectable.

◆ **Romantic Warning:** Another well-known restaurant in the Mauna Lani Resort is **THE GALLERY**, Kohala Coast, (808) 885-7777, (Moderate to Expensive), offering northern Italian dishes that incorporate fresh Hawaiian ingredients. The catch of the day is usually a good selection at any restaurant, but here the preparations are a disappointment. Sadly, the seafood tends to be overcooked and vegetables are undercooked. If the ambience were warmed up a bit we might recommend this place for dessert, but the shiny black tables topped with a single tropical flower, the bright lighting, and the impersonal service made us give this place a thumbs (as well as lips) down.

THE DINING ROOM, Kohala Coast   ❤ ❤ ❤ ❤
One North Kaniku Drive, in the Ritz-Carlton Mauna Lani
(808) 885-2000
Very Expensive to Unbelievably Expensive
Wedding facilities are available for a maximum of 25 people.

From the Keahole Airport, drive north up the Queen Kaahumanu Highway (Highway 19) for approximately 15 miles. The Ritz-Carlton is located in the Mauna Lani Resort on the left; Follow the signs.

Handsome wood paneling; distant water views; beautiful linens; formal place settings shining with silver, crystal, and china; and, most notably, flawless service. As lovely as that all sounds, it wouldn't count for much if the food weren't some of the most innovative and delicious we've had in all of the Hawaiian Islands, but it absolutely was. Savor perfectly prepared, remarkably fresh island fish, either broiled, sautéed, or grilled, with asparagus, capers, and olive vinaigrette; saffron herb sauce; or banana curry and ti leaf–wrapped banana, among other unique choices. And dessert will make you blush with the sweetness of the moment. Every detail makes this an indulgent, ecstatic dining experience for two.

◆ **Romantic Note:** Best of all, in The Dining Room's lounge, you can sway arm-in-arm to soft jazz late into the night, performed by exceptionally talented local musicians.

THE GRILL, Kohala Coast ❤ ❤ ❤ ❤
One North Kaniku Drive, in the Ritz-Carlton Mauna Lani
(808) 885-2000
Very Expensive
Wedding facilities are available for a maximum of 25 people.

From the Keahole Airport, drive north up the Queen Kaahumanu Highway (Highway 19) for approximately 15 miles. The Ritz-Carlton is located in the Mauna Lani Resort on the left; follow the signs.

Combine rich dark koa wood, sparkling crystal chandeliers, crisp linens, and plush upholstered chairs, and what do you get? The Grill, an alluring restaurant that meets the Ritz-Carlton's ever-so-high standards. Add to this regal atmosphere excellent service and an incredible chef who serves world-class cuisine, and what do you get? A four-lip dining destination that meets *our* ever-so-high, romantic-minded standards.

Traditional grilled fare with innovative Mediterranean flair graces the menu. The risotto with Gorgonzola, fontina, and Parmesan cheese is delightful, and the fresh pastas are heavenly, especially the mushroom ravioli with herb-marinated chicken and leek cream, but save room for more. Oven-roasted Kona Maine lobster stuffed with sea scallops and prawns, topped with a tarragon-tomato beurre blanc, is to die for. Desserts are equally irresistible.

Remember, all beaches are public in Hawaii. As long as you can find public access, you are welcome to enjoy the beaches everywhere.

Miscellaneous Kissing

KONA VILLAGE LUAU, Kailua Kona ◆ ◆ ◆
Queen Kaahumanu Highway (Highway 19)
(808) 325-5555
(800) 367-5290 (mainland), (800) 432-5450 (inter-island)
$65 per person

From the Keahole Airport, drive north six miles up the Queen Kaahumanu Highway (Highway 19). Kona Village is on the left (watch for a cluster of flagpoles and a small tollbooth with a thatched roof).

Kona Village has the best luau in Hawaii, and we don't mean just on the Big Island, we mean it is the best luau in the *entire state.* Judging from the number of locals who frequent this weekly event for special occasions or just to reunite themselves with Hawaii of old, this luau is the real deal. Polynesian dancers and entertainers perform on a stage beyond a pond area, so the experience isn't "in your face" like most other luaus (see "To Luau or Not To Luau" in the introduction for our thoughts on this activity). The high-energy entertainment is excellent, and the food was one of the most memorable parts of our trip.

Our senses were first dazzled by the smoky aroma of the *kalua* pig as it was lifted from the *imu* (an underground oven that is six feet wide and four feet deep and is lined with burning wood and hot lava rocks). This delicious, traditionally prepared meat is the main dish of the feast, and, unlike other luaus where you might get only a taste, there is plenty of it to go around. Other authentic Polynesian favorites from the intriguing menu include *poi,* which is mashed taro root and crucial to any Hawaiian meal; *laulau,* seasoned pork with salted butterfish wrapped in taro leaves; *poisson cru,* fresh chunks of fish and thin slices of vegetables marinated in lime juice and coconut milk; and banana and papaya *po'e,* mashed bananas and papayas baked with pineapple juice and coconut milk. At Kona Village, this luau is an event not to be missed.

Reserve your rental car in advance. During high season, cars may not be available when you arrive.

Waikoloa

Hotel/Bed and Breakfast Kissing

HILTON WAIKOLOA VILLAGE, Waikoloa   ❤ ❤ ❤
69-425 Waikoloa Beach Drive
(808) 885-1234, (800) 221-2424
Moderate to Unbelievably Expensive and Beyond
Wedding facilities are available for a maximum of 2,000 people.

From the Keahole Airport, head north on the Queen Kaahumanu Highway (Highway 19) for approximately 30 miles. The entrance to the Hilton is on the left; follow signs to the hotel.

Sixty-two oceanfront acres (but, alas, no natural beach) envelop this palatial wonderland, which includes eight restaurants, 12 lounges, 1,241 guest rooms, meeting facilities, three swimming pools, a lagoon, a golf course, several twisting water slides, shopping, a health spa, trained dolphins, and more. So how do you make your way across this gargantuan property? It's easy! Hop on the small ferryboat that winds through the connecting waterways or get whisked to your destination in an electric tram. Either option can be delightful once or twice, but both grow tiresome quickly, especially when there are crowds. Instead, set out on foot (don't forget your map), and wander along flagstone walkways that meander past the stunning Oriental and Pacific art pieces that grace this Polynesian palace. Although there are acres upon acres of property to explore, most of it is man-made (waterfalls and lagoon included), and you may find yourselves longing for open stretches of untouched beach and sky. (Isn't that why you came to Hawaii?) To satisfy your cravings, take a shuttle bus from the hotel to the public beach next door.

Once you've finally found your suite, located in either the Ocean, Lagoon, or Palace towers, you can bask in stately (although pricey) comfort and ocean views. The Club Bay Suites are especially luxurious, with Oriental motifs, unusual pottery, magnificent view lanais, queen-size koa wood beds, marble baths, and Jacuzzis. The Regency Club Suites include exemplary concierge service, breakfast and the morning paper, and evening cocktails with hors d'oeuvres. If your budget can handle it and you're in the mood for miles of hotel and lots of outdoor recreation, you've found heaven. Otherwise, you'll be looking frantically for the exit.

◆ **Romantic Note:** The Hilton has eight different restaurants to choose from, all just a ferryboat (or tram) ride away. **IMARI**, (808) 885-2893, (Moderate), set in a lovely tea garden highlighted by waterfalls, offers innovative Japanese cuisine and a sushi bar with some of the best bite-size creations around. Another option is the **PALM TERRACE**, (808) 885-2893, (Moderate), an open-air dining room beside a plunging waterfall. Delectable baked goods, fruits, and traditional American and Japanese dishes are served at deluxe breakfast and dinner buffets. **DONATONI'S** and the **KAMUELA PROVISION COMPANY** (both are reviewed in "Restaurant Kissing") are also quite good.

Restaurant Kissing

DONATONI'S, Waikoloa   ❤ ❤
69-425 Waikoloa Beach Drive, in the Hilton Waikoloa Village
(808) 885-2893
Expensive

From the Keahole Airport, drive north up the Queen Kaahumanu Highway (Highway 19) and turn left onto Waikoloa Drive. Follow signs to the Hilton Waikoloa Village.

With its elegant house-like setting and old-world charm, this cozy restaurant is clearly a favorite of the rich and famous (photographs of happy celebrities cover the entryway). The northern Italian cuisine served here ranges from gourmet pizzas and pastas to savory meat dishes. Swift and friendly service, large overstuffed brocade chairs, romantic lighting, and views of the hotel's waterways and surrounding garden create an intimate atmosphere in which to dine in bliss.

KAMUELA PROVISION COMPANY, Waikoloa
In the Hilton Waikoloa Village
(808) 885-2893
Moderate to Expensive

From the Keahole Airport, drive north up the Queen Kaahumanu Highway (Highway 19) and turn left onto Waikoloa Drive. Follow signs to the Hilton Waikoloa Village.

After you've worked up an appetite exploring the amusement park–like grounds of the Hilton Waikoloa Village, hop on the electric tram (be sure to ask if you're headed in the right direction) and go to the Kamuela Provision Company for steak and seafood. (Asking for directions is a must at this 64-acre resort.)

The Kamuela Provision Company is located at a quiet edge of the resort, and you might even forget the rest of this massive property. Outdoor seating is especially nice because of the surrounding tropical ambience, and from 6 P.M. to 10 P.M. a guitarist sends soft melodies into the open night air. Inside, tall French doors separate several quaint dining rooms, each holding tables with floral linens and glowing candles, black-and-cream-checked chairs, and hardwood floors. Service is prompt and friendly, and the menu, although small, offers hearty choices like macadamia nut rack of lamb and roasted chicken marinated with ginger and soy sauce. For dessert, consider sharing a generously sized slice of mud pie served with hot fudge sauce and whipped cream. Heavy and heavenly!

Kawaihae

Hotel/Bed and Breakfast Kissing

MAKAI HALE, Kawaihae
Reservations through Hawaii's Best Bed and Breakfasts
(808) 885-4550, (800) 262-9912 (mainland)
Inexpensive

Call for reservations. Address and specific directions are provided upon confirmation.

As you wind up the hillside toward Makai Hale, the stunning splendor of the Kohala Coast becomes more apparent. Across the expanse of horizon, the crystal blue Pacific dazzles your eyes while the mountain peaks of Mauna Lani and Mauna Kea rise majestically to meet the sky. Vast black lava beds below drop suddenly to the raging sea. Makai

Hale takes full advantage of this view, and guests can take in the heavenly surroundings in a detached two-bedroom suite. Floor-to-ceiling windows, a comfy white wicker bed with floral linens, a standard, rather small bathroom, and unhindered views from the front bedroom are yours alone. To fully embrace views of Kohala, slip out the sliding glass door of your suite onto a sweeping cement deck with a large black-bottomed swimming pool, Jacuzzi, and picnic tables where you can relax for hours and contemplate the breathtaking panorama. Breakfast provisions are left in the small kitchenette by the hosts, who live in the adjacent house and leave your privacy undisturbed.

Restaurant Kissing

CAFE PESTO, Kawaihae
In the Kawaihae Shopping Center
(808) 882-1071
Inexpensive
Wedding facilities are available for a maximum of 90 people.

Drive east on Highway 19 to Highway 270, turn left, and continue to the Kawaihae Shopping Center at the Kawaihae Harbor. The restaurant is located in the shopping center.

Tucked, or trapped, in the middle of a small shopping center, this casual cafe, distinguished by a black-and-white-checked floor and bright contemporary art, is the perfect place for a quick lunch or dinner. The menu lists a wide variety of salads, calzones, hand-tossed pizzas, hot sandwiches, pastas, and risottos, and fresh seafood prepared in three tantalizing styles. The service rates among the friendliest and most efficient on the island, and we know your lips won't be disappointed.

Waimea

Up here, at 2,200 feet above sea level, the days can be hot, with warm afternoon rains and cool breezes that blow through gently swaying trees and over idyllic green pasture land. The ocean is only eight miles away, but another world exists at this elevation, and it is worth discovering for yourselves. Waimea is a thriving, quiet country town, home to 8,000 islanders. You'll find only a handful of restaurants and shops, but acres and acres of visual enchantment.

For well over a hundred years, the pivotal business of the region has been the **PARKER RANCH**, the largest family-owned ranch in the United States. Currently, more than 225,000 acres are in a charitable trust serving the town of Waimea, but it began as a two-acre land grant back in 1837 from King Kamehameha I to John P. Parker. For a more detailed historical retrospective, tour the two museums, one of which is in the owners' ranch house.

Instead of spending just a day in this peaceful countryside, you should consider a longer romantic sojourn. Waimea isn't the tropical Hawaii you usually think of, but it also isn't as crowded or as expensive as the coastal areas.

Hotel/Bed and Breakfast Kissing

PUU MANU COTTAGE, Waimea   ❤ ❤ ❤
Reservations through Hawaii's Best Bed and Breakfasts
(808) 885-4550, (800) 262-9912 (mainland)
Inexpensive

Call for reservations. Detailed directions are provided upon confirmation.

What a remarkable little hideaway this is, nestled in the middle of a vast rolling meadow dotted with Rousseau-esque clusters of trees, in the foothills of Mauna Kea. Unbelievably, this immaculate, meticulously refurbished cottage was once a barn that served the nearby country home of the owners. Now it is a cozy respite for those who want secluded country life and the warm Hawaiian sun. French doors that open onto a wide deck, a charming living room warmed at night by a glowing fireplace, two genial bedrooms, and a handsome open kitchen supplied with a generous morning meal are all part of the tranquil, serene indulgences you can enjoy here. Yes, the beach is a 25-minute drive away, but you get to come back to your mountain hideaway, so it doesn't really matter.

◆ **Romantic Note:** A five-night minimum stay is required.

WAIMEA GARDENS COTTAGE, Waimea   ❤ ❤ ❤ ❤
Reservations through Hawaii's Best Bed and Breakfasts
(808) 885-4550, (800) 262-9912 (mainland)
Inexpensive

Call for reservations. Detailed directions are provided upon confirmation.

As you've thumbed through the "Hotel/Bed and Breakfast Kissing" selections in this guide, you probably have noticed references to Hawaii's Best Bed and Breakfasts, a reservation service. Well, the owners of that select business have created a "best" bed and breakfast of their own. An impeccably renovated duplex cottage adjacent to the main house holds two lovingly decorated units bordered by a rushing creek, forest, sweeping lawn, and well-maintained English garden. The shingled red exterior is punctuated by forest green windows and a picket fence. The country-inspired interiors are flawless, with marble wood-burning fireplaces, hardwood floors, alcove bedrooms, down comforters, charming kitchens, stereos, and TVs. Every amorous detail has been attended to, so all you have to do is snuggle together and enjoy.

Restaurant Kissing

MERRIMAN'S RESTAURANT, Waimea
Highway 19 and Opelo Road
(808) 885-6822
Moderate to Expensive
Wedding facilities are available for a maximum of 110 people.

Just off Highway 19 in the heart of Waimea, in the small Opelo Plaza.

Lunches are reliably good at this fine restaurant, one of the Big Island's best, but evenings are when the unique style of the chef takes flight. Our wok-charred ahi was perfectly done, and the fresh catch of the day, sautéed in a sesame crust and topped with a mango-lime sauce, was outstanding. Fresh local meats are equally savory and masterfully prepared; the filet mignon in brandy cream sauce is superb. Tables are situated a little too close to one another for any privacy, but the food is so good it is easy after a few moments to forget this one shortcoming. You can save the kissing until you get home, full and satisfied from a delightful meal.

Pack insect repellent. Hawaii's trade winds tend to keep bugs on the move, but in the more tropical, jungle-like areas, mosquitoes are a problem.

Waipio

Outdoor Kissing

WAIPIO VALLEY, Waipio
Waipio Valley Shuttle, (808) 775-7121
Waipio Valley Wagon Tours, (808) 775-9518
Prices are between $25 to $35 per person for a one-and-a-half-hour tour.

Call for reservations and directions.

Looking down into the breathtaking Waipio Valley from the lookout is an awesome experience, but an excursion through the valley itself, in a mule-driven wagon, provides passage to gorgeous tropical vegetation, cascading waterfalls, wet taro fields, and a striking black sand beach. It is also a journey through history. King Kamehameha I established his long reign over the islands from this location. Formidable battles, human sacrifices, and peaceful agriculture have all been part of life in this mesmerizing valley. The softly wafting breezes here seem to whisper of Hawaii's past—take a moment to contemplate the ancient stories this area could share.

◆ **Romantic Note:** If you are interested in a more intimate trek and are also capable of handling a fairly steep ascent out of the valley (going in is downhill, so that part is easier), hiking is definitely an option. Watertight shoes are a necessity, along with a backpack and light rain gear. Remember, this is the rainy part of the island.

Volcano

There aren't many places in the great state of Hawaii where snuggling up beside a warm fireplace sounds like a good idea. Taking a refreshing swim or cranking up the air-conditioning is more likely to appeal to mainlanders not used to heat and humidity. But in the tiny two-store town of Volcano ("town" actually feels like a misnomer; "village" or "neighborhood" might be more accurate), cool weather and rainy days prevail most of the year. This could be seen as a drawback (and to visitors looking forward to palm trees, warm ocean waves, sunny skies, and hot days, it is), but such conditions can inspire cozy, romantic inclinations.

Volcano can be a moving experience—literally. Don't be surprised if you awaken to a small earthquake in the middle of the night. Rumbling earth is just an accepted part of life in Volcano (along with events such as lava flows closing down sections of roadway). Everything in Volcano, including a bevy of bed and breakfasts, is just minutes away from **HAWAII VOLCANOES NATIONAL PARK** (reviewed in "Outdoor Kissing"), the area's main attraction. Kilauea, the unpredictable volcano, continues its eruptive activity with majestic but destructive glory. Past lava flows have covered a newly built visitor center, annihilated main roads, and demolished the popular local black sand beach. Nevertheless, if you can calm your apprehensions (locals don't seem worried and say that living in any mainland city is far more dangerous), witnessing the tremendous power of the earth's miraculous birth process is a must. Walk through extinct lava tubes, drive around the volcano's steaming crater, or, if your timing is lucky, survey momentous views of flowing red hot lava.

Hotel/Bed and Breakfast Kissing

CARSON'S VOLCANO COTTAGE, Volcano
505 Sixth Street
(808) 967-7683, (800) 845-LAVA
Inexpensive

Heading south on Highway 11 from Hilo, take the second left after mile marker 25, onto Jade Street. Turn right onto Sixth, drive about a half mile, and park immediately after the Carson's sign on the right.

Sheltered by a lush tropical forest of camellias, cedars, and Japanese maples, Carson's offers three secluded rooms and a separate cottage decorated with great attention to detail. Of the three rooms, one is done up in Hawaiian monarchy period style, replete with appropriate antiques and lace curtains; one reflects Hawaii in the 1940s, with bright colors and period collectibles; and the last features a Japanese theme, with shoji screens and Oriental art. While the rooms are not outstanding, they are intriguing and have inviting personalities of their own. The cottage, although it lacks a discernible theme, is packed full (almost to overflowing) with antique knickknacks.

Each unit, including the cottage, is equipped with a refrigerator, microwave, and private bath. Regardless of where you stay, breakfast is brought to your room each morning, and may consist of coffee, tea, tropical juices, fresh fruits, French toast, and bagels with cream cheese, lox, and capers. After breakfast, take a relaxing soak in the outdoor hot tub, tucked in a wooden gazebo; it's open for romance 24 hours a day.

CHALET KILAUEA—THE INN AT VOLCANO,
Volcano
Wright Road and Laukapu Road
(808) 967-7786, (800) 937-7786
Inexpensive to Expensive

Heading south on Highway 11 from Hilo, turn right after mile marker 26 onto Wright Road. The inn is on the right.

Chalet Kilauea is one of Volcano's many secret treasures. This eclectic two-story home, with a connected tree house, is ensconced in deep woods and fragrant flowers. The inviting common area is filled with exceedingly comfortable, contemporary furnishings and affectionate detailing, which will pique your curiosity about your own accommodations. The delightful Oriental Jade Room is done, of course, in deep green hues, with a green marble Jacuzzi tub in the private bathroom and a queen-size bed in the bedroom. The Out of Africa Room features warm earth tones, while the lovely Continental Lace Room (which the owners also refer to as the Bridal Suite) is romantically done up in white and pink and offers a large soaking tub surrounded by white tile. Adjacent to the main house is the more private, two-level Tree-House Suite, with a king-size bed and windows that look out to nothing but thick forest. An outdoor kitchenette, with a small refrigerator and microwave, is available for guests' use.

Don't oversleep and miss your first meal of the day: the owners here go all out. Seated at one of three private two-person tables, under a twinkling chandelier, you'll savor a full breakfast served on antique Victorian china. Sample items include a smoked salmon and bagel plate, hot omelets with ham and cheese, fresh muffins, fruit, and coffee and juice. Later in the day, when the customary late-afternoon fog rolls in, relish complimentary high tea in the common room, followed by a dip in the outdoor hot tub.

◆ **Romantic Note:** You would be doing yourselves a huge disservice if you neglected to ask about Chalet Kiluea's six other vacation homes, set off the property. Decorated in a variety of styles and colors, these are excellent options for a more private getaway, and prices for the homes include high tea at the main house and use of the Jacuzzi.

HALE IKI, Volcano
Reservations through Hawaii's Best Bed and Breakfasts
(808) 885-4550, (800) 262-9912 (mainland)
Inexpensive

Call for reservations. Address and detailed directions are provided upon confirmation.

When it's wet and chilly outside (as it can frequently be in Volcano), Hale Iki is just the kind of place you'll long for. This cozy little cedar cabin is tucked into lush forest surroundings, and it's all yours (at least for the nights that you book in advance—at least two are required).

Knotty pine walls, hardwood floors, and a wood-burning fireplace hint of Aspen, but the rattan furniture and tropical prints help remind you this is Hawaii (a fact you probably don't want to lose touch with). The bedroom is set in a loft, and the main floor consists of a snuggling area next to the fireplace, full kitchen, dining area, and a bathroom with a huge soaking tub for two set next to windows facing lush forest. The dense shrubbery all around keeps your bath, and your whole time here, private. Breakfast, a private affair as well, is left in the kitchen.

◆ **Romantic Alternative:** Nestled in the woods nearby is **LOKAHI LODGE BED AND BREAKFAST**, Kalanikoa Road, Volcano, (808) 985-8647, (800) 457-6924, (Inexpensive). The two double beds in each of their four guest rooms don't necessarily suggest romance, but the price is certainly right (we haven't found cheaper lodgings anywhere else on the islands), the rooms are spacious and immaculate, and the welcoming charm of the innkeepers and their lively pets (two dogs and a cat) assure you of a pleasant stay. Experience quiet country living and a good healthy breakfast for an extremely agreeable price.

KILAUEA LODGE, Volcano
Old Volcano Road
(808) 967-7366
Inexpensive

Wedding facilities are available for a maximum of 70 people.

Heading south on Highway 11 from Hilo, turn right onto Wright Road, then left onto Old Volcano Road. The lodge is on the right.

Known best for its restaurant (reviewed in "Restaurant Kissing"), Kilauea Lodge also has some charming rooms to choose from. This simple country inn offers 12 units in three adjoining buildings, but we recommend the newer suites in the Hale Aloha Building. We especially liked the upstairs suites, with their cathedral ceilings, wood beams, king-size beds with Ralph Lauren linens, fireplaces, stained glass windows, and private baths. Our only complaint is that the walls are thin and voices can be heard through them.

Accommodations in the two original buildings are less fresh and inviting, although they are graced with fireplaces and homey country ambience. Fortunately, all of the rooms have central heat, a must for Volcano in the winter, and a simple but filling complimentary breakfast is served every morning in the lodge's handsome restaurant.

◆ **Romantic Alternative:** Another property nearby with a similar 1930s lodge charm is **HALE OHIA,** Volcano Village, reservations through Hawaii's Best Bed and Breakfasts, (808) 885-4550, (800) 262-9912, (Inexpensive). The inn has been in operation for over 60 years, and the six guest rooms show their age; a few display a considerable amount of wear and tear. The private little Ihilani Cottage, with a wood-burning fireplace and enclosed garden area with a fountain, is your best bet. The Dillingham Suite in the main house, with hardwood floors and antiques, is another option. It may not be luxurious, but the history of the property, the lovely gardens, and undeniable rustic charm make Hale Ohia worth considering.

MOUNTAIN HOUSE AND HYDRANGEA COTTAGE, Volcano   ❤ ❤ ❤
Reservations through Hawaii's Best Bed and Breakfasts
(808) 885-4550, (800) 262-9912 (mainland)
Inexpensive to Expensive

Call for reservations. Address and specific directions are provided upon confirmation.

Informed couples know just where to find real romance in Volcano: hidden among the ohia trees, hapu'u ferns, orchids, magnolias, and hydrangeas of the Mountain House. This once-private estate and an adjacent cottage have been lovingly converted into an elegant bed and breakfast that provides guests with sumptuous surroundings and utter seclusion.

Depending on your means, the Hydrangea Cottage might be the better choice of the two. For a phenomenally low price, you get an entire luxury cottage with views of the surrounding woods all to yourselves. The spacious living room has plush modern furnishings, a large kitchen area stocked with breakfast foods, extensive windows that allow an infusion of natural light, a wood-burning fireplace, and a VCR (upon request). The bedroom and private bath are equally special. It's hard to believe they don't charge more, but we won't tell the owners if you won't.

Even more intriguing is the Mountain House, where the owners once lived. Two bedrooms, placed at opposite ends of this colossal home to ensure the utmost privacy, are graced with lovely color schemes, handsome linens, and spacious private baths. An extravagant gourmet kitchen, so large it almost looks like it's been transplanted from a restaurant, sits in the middle of the home. Cook to your hearts' content, or enjoy the complimentary breakfast provided for you. The house's spare Asian-influenced decor, koa wood details, and beautiful views of the surrounding woodland and gardens encourage long hours of rest and relaxation. If your budget allows, an evening at the Mountain House might tempt you into staying a day or two longer in Volcano.

Restaurant Kissing

KILAUEA LODGE RESTAURANT, Volcano
Old Volcano Road
(808) 967-7366
Moderate
Wedding facilities are available for a maximum of 70 people.

Heading south on Highway 11 from Hilo, turn right onto Wright Road, then left onto Old Volcano Road. The lodge is on the right.

People come to Volcano to see the works of Pele, the Hawaiian fire goddess, but that doesn't mean they lose their appetites. Much to tourists' dismay, there are relatively few dining options in Volcano. In fact, the Kilauea Lodge is considered by most to be not only the best, but the *only* dining option here. Despite its lack of competition, the restaurant maintains its reputation by consistently preparing excellent dishes with a well-balanced mixture of European and Hawaiian flair.

Cozy up in the provincial dining room next to the Fireplace of Friendship, which pays tribute to Kilauea Lodge's past as a YMCA camp with a collection of artifacts from children's groups around the world. Hardwood floors, koa wood tables, fresh flowers, and artistic renditions of Pele's fiery temper enhance your dining enjoyment. It isn't exactly fancy, but the atmosphere is warm and the service is friendly. Begin your meal with warm Brie cheese coated in herb batter and coconut flakes, served with fresh hot bread, then sample the fresh local fish or one of the nightly specials, such as rack of lamb with apple-papaya-mint sauce. The delightful aromas and flavors may even distract you from the brooding volcano, at least for the moment. Kilauea Lodge Restaurant is open only for dinner (unless you are a guest at the lodge, in which case breakfast is included with your stay).

◆ **Romantic Alternative:** Finding lunch in Volcano is a bit of a challenge. Packing a picnic or munching on snacks until dinner time is an option, but if you would prefer to eat in a restaurant, consider the **VOLCANO GOLF AND COUNTRY CLUB RESTAURANT**, Hawaii Volcanoes National Park, (808) 967-8228, (Inexpensive to Moderate). Their soups, salads, and sandwiches aren't exactly gourmet and the plastic table coverings are less than romantic, but it is pretty much the only game in town when it comes to lunch, and the food, service, and casual atmosphere aren't all that bad.

◆ **Romantic Warning:** Avoid the **VOLCANO HOUSE**, located in Hawaii Volcanoes National Park, at all costs. It is set up to cater to busloads of tourists who tour the park. Although it is one of the only other dining options in Volcano, its grim and greasy atmosphere can spoil anyone's appetite for food and romantic possibilities.

Outdoor Kissing

HAWAII VOLCANOES NATIONAL PARK,
Volcano
(808) 967-7311
Entrance fee is $5 per car.

Heading south on Highway 11 from Hilo, go about 28 miles, then look for signs to Volcano and to the park's entrance.

If capricious Kilauea is in the mood to erupt, don't hesitate to wit-ness it for yourself. Without question, it is a once-in-a-lifetime event. Unlike any other natural wonder, a volcano (and the power of the fire goddess Pele, according to legend) moves the soul in a way that is hard to describe.

At various times over the past millennium, but more specifically in the past 100 years, and in varying intensities, Kilauea has displayed its awesome force in a passionate fury that gurgles up from the earth in rivers and fountains of 2,000-degree molten lava. Thick flaming red fingers move across the land through an array of lava tubes, then spill into the sea in hissing explosions that turn the liquid fire into black powder and rock.

There are two ways to experience this phenomenon. One is to drive to the end of **CRATER RIM DRIVE** at night to see fountains of molten rock shooting up from the earth. When conditions are safe enough, you can even hike down to the ocean over a well-marked lava field to take a closer look (warm clothes, water, snacks, and flashlights are essential for this excursion). For the less hardy, or for those with a more liberal expense account, a helicopter tour is a must. Several flight services will take you aloft to survey the devastation from above it all. (**VOLCANO HELI-TOURS** is one option, (808) 967-7578, about $125 per person). The pools of bubbling, fiery lava moving through collapsed caverns and open fissures are literally astounding. Sit tight and clasp hands; you're going on the ride of your lives.

Romantic Note: After all this, we must warn you that Kilauea is unpredictable; depending on all kinds of geological forces, you may not see as much volcanic activity as you hoped for. Fortunately, even if the lava flow has slowed down, you can at least witness the orange glow of the lava's path from the end of Crater Rim Drive after dusk. Visibility and safety conditions are posted at the park's visitor center, and the staff there is extremely helpful.

Lanai

• LANAI CITY

> *"Women still remember the first kiss after men have forgotten the last."*
> Remy de Gourmont

LANAI

Most of the 7 million visitors who come to Hawaii each year never visit the island of Lanai, and their absence is one of its most alluring features. A tiny island 18 miles long and 13 miles wide, just 7 miles west of Maui, with a resident population of only 2,400, Lanai has all the tantalizing details of paradise you may be looking for, especially solitude and conspicuous tranquillity. Completing this dream come true are accessible but hard-to-reach sandy beaches where you and your loved one will be the only strollers for miles around, meandering trails to hike, gentle island people who love their land and welcome visitors, truly remote resort hotels with all the sumptuous, accommodating services you would expect from the most elegant of destinations, and no tourist attractions. We'll repeat that because we know it's hard to believe—*no tourist attractions.* Romance is the very soul of Lanai.

You won't find the lush vegetation of the other islands here, but every other facet of a blissful tropical paradise awaits. Pine-covered highlands, rocky cliffs, rolling red clay hillsides dabbed with green, and pineapple fields healing from years of operation cover Lanai's arid interior, where there's not enough surface water to duplicate the lavish rain forests found on the other islands. Only one road leads from the boat landing up to Lanai City, 2,000 feet above sea level. This same road wanders around a short distance and splits into two branches that take you to roads suitable for four-wheel-drive vehicles only. Car rentals are expensive ($100 a day), but worth it for a long day of exploration.

Lanai has a fascinating recent history. In the 1920s, 98 percent of the island was purchased by Jim Dole, who developed and planted the illustrious pineapple crop canned by his plantation. For years virtually all of Lanai's usable land was covered in cultivated fields. Eventually, U.S. costs grew too high, and South America became the new center of pineapple production. The last pineapple harvest here was in 1993. Employment prospects in this innocent corner of the world would have been devastating had the Dole Food Company (also flirting with financial woes) not built two of the most charming, exclusive hotel properties in all of Hawaii. Now tourism is the major industry on tiny Lanai, with additional controlled development coming.

Is paradise lost? Far from it. For now, Dole is the only developer and thankfully they are moving slowly. In the meantime, Lanai awaits in all of its original glory.

◆ **Romantic Note:** All the inter-island airlines offer daily flights to and from Lanai. There is also daily passenger-only ferryboat service from Lahaina, Maui, to Hulope Bay, Lanai, via **EXPEDITIONS**, (808) 661-3756. If you take the boat between December and March, hang on tight and watch for whales—they often accompany the crossing.

Lanai City

Hotel/Bed and Breakfast Kissing

THE LODGE AT KOELE, Lanai City
Reservations through Lanai Resorts
(808) 565-7300, (800) 321-4666
Expensive to Unbelievably Expensive and Beyond
Wedding facilities are available for a maximum of 60 people.

Call for reservations. Directions and arrival information are provided upon confirmation.

Unlike any other destination in Hawaii, the architecture and the mood at The Lodge at Koele may make you feel you're in the wrong state. Unmistakable Pacific Northwest flair marks this lodge standing proudly on top of an idyllic verdant hillside. The building resembles an incredibly luxurious ski lodge, and a casual alpine spirit envelopes you as you cross the threshold. Inside, the enormous great hall, with its high-beamed ceilings and two formidable stone fireplaces, is adorned with plush furnishings and beautiful antiques from all over the world. An opulent Hawaiian plantation feeling is evident in a series of luxurious sitting rooms where guests can have high tea, watch television, or while away the hours playing billiards or other games. A long hallway leads to an adjacent building where each uniquely decorated room is utterly charming and cozy. Four-poster beds, wicker chairs, pine furniture, large soaking tubs, and private lanais are all affection-inspiring. Outdoors you'll find immaculate gardens bordered by evergreen forest, with the endless Pacific in the distance. Centered in the midst of all this lushness are a large pool and a hot tub.

The restaurants display the same high standards and attention to details. Of particular interest are both the **KOELE TERRACE,** (Moderate to Expensive), and the **FORMAL DINING ROOM,** (Expensive to Very Expensive), where sumptuous meals are served with a mastery almost unparalleled on any of the islands. Every meal seemed more remarkable than the last. The menu offers a creative commingling of Mediterranean and Pacific Rim cuisines, and every bite is a memorable experience.

THE MANELE BAY HOTEL, Lanai City
Reservations through Lanai Resorts
(808) 565-7700, (800) 321-4666
Expensive to Unbelievably Expensive and Beyond
Wedding facilities are available for a maximum of 200 people.

Call for reservations. Directions and arrival information are provided upon confirmation.

You may not know how to describe paradise, but you definitely know it when you see it. At The Manele Bay Hotel, in addition to paradise, you'll also encounter luxury, grandeur, and gracious, sincere hospitality. From the moment you arrive, you are the focus of unsurpassed and attentive service as you are escorted through the magnificent two-story lobby. Towering etched glass doors open out to a grand pool area; in the distance, a rocky bluff outlines the ocean, nearby beach, and pristine countryside. Add to all this exquisite furnishings, poshly decorated dining rooms, a fire-warmed game room, and a variety of stately terraces.

In the guest rooms, European comfort and refinement impart serene relaxation. Each large room features expansive sliding glass doors that open to a private lanai overlooking either a sculpted Japanese garden or the pounding surf. Bright yellow English floral fabrics, plantation-style furnishings, and attractive baths further enhance each interior.

Both of the dining rooms here are pleasantly sophisticated and surprisingly excellent (a real relief considering that they are pretty much the only game in town besides the two dining rooms at The Lodge at Koele). Share a casually elegant breakfast, lunch, or dinner at the Mediterranean-inspired **HULOPO'E COURT** dining room, (Expensive), where Hawaiian regional cuisine is the specialty. For a more intimate interlude, schedule an evening at the **IHILANI DIN-ING ROOM**, (Expensive to Very Expensive). The menu is French Mediterranean and the room is tastefully adorned in a Hawaiian monarchy theme. Shuttles transport guests between the sister prop-erties and to and from the panoramic 18-hole golf course. For super-lative solitude and a pampered interlude together, The Manele Bay Hotel is every inch a taste of paradise.

♦ **Romantic Note: HOTEL LANAI**, (800) 321-4666, (Inexpen-sive to Moderate), is the only other available place to stay on Lanai. In comparison to the Manele and the Koele, it is too disappointing for words, but even judged on its own merits it isn't anything to write home about. Built in 1923, it has been modestly refurbished. Rooms are small and spartan, with few windows. Its casual restaurant was too smoke-filled for us to eat in, but it seemed on par with everything else—just OK. The price tag is infinitely lower than the other two proper-ties', but that's where its attraction stops.

Molokai

KALUAKOI

KALAUPAPA

MAUNALOA

KAUNAKAKAI

WAIALUA

"When kisses are repeated and the arms hold there is no telling where time is."
Ted Hughes

MOLOKAI

Formerly known as "The Forgotten Isle" and "The Lonely Isle," Molokai has been trying to change its image over the years to "The Friendly Isle." Molokai will seem most friendly to those searching for very little commercialism, relative isolation, and a slow-paced vacation. Since the demise of its extensive pineapple-farming operations in 1988, the island has come to rely on tourism as the major industry. Even so, many islanders are strongly opposed to promoting tourism for fear that Molokai will become another Oahu. Fortunately, at the current rate of development (virtually none), we don't foresee that happening any time soon, and the feeling of "old" Hawaii is still prevalent on Molokai.

The arid western side of the island is mostly dry, dusty roads, rolling cattle pastures, and former pineapple fields dotted with leafless gray trees, but the east end is a true tropical fantasy. The magnificent rugged coastline is hemmed with palm trees, which are nowhere else to be found on this island, and the surrounding jungle-like countryside is luxuriously thick and green. Alas, the beach area is limited, because the water comes right up to the land, with very little, if any, sand between the ocean and grassy or rocky shores.

Molokai is only 38 miles long, but it takes nearly an hour to get to the east shore from the west end (which is where you're likely to be staying). The dramatic change of scenery and gorgeous vistas make every second in the car worthwhile. Take turns driving each way so you can both enjoy the views; the narrow, curving road demands all of the driver's attention.

An unusual point of interest on the island is **PHALLIC ROCK**, located in **PALAAU STATE PARK**. You'll have to use quite a bit of imagination to see the phallic likeness, but according to legend, women who could not get pregnant would spend the night at the base of the stone, then return home pregnant. (We didn't see anyone camping out when we were here, but if you're hoping to conceive on your honeymoon, it might be a worthwhile stop.)

Some of the most dramatic scenery (and intriguing history) is found on the **MAKANALUA PENINSULA**, better known as the site of **KALAUPAPA**. From a distance, this lovely green peninsula, set beneath Molokai's majestic seaside cliffs (some of the highest in the world) and surrounded by turbulent ocean surf on the remaining three sides, bears no traces of its poignant past. Closer up, mile after mile of gravestones reveal the final resting place for patients of the state's Hansen's Disease Leprosy Treatment Center. People suffering from leprosy (properly known as Hansen's disease) were first cruelly exiled here by fearful governments in 1866, in an attempt to keep the disease under control. People afflicted with Hansen's disease were essentially left here to die and were not provided with even the most basic necessities. In 1873, Father Damien Joseph de Veuster, a Belgian priest who was deeply concerned about the misery of the people at Kalaupapa, settled his ministry here, and brought hope and healing to this lonely peninsula. Father Damien was the first person to recognize the needs of the people at Kalaupapa, and he spent the remainder of his life serving this community. Today, many refer to Father Damien as a saint and a martyr; sadly, he contracted Hansen's disease himself and died of the disease in 1889.

Thanks to sulfone drugs developed in the 1940s, Hansen's disease is now curable (and not contagious). Yet many recovered patients have chosen to remain in Kalaupapa; today, fewer than 100 people live in this small community. They encourage visitors to learn more about their private peninsula and its past. Despite its somber history, Kalaupapa is a powerful place to behold and a true testament to the strength of the human spirit.

◆ **Romantic Note:** This peninsula is accessible only by foot (it's a steep and strenuous four-hour round-trip hike) or by plane. You are required to call **DAMIEN MOLOKAI TOURS**, (808) 567-6171, for entrance permission. The tour alone is $25; the tour plus plane fare is $80. Mule rides into the valley used to be available, but due to insurance problems this is no longer an option.

Maunaloa

Hotel/Bed and Breakfast Kissing

PANIOLO HALE, Maunaloa
Kakaako Road
(808) 552-2731, (800) 367-2984
Inexpensive to Expensive

From the airport, travel west on Highway 460 and turn right at the Kaluakoi Resort sign. These condos are several miles down; watch for signs.

After you've followed a long, winding driveway through somewhat barren scenery, Paniolo Hale's well-tended grounds and spacious condos are a pleasing sight. All of the studio, one-, and two-bedroom units have one outstanding feature: a large, fully screened-in porch, perfect for letting the blustery trade winds refresh the rooms. Every unit also comes equipped with a full kitchen and a washer and dryer; in some of the two-bedroom units, a Jacuzzi tub is available for an additional daily charge. Although the decor throughout the condos tends to be Hawaiian-inspired, some are decorated more elaborately than others. If you're looking for something extra-special and have flexible travel dates, describe your preferences to the amiable staff and they will gladly accommodate you.

Other noteworthy features of the resort are a swimming pool, golf course, tennis courts, barbecue grills, and picnic tables. In addition, it is right next to Kepuhi and Papohaku beaches. Although swimming is not recommended because of strong currents, Papohaku is the longest sandy beach in Hawaii, and the scenery is brilliant.

◆ **Romantic Note:** The only other lodging options on the island are various condominium complexes or the **KALUAKOI HOTEL AND GOLF CLUB**, Maunaloa, (808) 552-2555, (800) 777-1700 (mainland), (800) 435-7208 (inter-island), (Moderate to Very Expensive). Unfortunately, the rooms are small and plain, and the entire hotel is in desperate need of renovation. Until that happens, we cannot recommend staying there. The condominium properties can be a bargain, but also tend to be run-down.

Restaurant Kissing

OHIA LOUNGE, Maunaloa
1131 Kaluakoi Road, in the Kaluakoi Resort
(808) 552-2555
Moderate to Expensive

From the airport, travel west on Highway 460 and turn right at the Kaluakoi Resort sign. Follow signs to the resort, where you will find the restaurant.

If you time your reservations right, you can witness a glorious sunset and look out over the sparkling Pacific from a table at the Ohia Lounge. Unfortunately, this is the only romantic reason to come here. The dining room's island motif is attractive enough, but the standard American fare is terribly disappointing, as is the service. We only recommend drinks and appetizers at sunset here.

◆ **Romantic Alternatives:** Dining options on Molokai are limited and not what we would typically deem romantic, but we did find several places worth recommending. Decent meals are served at **JOJO'S CAFE**, the only restaurant in the village of Maunaloa, (808) 552-2803, (Inexpensive), where the fresh fish and curry are good; the **KUALAPUU COOKHOUSE**, Farrington Road, Kualapuu, (808) 567-6185, (Inexpensive), where you must try the chocolate macadamia nut pie; and the **MOLOKAI PIZZA CAFE**, Wharf Road, Kaunakakai, (808) 553-3288, (Inexpensive), which also delivers its good pizzas.

Halawa

Outdoor Kissing

MOAULA FALLS FOOTPATH

The trailhead is located at the easternmost end of Highway 450.

The footpath begins at a small tumble-down snack shop, whose friendly owners provide maps and parking for $5. You can probably do the hike without the map and park elsewhere, but rental cars on Molokai are prone to theft and it's nice not to have to worry about your belongings. The two-hour (round-trip) hike takes you into the heart of the lush Halawa Valley. It is hard to believe because of the dense jungle surroundings, but hundreds of families once lived here, and you can spot the remains of a number of homes. The valley was deserted in 1946 after a massive tsunami (tidal wave) flattened the area. Trail markers are sometimes difficult to find, so take it slow and savor the incredible jungle scenery. You will feel as if you are in a movie when you finally emerge from the forest and come to a surging waterfall tumbling into a calm green pool of water surrounded by rocks. Share a kiss under the spray of the falls while celebrating your find and swimming together (watch out—the water's cold and can be algae-filled, depending on the season).

♦ **Romantic Warning:** This path is fairly easy to maneuver when it's dry, but can be quite dangerous after a rainfall, due to slippery mud and hidden roots. You have to cross two rivers, an easy skip and a jump over rocks when the water level is low, but excessive rain can bring the water levels knee-deep or higher, which is intimidating, not to mention dangerous. Also, mosquitoes seem to like this jungle paradise as much as you will, so don't forget bug repellent.

♦ **Romantic Suggestion:** The long drive and the walk to the falls might be too tiring for you to try snorkeling in the same day. If you still have energy or care to snorkel another time, though, the string of beaches from **MILEPOST 17 TO MILEPOST 21** on Highway 450 are rimmed with vast reefs full of fish. Unfortunately, seclusion is out—everyone seems to know about these small strips of beach that are right along the main highway.

"Press yourself into a drop of wine, and pour yourself into the purest flame."
Rainer Maria Rilke

INDEX

A

A Pacific Cafe (Kauai), 142
A Pacific Cafe (Maui), 88
Aihualama Trail, 46
Alan Wong's Restaurant, 36
Aloha Cantina, 82
Aloha Tower
   Marketplace, 27
ANAHOLA, 137
Anini Beach Vacation
   Rentals, 137
Anue Nue, 105
Arizona Memorial, 24
Aston Kauai Beach
   Villas, 144
Aston Royal Sea Cliff
   Resort, 169
Aston Waikiki Beach
   Tower, 27
Aston Waikiki Beachside
   Hotel, 28
Avalon, 83
Azul, 26

B

Bali by the Sea, 37
Bali Hai Restaurant, 159
Banyan Tree, The, 65
Banyan Veranda, 38
Bay Club, The, 65
Beach House, The, 64
Bistro, 183
Black Rock, 59
Bloom Cottage, 102

C

Cafe Hanalei, 160
Cafe Pesto, 194
Cafe Restaurant and
   Lounge, 187
Canoe House, The, 187
Captain Cook's
   Monument, 178
Captain Zodiak Tours, 151

Car Rentals, 4
Carson's Volcano Cottage,
   198
Casa De Mateo, 86
Casa Di Amici, 156
Casanova, 101
Cascada by the Waterfall, 38
Chalet Kilauea —The Inn
   at Volcano, 199
Ciao, 96
Ciao Mein, 31
Coast Grille, 183
Colony Surf Hotel, 48
Colony's Poipu Kai
   Resort, 129
Contemporary Cafe, The, 39
Contemporary Museum,
   The, 39
Crater Rim Drive, 204

D

Damien Molokai Tours, 214
David Paul's Lahaina
   Grill, 83
DIAMOND HEAD, 47
Diamond Head Crater, 47
Dining Room, The, 188
Donatoni's, 192
Dondero's, 132

E

EAST MAUI, 105
Ekena, 110
Embassy Suites, 73
Embassy Vacation Resort,
   Poipu Point, 125
Expeditions Cruise
   Service, 208

F

Fern Grotto, 145
Fisherman's Landing, 175
Five Palms Beach Grill, 87
Fleming Beach, 69

Fogelstrom House, The, 137
Formal Dining Room, 209
Four Seasons Resort, 89

G

Gallery, The, 188
Garden Restaurant, The, 66
Gaylord's at Kilohana, 145
Gerard's, 84
Gloria's Spouting Horn
   Bed and Breakfast, 126
Golden Bamboo Ranch, 106
Golden Dragon
   Restaurant, 39
Grand Dining Room, 91
Grand Wailea Resort, 90
Grantham Resorts, 126
Grill, The, (The Big
   Island), 189
Grill, The, (Kapalua), 66
Grove Dining Room,
   The, 121

H

HAENA, 149
Haena Beach Park, 151
HAIKU, 105
Haikuleana, 106
Hakone, 95
HALAWA, 216
Hale 'Aha, 157
Hale Hana Bay, 111
Hale Hoku, 127
Hale Iki, 200
Hale Makai Beach
   Cottages, 151
Hale Malia Bed and
   Breakfast, 169
Hale Ohia, 201
Hale O'Honu, 54
Hale O' Wailele, 138
Haleakala National
   Park, 104
Halekulani, 28

HALIIMAILE, 100
Haliimaile General
  Store, 100
Hamoa Bay Bungalow, 110
Hamoa Beach, 109
HANA, 108
Hana, Road to, 114
Hana Alii Holidays, 111
Hana Hale
  Malamalama, 112
Hana Plantation Houses, 112
Hanakapiai Beach, 151
Hanakapiai Falls, 151
HANALEI, 151
Hanalei Bay Resort and
  Suites, 158
Hanalei Gourmet, The, 153
Hanalei National Wildlife
  Refuge, 149
Hanalei North Shore
  Properties, 159
Hanalei Sea Tours, 150
HANAMAULU, 143
Hanamaulu Cafe, 143
Hanatei Bistro, 52
Hanauma Bay, 52, 53
Hanohano Room, 40
Hapuna Beach Prince
  Hotel, 182
Harlequin Restaurant, 40
Hau Tree Lanai, 50
HAWAII (The Big
  Island), 165
HAWAII KAI, 51
Hawaii Visitors Bureau, 3
Hawaii Volcanoes National
  Park, 203
Hawaii's Best Bed and
  Breakfasts, 12
Hilton Hawaiian Village, 29
Hilton Waikoloa
  Village, 191

HOLUALOA, 179
Holualoa Inn, 179
Honokahua to Kahakuloa
  Drive, 68
Honokalani Cottage, 111
Honokeana Cove, 70
Honolua Bay, 69
HONOLULU, 26
Honolulu Mauka Trail
  System, 46
Hookipa Park, 60
Hotel Hana-Maui, 113
Hotel Lanai, 210
House of Seafood, The, 133
House Without A Key, 45
HUELO, 107
Huelo Point Lookout Bed
  and Breakfast, 107
Hulopo'e Court, 210
Humuhumunuku-
  nukuapua'a, 91
Hurricane Iniki, 119
Hyatt Regency (Waikiki), 30
Hyatt Regency (Kauai), 127
Hyatt Regency (Maui), 74

I
Iao Needle, 59
Iao Valley State Park, 59
Ihilani Dining Room, 210
Ihilani Resort and Spa, 24
Ilima Terrace, 133
Imari, 192
Indigo, 41
Inn Paradise, 146
International Marketplace,
  27
Island Glass Blowers Studio
  and Gallery, 100
Island Helicopters, 150
Island Hopping, 3
Islands at Mauna Lani,
  The, 183

J
Jasmine House, 92
Jojo's Cafe, 216

K
Ka Hale Kea, 111
KAANAPALI, 72
Kaanapali Alii, 75
Kaanapali Beach, 79
Kacho, 36
Kaena Point State Park, 23
Kahala Mandarin Oriental
  Hotel, 48
Kahala Moon Cafe, 42
KAHANA, 71
Kai Mana, 153
KAILUA, 53
Kailua Beach Park, 53
KAILUA KONA, 168
Kailua Plantation House, 170
Kalahiki Cottage, 171
Kalalau Trail, 151
Kalani Aina, 159
Kalaupapa, 213
Kaluakoi Hotel and Golf
  Club, 215
Kamuela Provision
  Company, 192
KANEOHE, 54
KAPAA, 138
Kapaa Sands, 139
KAPALUA, 61
Kapalua Bay Hotel and
  Villas, 61
Kapalua Beach, 62
Kapalua Villas, The, 62
KAPOLEI, 24
KAUAI, 117
Kauai Division of State
  Parks, 119
KAUAI EAST SHORE, 136
KAUAI NORTH
  SHORE, 148

KAUAI SOUTH
  SHORE, 124
Kauai State Parks Visitor
  Information, 119, 123
KAUAI WEST SHORE,
  120
Kauapea Beach (Secret
  Beach), 156
KAWAIHAE, 193
Kaweonui Point Beach
  (Sealodge Beach), 161
Kayak Kauai Outfitters
  (Hanalei), 152
Kayak Kauai Outfitters
  (Kapaa), 146
Kea Lani Hotel, 92
Kea Lani—The
  Restaurant, 96
KEALAKEKUA, 177
Kealakekua Bay, 178
Kealakekua Bay Bed and
  Breakfast, 177
Kealoha Rise, 147
Kee Beach, 149
Keo's Thai Bar & Grill, 43
Keo's Thai Cuisine, 42
Kiahuna Plantation, 128
Kiele V, 69
KIHEI, 86
KILAUEA, 153
Kilauea Lodge, 200
Kilauea Lodge
  Restaurant, 202
Kimo's, 84
Kincha, 91
Koele Terrace, 209
KOHALA COAST, 181
Kokee Lodge, 121
Kokee State Park, 122
Koko Head District Park, 52
KONA DISTRICT, 168
Kona Inn Restaurant, 174
Kona Village, 184

Kona Village Luau, 190
Koolau Mountain Range, 23
Kualapuu Cookhouse, 216
Kuhio Highway (Highway
  56), 149
KULA, 102
Kula Lodge Restaurant, 103
Kumulani Chapel, 65

L
La Cascata, 161
La Mer, 43
LAHAINA, 80
Lahaina Coolers, 82
Lahaina Inn, 80
Lahaina Shores Beach
  Resort, 81
LANAI, 205
Lanai City, 208
Lanikai, 140
Lanikai Beach, 54
Leis, 14
LIHUE, 144
Liko Kauai Cruises, 150
Lodge at Koele, The, 208
Lokahi Lodge Bed and
  Breakfast, 200
Luaus, 14
Lyon Arboretum, 47

M
Mahana at Kaanapali, 76
Mahaulepu Beach, 136
Mai Tai Bar, 34
Makahuena, 127
Makai Hale, 193
Makana Inn, 141
Makanalua Peninsula, 213
MAKAWAO, 100
Makena Surf, 93
Mama's Fish House, 109
MANA, 123
Mana Kai-Maui, 86

Manele Bay Hotel, The, 209
Manoa Cliff Trail, 46
Manoa Valley, 46
Manoa Valley Inn, 31
Manu Mele Bed and
  Breakfast, 53
MAUI, 57
Maui Inter-Continental
  Resort, 93
Maui Kai, 76
Maui Prince Hotel, 94
Maui Princess, 3
Maui Visitors Bureau, 60
Mauna Kea Beach Hotel, 185
Mauna Lani Bay Hotel and
  Bungalows, 185
Mauna Lani Point, 183
MAUNALOA, 214
Merriman's Restaurant, 196
Merryman's Bed and
  Breakfast, 177
Michaelangelo's, 175
Michel's, 50
Milepost 17 to Milepost 21
  (Molokai), 221
Moaula Falls Footpath, 216
MOLOKAI, 211
Molokai Pizza Cafe, 216
Molokini, 60
Mountain House and
  Hydrangea Cottage, 201

N
Na Pali Coast State
  Park, 150
NAPILI, 70
Naupaka Restaurant, 25
New Otani Kaimana Beach
  Hotel, The, 49
Nicholas Nickolas, 44
Nick's Fishmarket, 44
Nihi Kai Villas, 127

O

OAHU, 21
OAHU NORTH SHORE, 54
Ohana Helicopter
   Tours, 150
Oheo Gulch, 109, 114
Ohia Lounge, 215
Old Lahaina Cafe, 85
Olinda Country Cottage, 101
One Napili Way, 71
Opaekaa Falls Hale, 147
Orchids, 45
Outrigger Beach Hotel, 144
Outrigger Hotels
   Hawaii, 32

P

Pacific Cafe, A (Kauai), 142
Pacific Cafe, A (Maui), 88
Pacific Grill, 90
Pacific Whale Watching
   Foundation, 17
Pacific-O, 85
Palaau State Park, 213
Palm Cafe, 176
Palm Court, 95
Palm Terrace, 192
Paniolo Hale, 214
Pavilions at Seacliff, 154
Phallic Rock, 213
Pilialoha, 107
Pineapple Hill Restaurant, 67
Plantation House
   Restaurant, 67
Plantation Inn, The, 81
POIPU, 125
Poipu Shores Oceanfront
   Condominiums, 129
Polihale State Park, 123
Polo Beach, 98
Polynesian Cultural
   Center, 23
Prince Court, 95

PRINCEVILLE, 157
Princeville Hotel, 160
Puanani, 172
Puu Manu Cottage, 195
Puu Ohia Trail, 46

R

Raffles, 96
Ritz-Carlton, Kapalua
   (Maui), 63
Ritz-Carlton, Mauna Lani
   (The Big Island), 186
Road to Hana, The, 114
Rosewood Bed and
   Breakfast, 148
Rosy's Rest, 180
Royal Garden Hotel, 32
Royal Hawaiian, The, 33
Royal Kona Resort, 172
Royal Lahaina Resort, 77
Roy's Kahana Bar and
   Grill, 71
Roy's Nicolina, 72
Roy's Poipu Bar and
   Grill, 134
Roy's Restaurant (Oahu), 51

S

Sandy Beach, 23
Sea Village, 173
Sea Watch Restaurant at
   Wailea, The, 97
Sealodge Beach (Kaweonui
   Point Beach), 161
Seasons, 97
Seaview Terrace, 135
Secret Beach (Kauapea
   Beach), 156
Secret Beach Cottage, 155
Seven Pools, 109, 114
Sheraton Moana
   Surfrider, 34
Ship's Tavern, 45
Shipwreck Point, 136

Silver Cloud Upcountry
   Guest Ranch, 102
Sound of the Falls, 78
SOUTHEAST OAHU, 51
Spa Grande, 99
Stouffer Renaissance
   Wailea Beach Resort, 95
Sugar Beach Resort, 87
Sunset Beach, 23
Sunset Makai Hale, 130
Surf Room, 34
Swan Court, 79

T

Tassa Hanalei, 162
Tedeschi Vineyards, 99
Teralani, 69
Tidepools, 135
Tunnels Beach, 149
Tutu's Country Cottage, 152

U

Under the Palm, 176
UPCOUNTRY (Maui), 99

V

Victorian Garden
   Cottage, 131
VOLCANO, 197
Volcano Golf and Country
   Club Restaurant, 203
Volcano Heli-Tours, 204
Volcano House, 203

W

Wai Ola, 82
Wai'anapanapa State
   Park, 109
WAIKIKI, 26
Waikiki Joy Hotel, 35
Waikiki Parc Hotel, 36
WAIKOLOA, 191
Waikomo Stream Villas, 127
WAILEA, 89

Wailea Beach, 98
Wailea Golf Course, 89
Wailea Point, 98
Wailea Tennis Club, 89
WAILUA, 145
Wailua Bay View
    Condominiums, 141
Wailua Falls, 109
WAILUA HOMESTEADS,
    146
WAIMEA (The Big
    Island), 194
WAIMEA (Kauai), 120
Waimea Beach, 23
Waimea Canyon State
    Park, 122
Waimea Falls Park, 23
Waimea Gardens Cottage, 195
Waimea Plantation
    Cottages, 120
Wainae Mountain Range, 23
WAINIHA, 162
WAIOHINU, 181
WAIPIO, 197
Waipio Valley, 197
Waipio Valley Shuttle, 197
Waipio Valley Wagon
    Tours, 197
WEST MAUI, 61
WEST OAHU, 24
Westin Maui, The, 77
Whaler's Cove, 131
Whaling's Hobbit House, 181

The Best Places To Kiss In Hawaii

KISS AND TELL FORM

Please consider my comments about the following establishment for the next edition of **The Best Places To Kiss In Hawaii**.

Name of Establishment: _____

Address/City: _____

_____

Phone Number: _____

The above establishment does/does not deserve to be listed as a *Best Place To Kiss* because . . .

_____

_____

_____

_____

_____

_____

_____

I am not connected (directly or indirectly) with the management or ownership of this establishment.

My name: _____

Address/City: _____

_____

Phone Number: _____

Date: _____

Please send this form or a letter with your comments to:
Beginning Press
5418 South Brandon
Seattle, WA 98118

The Best Places To Kiss In Hawaii

KISS AND TELL FORM

Please consider my comments about the following establishment for the next edition of **The Best Places To Kiss In Hawaii**.

Name of Establishment: _____

Address/City: _____

_____

Phone Number: _____

The above establishment does/does not deserve to be listed as a *Best Place To Kiss* because . . .

_____

_____

_____

_____

_____

_____

_____

I am not connected (directly or indirectly) with the management or ownership of this establishment.

My name: _____

Address/City: _____

_____

Phone Number: _____

Date: _____

Please send this form or a letter with your comments to:
Beginning Press
5418 South Brandon
Seattle, WA 98118